The Great Batt[

The Great Tribulation
The Great Apostasy
The Great Havoc of War & Disaster
The Great Warning & Miracle
The Great Renewal
The Great Persecution
The Great Chastisement
The Great Victory

How to Approach the End of Our Times with Peace

A Modern Commentary on the Book of Revelation

by

Dr. Kelly Bowring

Author of the best-selling, highly-acclaimed book:

The Secrets, Chastisement, & Triumph

Two Hearts Press, LLC
www.TwoHeartsPress.com

Library of Congress Control Number: 2012955643

Published by: Two Hearts Press, LLC, Cumming, GA, USA

Printed in the United States of America

ISBN-13: 978-0-9802292-0-2

ISBN-10: 0-9802292-0-0

To order copies of this book:

Please call toll-free (24/7)

1-800-BookLog (266-5564)

Or fax orders to:

1-419-281-6883

Or order **book or e-book** on our website at:

TwoHeartsPress.com

D E D I C A T E D

T O

The faithful of the Church and all people of good will –

those modern apostles and missionaries,

filled with light,

who today have eyes to see the signs of the times,

and who strive faithfully to read, live, and spread

the biblical prophecy and the heavenly messages

of the latter times

with hope

*Children, **it is the last hour;***
and just as you heard that the antichrist was coming,
so now many antichrists have appeared.
*Thus we know **this is the last hour**.*
1 John 2:18

CONTENTS

PART 1: REVELATION 4-11

PART 2: REVELATION 12

PART 3: REVELATION 13-19

PART 4: REVELATION 20-22

How to Approach the End of Our Times with Peace

Chapter One

The Signs of Our Time

ॐ

When you see a cloud rising in the west you say immediately that it is going to rain—and so it does;
and when you notice that the wind is blowing from the south you say that it is going to be hot—and so it is...
You know how to interpret the appearance of the earth and the sky;
Why do you not know how to interpret the present time?
Luke 12:54-56

*Know how to read **the signs of the times***
through which you are living
and which are announcing to you Jesus' immanent return.
Gobbi

We are now living in the most important moment in history, since the time of Christ. The world is beginning to experience **the biggest shift in its history**. Changes are beginning to occur the likes of which man has never seen or experienced. When all the events of prophecy commence, it will be too late to prepare. The purpose of this book is to educate, to warn, and to call you to respond. From analyzing the heavenly messages, one can see that the Lord's goal is for His people of good will to 1) read His heavenly messages; 2) live them and apply them to their life; and 3) to spread His messages to others.

This book highlights some of the biblical and credible heavenly messages about the times that are upon us. It is an analysis of those biblical and heavenly messages, which seeks to systematically report the messages themselves, to discuss their main themes and multiple sources, and to demonstrate how they all fit together to give us a complete picture of the latter times event.

Prophecy foretells **an end-time period of war** the likes of which the world has never known, a war that is partly spiritual and partly physical; and it is telling us that this period of great battle is coming, that it is upon us even now, and in fact that it has already begun. Relying on divine revelation and upon private revelations, this book discusses this great battle, not from speculation but from God's perspective (and divine knowledge). It shows how He has foretold the full course of the battle itself. It tells us **how He wants us to fight** the great battle with Him so as to win the great victory He promises us will be granted to those who read these messages, who use them to move into the light, and who seek His aid moving forward in His peace and protection. This book is a handbook that reveals all the secrets of the great and final battle, step-by-step, and your role in its final outcome as the apostles of the latter times.

My first book on this subject, *The Secrets, Chastisement, and Triumph* (Two Hearts Press, 2009), a best-selling 'Book of the Year', discusses **the big picture of the whole unfolding of the latter times**. While I occasionally reference that book in this book, as it is helpful, that book too is well worth reading so as to assist in understanding our times.

This book, on the other hand, presents **the details of the latter times event AND how we can approach the end of our times with peace**.

Reading heavenly messages can do much good and people who respond to them experience a rich blessing. The outcome to this battle is already assured and promised to those of good will and faith. To get to the promised victory though requires divine power and a cooperating trust. As we learn God's plan, He can pour out His power on us to participate in the victory. But, for those who choose not to believe or are simply blind to see, their incredulity leads them to obstinacy and a hardness of heart, and to a dire end.

On the other hand, belief is helpful, as it softens the heart and disposes it to let itself be subdued by grace, and receive the sight to see, and thus to comprehend the meaning of the heavenly messages and how best to respond to them. I pray that you the reader will have eyes to see and ears to hear. When you read these biblical and heavenly messages, do not doubt. They are credible and trustworthy. And **these messages are for the whole world, for everyone, for you**. As one who has been researching these sources and writing on them for several years, including in my book, *The Secrets, Chastisement, and Triumph (with imprimatur)*, I propose to the reader the credibility of these sources. My work of analyzing and synthesizing biblical and credible heavenly messages has brought me to see how they all fit together, one with the other, to confirm each other in a balanced and proper context and to give us a full picture of the latter times which we are living in. For more background and information about the solid sources used in this book, see the end of the book where I discuss them in more detail.

How to Read This Book

I would like to offer you, the reader, a proposal: Read this book with an open mind seeking the grace of God's truth and then decide how you shall prayerfully respond. I think you will discover that this book offers a treasure of inestimable value and find yourself wanting to seek to live and share its message with **great joy and peace**. You will not be able to read this book without being enlightened and encouraged. I only propose that you read it entirely and while seeking God's grace of discernment. Three things are being asked of you: to listen, follow, and spread the biblical and heavenly message of our times, which are contained in summary in this book. As the heavenly message of one locutionist invites:

*I address this message of mine **to you**... **Listen** to it, and you will be saved. **Follow** it, and you will find peace of heart. **Spread** it everywhere, and you will help to prepare, for all, days, not of misfortune and affliction, but of hope and peace.[1] (Gobbi)*

A Hint of What Is Coming

I will draw the picture clearly. Soon, so very soon, the powers of hell will be unleashed against the whole world. All will experience these powers, in one degree or another. There will be a series of events, one following another, that will totally change the face of the earth.[2]

*No one can even imagine the destruction, the loss of life and the complete ravaging of the earth which **Satan** wants to bring about. This is as complete and as powerful a destruction as he is able to mount. Even those areas which do not experience the destruction directly will be shaken by the events. The whole world will be terrified and seemingly no relief will be in sight... **All of that can change and will change if only mankind** [3] cries out to God for help.*

We are free, and we must choose Heaven or hell. Our choices have consequences, and we cannot choose our consequences. God is merciful, but He is also just. God wants to intervene to help us, but we must ask Him.

God is sending messengers in preparation for these events for three reasons:

1) The first is **to remind mankind of the truth contained in the Book of Revelation.**

2) The second is **to make man alert to the times he is living in so that he can rekindle his faith.**

3) The third is **to help spread conversion so that [Christ's] followers can form the biggest army of all in order to save souls**... so that [His] word is heard in every corner of the world.[4]

Jesus says to us:
*The prophecies predicted in the **Book of Revelation** are now unfolding. **Spread the truth** of My teachings...Be brave. Preach the truth.*[5]

Turn to God, have faith, and move forward in His peace.

PART 1: REVELATION 4-11

ଓଃ

Chapter Two

The Final Confrontation

ଓଃ

I, John, heard the Lord saying to me:
Write this:
I know your works,
that you have the reputation of being alive, but you are dead…
I know your works;
I know that you are neither cold nor hot.
I wish you were either cold or hot.
So, because you are lukewarm, neither hot nor cold,
I will spit you out of my mouth.
For you say, 'I am rich and affluent and have no need of anything,'

and yet do not realize that you are wretched,
pitiable, poor, blind, and naked...

Those whom I love, I reprove and chastise.
Be earnest, therefore, and repent.
Behold, I stand at the door and knock.
Revelation 3:1-6, 14-20

We are now standing in the face of
the greatest historical confrontation
humanity has gone through.
I do not think that wide circles of the American society
or wide circles of the Christian community realize this fully.
*We are now facing **the final confrontation***
between the Church and the anti-Church,
of the Gospel versus the anti-Gospel.
This confrontation lies within the plans of Divine Providence...
Bl. John Paul II, just before he became pope, in Philadelphia

The vision awaits its time;
It hastens to the end – it will not lie.
If it seem slow, wait for it;
It will surely come, it will not delay.
Habakkuk 2: 2-3

Jesus said to his disciples:
Beware that your hearts do not become drowsy
from carousing and drunkenness
and the anxieties of daily life,
*and **that day** catch you by surprise like a trap.*
*For **that day** will assault everyone*
who lives on the face of the earth.
***Be vigilant** at all times*
***and pray** that you have the strength*

to escape the tribulations that are imminent
and to stand before the Son of Man.
Luke 21:34-36

All Prophecy Eventually Comes True

All authentic prophecy is conditional, but otherwise eventually comes true. The 3 Secrets of Fatima given in 1917 came true… they have actually occurred. Today, God is giving us new and final secrets for our time. Sister Lucia, one of the Fatima visionaries, said that Jesus appeared to her and made this complaint:

> *They did not wish to heed My request! ...*
> *They will repent of it, and they will do it (Consecrate Russia to the Immaculate Heart),*
> *but it will be late.*
> *Russia will have already spread its errors in the world,*
> *provoking wars and persecutions against the Church.*
> *The Holy Father will have much to suffer.*

This Fatima prophecy is not completely fulfilled yet either. When Pope Benedict XVI visited Fatima in 2010, he declared: *"It would be mistaken to consider the prophecy of Fatima complete."* He added: *"Today, God is seeking righteous persons to save the city of man... May the next seven years (2010-2017) see the fulfillment of the Triumph of the Immaculate Heart."* What a commissioning… what a hope!

All prophecy, while conditional, eventually comes true. For over 2000 years, God has been giving humanity prophecy about the latter times and the last great battle, and now such times are upon us in this generation. All of the prophecies are about to come true. And did you know that there is not a single biblical or heavenly prophecy about any time in the future beyond this generation, except the last chapter of

Revelation which has to do with the Final Coming of Christ at the end of time.

These Are the Latter Times

What does Scripture say about the latter times?

*Now the Spirit expressly says that **in latter times** some*
will depart from the faith
*by giving heed to **deceitful spirits***
*and doctrines of **demons** through the pretensions of liars...*
But understand this,
*that in **the last days** there will come times of stress.*
*For men will be **lovers of self, lovers of money,***
[and] lovers of pleasure
rather than lovers of God,
holding the form of religion but denying the power of it.
1 Timothy 4:1-2, 2 Timothy 3:1-5

Do not be terrified...
Nation will rise against nation...
there will be great earthquakes,
and in various places famines and pestilences;
and there will be terrors and great signs from heaven...
and upon the earth distress of nations in perplexity
at the roaring of the sea and the waves,
men fainting with fear...
*for the powers of **the heavens will be shaken.***
Luke 21:9-28

The 7 seals are now being broken, the Book, which was sealed, is now being opened, and the secrets are being revealed for the whole world to see and understand. They include:

- A great apostasy that splits the Church in two.

- The Middle East attack against Jerusalem, and war spreading.

- Economies collapsing, while Communism rises again.

- God intervening with signs and wonders, including with the Warning and the Miracle.

- Many then converting.

- But sadly, many others then turning away from the truth and trying to continue to inflict power and control over the rest of God's children.

- *Right after the Warning, the antichrist and his group, although weakened as a result of the global confession,* **will begin to plan his seizure of My Holy Church from within.** (MDM)

- The **false prophet ruling over the Vatican and Rome.**

A time of great devastation will now begin on earth, affecting in may cases **a third of humanity** and **a third of the world** (see Revelation 8-11).

Chapter Three

The Seven Seals

CZ

I, John,
saw a scroll in the right hand of the one who sat on the throne.
*It had writing on both sides and was sealed with **seven seals**.*
Then I saw a mighty angel who proclaimed in a loud voice,
"Who is worthy to open the scroll and break its seals?"
But no one in heaven or on earth or under the earth
was able to open the scroll or to examine it.
I shed many tears because no one was found worthy
to open the scroll or to examine it.
One of the elders said to me, "Do not weep.
The lion of the tribe of Judah, the root of David, has triumphed,
*enabling him to **open the scroll with its seven seals**."*
Revelation 5:1-5

Many identify the Great Tribulation with a final period of persecution shortly before the Second Coming. While thus is so, the whole period of the Apocalypse can rightly be characterized as the tribulation (2 Thess. 1:5-6; 2 Tim. 3:1, 12). The "great tribulation" refers to the time of the great crisis at the close of the age of man.

Jesus spoke of "great tribulation" in Matthew 24:21 and told John to write of it in Revelation 7:14.

We must begin to understand the Book of Revelation to understand the modern heavenly messages, and in turn, the modern heavenly messages help us to understand the Book of Revelation and its meaning for our times:

The Book of Revelation was given to all My children to help them understand the turmoil which will be caused towards the end times by the spread of lies created by Satan and his demons. Unless you understand the truth contained in the Book of Revelation then how can you possibly understand the messages I am bring to you today?[6] (MDM)

The two reasons for these modern heavenly messages are to prepare and to guide all people of good will:

I communicate to you now not just to prepare you all for this great act of My Mercy but to guide you through the maze of destruction planned by the Evil group whose King is the Evil One. My spiritual influence will block Satan's acts of destruction significantly. Hear My word. Follow My instructions.[7]

The Great Tribulation begins with the breaking of **the seven seals** of the Apocalypse. Let's examine the seven seals of Revelation:

1st SEAL: THE GREAT APOSTASY

Various **heresies have flourished and the light of faith has gone out in souls** because of almost total moral corruption. **Religious communities have been abandoned** and **many true vocations have been lost** for lack of prudent and skillful direction to form them. There has been **a spirit of impurity,** which floods the public places like a deluge of filth. The licentiousness is such that there are almost **no**

more virgin souls in the world. The New Age sects have **penetrated into the hearts of families and destroyed even the children.** The innocence of childhood has almost disappeared. Thus, many priestly vocations have been lost. **Priests have abandoned their sacred duties. The apostasy and the doctrinal errors, spread by misguided Church leaders, over the last four decades, has led to a divided Church and an ailing humanity.**

And soon, the Church will go through a dark night for lack of a Pope to watch over it. Satan will take control of the earth through faithless men. There will be **all sorts of chastisements**: plagues, famines, war, apostasy, and the loss of souls. There will be **a terrible war** and it will seem as though wickedness will triumph. **Men possessing great wealth will look with indifference while the Church is oppressed, virtue is persecuted, and evil triumphs.** They will not use their wealth to fight evil or to reconstruct the faith. The people will be swept away by all vices and passions. But, then will come the time of Our Lady and her Son. In astounding fashion, she will destroy Satan's pride, casting him beneath her feet, chaining him up in the depths of hell, leaving the Church freed from his cruel tyranny – so reports the messages of Our Lady of Good Success. Our Lady gives us details on this through Fr. Gobbi:

The spread of errors lead to the loss of faith and to apostasy. These errors are being propagated by false teachers, by renowned theologians who are no longer teaching the truths of the Gospel, but pernicious heresies based on errors and on human reasonings... It is because of these errors that the true faith is being lost and that the great apostasy is spreading everywhere...

*In the letter of Saint Paul to the Thessalonians, it is clearly announced that, before the glorious return of Christ, a **great apostasy** must take place. The loss of the faith is a true apostasy. The spread of the apostasy is therefore the sign which indicates that the **second coming** of Christ is, as of now, close at hand.*

At Fatima, I have foretold to you that a time would come when the true faith would be lost. These are the times. Your days are marked by this painful and significant situation, which was foretold to you in Holy Scripture: the true faith is in the process of disappearing in an ever increasingly greater number of my children.

*The **causes of the loss of faith** are:*

*(1) the spread of errors which are being propagated and are often taught **by professors of theology** in seminaries and in Catholic schools and which thus acquire a certain character of credibility and legitimacy;*

*(2) the open and public **rebellion against the authentic Magisterium** of the Church, especially against that of the Pope, who has from Christ the duty of preserving the whole Church in the truth of the Catholic faith;*

*(3) the **bad example given by those pastors**, who have allowed themselves to be completely possessed by the spirit of the world and who become propagators of political and sociological ideologies, rather than messengers of Christ and of his Gospel, thus forgetting the mandate received from Him: 'Go into the whole world and preach the Gospel to every creature.' (Mk 16:15)*

Thus, in these days of yours, apostasy on the part of many of my poor children is inundating you more and more. (Gobbi)

A WHITE HORSE Conquests by Way of Apostasy (Rev. 6:2)

The apostasy comes in 2 ways: from within the Church and from New Age practices. Scripture adds some details:

Take care that no one deceives you, because many will come using my name and saying, "I am the Christ," and they will deceive many. Matthew 24:4-5

But he said, "Take care not to be deceived, because many will come using my name and saying, 'I am the one' and 'The time is near at hand.'" Refuse to join them. Luke 21:8

The first seal is the apostasy, seen not only among unbelievers but among those who profess to know Christ and those who publicly proclaim their love for Him (from New Age influences and from within the Church). This is the time when the true faith is being twisted with a watered down doctrine that is an insult to the authentic teachings of the Church.

Jesus gives details about the evil of New Age practices and how quickly widespread they have become:

Any doctrine which teaches you the importance of putting yourself before everything else is a doctrine which springs from Satan... Any other god comes from Satan no matter how attractive the guise. Please do not waste your eternal life by pledging your allegiance to those faiths which honor new age **practices including Reiki, Yoga, new age meditation, tarot cards, clairvoyancy, psychic readings and angel worship connected with ascended masters.** *Slowly but surely these practices of the occult are being accepted not only by your society but by Catholic and Christian Churches. These false religious doctrines are spreading so fast they have consumed billions of God's children who have now found so much false solace within them that they no longer acknowledge the existence of the one true God. (Jesus)* [8]

Our Lady also explains through Maria Divine Mercy (MDM) what will happen because the apostasy has infiltrated the Church:

My child perseverance is needed by all God's children during this time of **apostasy in the world... Pope Benedict XVI is being plotted against within his own corridors by an evil sect... Pray that they do not drive the Pope away.** *Pray that the* **false prophet** *will not take the seat of the Holy Father so that he can spread lies. Pray that those sacred servants in the Vatican are strong enough to withstand this evil plot designed to destroy the Catholic Church.* **They plan to replace the**

Holy Vicar Pope Benedict XVI with a dictator of lies. He will create a new church in league with the anti-christ and his group in order to deceive the world... Great division will emerge within the ranks of priests, bishops, archbishops and cardinals. One side against the other. Those true disciples will have to hide and preach privately or else be killed. So hidden will the true church be that the true faithful will have to bind together in order to practice their allegiance to My Eternal Father. [9]

But, Jesus explains that He will lead a counter-attack:

Satan will attack the Church, in its external form throughout the world. How can this be, since the Church exists everywhere, with places of worship in many cultures? You will see surprising things. The Church is different in each country, and has a different relationship with the government and with the people. Satan will know the weakness of the Church and how it can be attacked and destroyed in each culture. However, he does not see that I am building a Church of faith and belief. (Jesus) [10]

2nd SEAL: WARS

The outbreak of wars and fratricidal struggles will commence.

A RED HORSE of Slaughter (Rev. 6:3-4)

Wars, revolutions and **bloodshed** on an unparalleled scale will involve many nations. Scripture adds some details:

You will hear of wars and rumors of wars; see that you are not alarmed, for this is something that must happen, but the end will not be yet. For nation will fight against nation, and kingdom against kingdom. Matt. 24:6-7

'And when you hear of wars and revolutions, do not be terrified, for this is something that must happen first, but the end will not come at

once.' Then he said to them, 'Nation will fight against nation, and kingdom against kingdom.' Luke 21:9-10

To assist us in the midst of the slaughter and wars, God the Father announces His seal of protection:

My Seal of Protection is foretold as the second seal is broken.

I gather My family together at this time so that we can unite in the final battle to slay the dragon who has tormented the earth for so long. Children do not be afraid. *No harm will come to those who* **wear My Seal, the Seal of the Living God** *(see Revelation 7). Satan and his fallen angels, who infest the world at this time,* **do not have the authority over those who have the mark of the Living God. You must listen to Me children and accept My Seal for it will save not only your lives but your souls.** *Recite the prayer to receive My Seal every day...*

My Seal of protection is foretold as the second seal is broken. *The* **rider of the red horse** *is the avenging dark angel who will slay My children in the* **many wars** *to come. But he will pass over those of My children with the seal on their foreheads. Prepare now for these wars are already happening and more are being planned in every corner of the earth and, especially, in the Middle East and in those lands upon which My precious Son, Jesus Christ, walked during His time on earth. (God the Father)*[11]

Seal of Protection Prayer to God the Father

O My God, My loving Father,
I accept with love and gratitude
Your Divine Seal of Protection.
Your Divinity encompasses my body and soul for eternity.
I bow in humble thanksgiving
and offer You my deep love and loyalty.
To You my Beloved Father,

I beg You to protect me and my loved ones with this special Seal.
And I pledge my life to Your service forever and ever.
I love You, Dear Father.
I console You in these times, Dear Father.
I offer You the Body, Blood, Soul and Divinity
of Your dearly beloved Son
in atonement for the sins of the world
and for the salvation of all Your children.
Amen.

www.thewarningsecondcoming.com

NATURAL CATASTROPHES – GREATER & MORE FREQUENT

3rd SEAL: FAMINES

A BLACK HORSE of Famine (Rev. 6:5-6)
Food at extremely high prices with worldwide **famines** when prices for even the barest of life's necessities will spiral out of control. Oil and wine are spared, indicating the partial nature of the famine. Scripture adds some details:

There will be famines and earthquakes in various places. All this is only the beginning of the birth pangs. Matt. 24:7-8

There will be great earthquakes and plagues and famines in various places; there will be terrifying events and great signs from heaven. Luke 21:11

4th SEAL: EPIDEMICS

A PALE, SICKLY HORSE of Death (Rev. 6:7-8)
The forces of Hell bring **pestilence** and **disease epidemics** of various kinds, which will lay low millions of people. **A fourth of the**

earth suffers the effects of death, famine, pestilence, and wild beasts. About the ecological catastrophes that will occur on earth during the Great Tribulation,[12] Our Lord says:

*Tell the world that the **ecological disasters foretold will now strike the earth.** All will commence now. So many. So quickly. And all due to the blind eyes turned on the word of God the Father by sinners wrapped up in their dens of iniquity... Do not be fearful. I will offer you My Divine protection at all times even when you are ridiculed in My name. Prayer will give you strength and courage as the Evil One and his minions now pour out their venom on My children. As their heinous acts of warfare on humanity begins to escalate through terrorism, monopoly of world currencies and the poisoning of the earth through deliberate contamination will occur.[13]*

*Countries all over the world are bubbling under the surface with unrest both in terms of the **hatred** being shown by man to man as well as **pending ecological upheavals.** This is where Mother Nature will unleash the unexpected soon to show man that he is not, irrespective of his arrogant assertiveness, in control of anything...*

*My warning to those leaders all over the world, whoever you are, is this. Inflict unfair practices and hardships on your people and the hand of My Eternal Father will fall swiftly **on those countries and locations** within which you reside. He will no longer tolerate your sinful deeds. Hide if you will but it will be useless. Your weapons of destruction will be destroyed. Your treatment of your fellow citizens will create a situation, whether you like it or not, where you will have to answer to God the Eternal Father. Your moral responsibilities must be adhered to because you will be judged by your actions eventually.*

*Lead your people with love, dignity and respect for their physical and moral welfare. Deny your people **the right to religious freedom** or inflict dictatorships of any kind which forces them to stop or curtail their religious practices in the name of Political unity, then you are doomed. Not only will you suffer for your actions but judgment will be harsh. Any of you who swears allegiance to your people in the name of God, the Eternal Father and orchestrates **unfair new laws** which deny* *them **the right to food, shelter and religious freedom** will face the wrath and the hand of God, the Father...*

*The time has come for **the battle** to rid the world of evil and the rule of Satan. God the Father is now about to unleash many **earthquakes, tsunamis** and **floods** in an effort to make you wake up. Your plots to overthrow world leaders, those in power of Religious groups and to introduce control measures including a **one world currency** will not be ignored...*

*Prayer will, as I have said before, help dilute disasters in the world as it now heads towards **a series of climate-related catastrophes**, never witnessed by man since the days of Noah. The world as you know it will suffer so many events all at once that **chaos and confusion will be the norm**.[14]*

*It is with great sadness that I must tell you that pending **ecological catastrophes** will result in a huge loss of life in **Asia, Europe, Russia and the United States of America**. The wrath of God, My Eternal Father will fall swiftly on this Global Alliance who are plotting underground organizations to inflict death on the rest of the world for their own gain.[15]*

*Tell the world that they are about to witness a number of **ecological disasters now**. They will occur in the most unusual and unexpected places and will be severe in their intensity. Man's **sinful behavior** has brought this about. Repent all of you and remember these climatic disasters will wake you up from your blind slumber and lack of faith. They are also taking place **to dilute the impact of the evil group of global alliances**.. These same groups have brought about the collapse of the Banking system and **will now destroy currencies** everywhere. This is so that they can control you... These people will now control each of you through **a global currency** and your country's indebtedness. No country will escape their clutches. Please heed My word.[16]*

5ᵗʰ SEAL: MARTYRS

MARTYRS AND SOULS Faithful to the Altar (Rev. 6:9-11)

The martyrs and faithful ones are heard crying for justice. They are told to wait for a while till a further martyrdom takes place (in phase two of the Apocalypse which begins in Revelation 13). Scripture adds some details:

Then you will be handed over to be tortured and put to death; and you will be hated by all nations on account of my name. And then many will fall away; people will betray one another and hate one another. Many false prophets will arise; they will deceive many, and with the increase of lawlessness, love in most people will grow cold; but anyone who stands firm to the end will be saved. This good news of the kingdom will be proclaimed to the whole world as evidence to the nations. Matt. 24:9-14

But before all this happens, you will be seized and persecuted; you will be handed over to the synagogues and to imprisonment, and brought before kings and governors for the sake of my name - and that will be your opportunity to bear witness. Make up your minds not to prepare your defense, because I myself shall give you an eloquence and a wisdom that none of your opponents will be able to resist or contradict. You will be betrayed even by parents and brothers, relations and friends; and some of you will be put to death. You will be hated universally on account of my name, but not a hair of your head will be lost. Your perseverance will win you your lives. Luke 21:12-19

Much of humanity is forming a group opposed to God. Humanity is divided into two groups: the people of God, whose citizenship is in heaven (Phil 3:20), and, in opposition to them, the rebellious people of the world (Rev. 6:15; 8:13; 11:10; 13:3, 8, 12, 14; 17:2, 8). Though in this seal, the focus is specifically on the martyrs, it applies to all the faithful believers. Jesus calls on all His followers to surrender their lives to His Will in order that they may gain eternal life (Matthew 16:24-26; Luke 9:23-26; John 12:25). Final judgment will not come immediately, but only in God's time (Rev. 11; 22:7, 10-12, 17; Luke 18:1-8). The final battle is just beginning.

6th SEAL: HEAVENLY SIGNS

CELESTIAL SIGNS (Rev. 6:12-17)

The sixth seal reveals the celestial signs that will shake up all humanity:

1. A great earthquake
2. The sun turns black
3. The moon turns blood-red
4. The stars (meteorites/comets) fall
5. The sky is rolled back as a scroll
6. The world's population becomes terrified

These are the literal signs that will occur. And when they occur, panic will overtake the inhabitants of the world. Some will think this is the end of the world. But, the Messiah does **not** return to earth in victory to reign anew during this seal, not until the end of the last battle in phase two of the Apocalypse (after the events of Revelation 13-20). Scripture adds some details:

*There will be **signs in the sun and moon and stars**; on earth nations in agony, bewildered by the turmoil of the ocean and its waves; men fainting away with terror and fear at what menaces the world, for the powers of heaven will be shaken.*
*And **then they will see the Son of man coming in a cloud with power and great glory**. When these things begin to take place, stand erect, hold your heads high, because your liberation is near at hand.' And he told them a parable, 'Look at the fig tree and indeed every tree. As soon as you see them bud, you can see for yourselves that summer is now near. So with you when you see these things happening: know that the kingdom of God is near.* Luke 21: 25- 26

During this seal, all dwellers on earth and the cosmos itself experience God's judgment. These verses give the first descriptions in

Revelation of events building up to the Second Coming. In Luke 21:25-27 and Mark 13:24-26, there is also mention of phenomena in the sun, moon, and stars. The mention of seven types of people (Revelation 6:15) suggests complete judgment, as does the characterization of *"the great day of their wrath"* (6:16-17). Since this world is to be so thoroughly shaken, the faithful must prepare now by placing their hopes on God (Heb. 12:25-29; Luke 12:32-34; 1 Cor. 7:29-31).

An earthquake indicates that God is coming, and that the very foundations of the creation respond to his presence (see Revelation 8:5; 11:19; 16:18; Mark 13:8; Exod. 19:18; Isa. 29:6; Matt. 27:54). Phenomena in sun, moon, stars, and sky show the shaking of the old order of the first creation, in preparation for the coming of the new creation (Revelation 21:1; 2 Pet. 3:10-14; Matt. 24:29-30; Isa. 13:10; 24:23). People of all types will recognize that this is the judgment of God. While all finally come to a point of fearing judgment, many will respond with terror rather than with repentance. As with Adam and Eve (Gen. 3:8), they will only think of fleeing and hiding to avoid exposure and punishment (cf. Luke 23:30; Hos. 10:8; Isa. 2:19). But, in this seal, God is calling all to repentance and to His mercy.

The faithful and people of good will, on the other hand, should look forward to this day with anticipation. It represents their vindication and the suppression of wickedness. It is **the great day of [God's] wrath**, not a mindless, arbitrary human anger, but the just anger of God against the evils and corruptions that have spread on earth (cf. Gen. 6), that He longs to replace with His mercy and forgiveness. Let us say now and always: **Jesus, I trust in You.**

The Warning and the Great Miracle

This is the period of the Warning and global illumination of conscience. As the sixth and seventh seals unfold, there will come the Warning, with great conversions. Then comes the Great Miracle. Marian prophecy says the Miracle will come within a year after the Warning.

Our Lady tells us through Fr. Gobbi that the world is in such dire straits due to sin today, and that the only hope for it is a divine intervention, of which it will soon receive in the form of the Warning:

*Today humanity... is sick because of its obstinate rejection of God... is it gravely ill because it has become incapable of loving. The world has been reduced to an immense desert, devoid of love. In it there flourish the bad weeds of hatred, of division, of sin, of unbridled egoism, of impurity, of violence and of war. **Only a great miracle of divine mercy** will be able to save this straying and dying humanity, which has even now touched the depths of its extreme misery.*[17]

Chapter Four

The Seven Trumpets

Ↄ℈

THE SEALING of God's Faithful

By divine authority, the devastation of the **earth**, the **sea** and the **trees** will be delayed until the servants of God are sealed in their foreheads and right hands (mind and actions). Yahweh seals his people who have persevered with **obedience**. The blessings of God are reserved for the obedient (Deuteronomy 28; Ezekiel 20:12-20; Exodus 13:9; Exodus 31:13-17; Ezekiel 9).

Our Lord warns us through Maria Divine Mercy:

*Many question and continue to question just as they did **during the time of Noah.** They were warned but would not listen. They blocked out the voice of My Father when He sent messages through Noah and the other prophets. **Only those who listened and obeyed were saved.**[18]*

We must listen and obey while we still can, so as to receive the Father's special seal of protection.

7th SEAL: THE SEVEN TRUMPETS (Rev. 8:2-11:19)

In the seventh seal, when the Trumpets begin to sound, a time of great devastation will begin on earth, affecting in may cases **a third of humanity** and **a third of the world**. The seven trumpets are:

1st Trumpet: Hail and Fire
2nd Trumpet: A Mountain Burning with Fire in the Sea
3rd Trumpet: Wormwood and Bitter Water
4th Trumpet: Darkness
5th Trumpet: Locusts
6th Trumpet: War
7th Trumpet: Storm

We will now briefly examine each trumpet of the seventh seal:

1st Trumpet

Hail and fire mingled with blood are cast upon the earth: and the third part of trees is burnt up, and all green grass is burnt up. (Rev. 8:7)

2nd Trumpet

A great mountain burning with fire is cast into the sea: and the third part of the sea becomes blood; and the third part of the creatures which were in the sea, and had life, die; and the third part of the ships are destroyed. (Rev. 8:8-9)

3rd Trumpet

A great star from heaven, burning as it were a lamp, falls upon the third part of the rivers, and upon the fountains of waters; and the name of the star is called Wormwood: and the third part of the waters became wormwood; and many men die of the waters, because they were made bitter. (Rev. 8:10-11)

4th Trumpet

The third part of the sun is smitten, and the third part of the moon, and the third part of the stars; so as the third part of them is darkened, and the day shines not for a third part of it, and the night likewise. (Rev. 8:12)

5th Trumpet: First Woe (Rev. 9)

The Bottomless Pit (Abyss) is now opened and an evil host led by Abaddon (Apollyon - Destroyer) the King of the Abyss comes forth. He and his followers proceed to torment mankind for five months - all except those who have received God's Seal at the time of the sealing. These believers were supernaturally protected from Abaddon's power, these who accepted the Seal of God in their foreheads and right hands (minds and actions) at the time of the sealing.

The fifth trumpet blast sets in motion a horrific army of locusts, energized by demonic sources (9:1-2). The imagery derives from Exodus 10:13-15 and from Joel 2:1-11, where a literal locust plague foreshadows even more devastating judgment coming from a divinely commissioned army (Joel 2:11). These infernal monsters attack only the wicked, not the faithful (9:4). The locusts operate for **five months** (v. 5). A normal locust swarm would move on after a few days. This demonic swarm stays for the whole period during which locusts might be seen, emphasizing the severity of this judgment.

6th Trumpet: Second Woe

Four mighty angels are then loosed from the Great River Euphrates (from the region of Iraq). Aided with a force of 200,000,000 they will kill **one third of mankind** by *"fire and smoke and brimstone"* – *"By these three was the third part of men killed, by the fire, and by the smoke, and by the brimstone, which issued out of their mouths"* (Revelation 9:17-18).

Jesus warns about the coming disaster through locutionist Maria Divine Mercy:

Pray that a Nuclear War, which would wipe out One Third of Humanity, can be averted.

*My dearly beloved daughter, My followers must unite together as one family and stay strong. I afford all My beloved and trusting followers the graces to keep calm amidst the storm... The seals have been broken, My daughter, and wars will emerge quickly. Pray that the global atrocity of **a nuclear war, which would wipe out one third of humanity**, can be averted. I need more prayer children. I realize how hard you pray but please, I implore you, invite as many prayer groups, friends and families to pray for peace. (Jesus)* [19]

Our Lady of America confirms this warning of the threat of nuclear war, and she also tells us just how it can be averted, saying:
***If** my warnings are taken seriously and enough of my children strive constantly and faithfully to renew and reform themselves in their inward and outward lives, **then there will be no nuclear war**.*

Prayer for Peace in the World
O My Jesus, I beg for mercy for those afflicted by terrible wars.
I plead for peace to be instilled in those tortured nations who are blind to the truth of Your existence.
Please cover these nations with the power of the Holy Spirit so that they will stop their pursuit of power over innocent souls.
Have mercy on all Your countries who are powerless against the evil atrocities which cover the whole world.
Amen.
www.thewarningsecondcoming.com

The End Times Messenger (Rev. 10)

"The seventh messenger", mentioned in Revelation 10, will take the (now) opened Book of Revelation and prophesy *"against many different nations and countries and languages and kings"* (Rev 10: 11) during this time of its fulfillment. When this happens, the angel of the Lord announces that this is the time of **no more delay** (Rev

10:6), for the consummation of all God's prophetic plans comes with the seventh trumpet.

In March 2012, Jesus told locutionist Maria Divine Mercy that she is *"the seventh messenger"* that is mentioned in Revelation. Jesus said to her:

This time has come for you to open the Book of Truth and reveal the contents therein for all of God's children to prepare their souls for eternal life.

The Book of Truth is being revealed to you, the seventh messenger for the end times.

By the sound of your voice the truth will finally be revealed and the mysteries contained in the Book of Revelation will be presented to a disbelieving world.

But not for long. Despite the apostasy, which will not only affect believers but those sacred servants within the Church, the time for the great confession (the Warning) is close.

Once this takes place great conversion will occur throughout the world.

Then they will be hungry for the truth contained in the unsealed book promised to the world for these, the end times.

*You are **the messenger** who has been given the task not only to prepare the world for the salvation of souls but who will also announce My reign.*[20]

Announcement that the Holy City Will Be Trampled (Rev. 11)

Sometime during this period, the "gentiles" will trample the holy city for 42 months (3.5 years). But, God will send the two witnesses to prophesy for 1260 days (almost 3.5 years).

The two witnesses symbolize two groups of the People of God more than human individuals. The city being trampled is the "city of God", which is "the people of God". It will be trampled by the "city of man" which Revelation calls "the people of the world" (Rev 11:10).

The Two Witnesses mentioned in Revelation (11:3-4) are also called the two olive trees and the two lamps stands. Therefore, it seems the two olive trees represent: **the Law & the Prophets**; while the two lamp stands represent: **Israel (the Jews) & the Church (particularly the Catholic Church)**. Thus, the teachings of the Faith and of the Church will be attacked and "killed" while the two great religions of the inspired Word will also be "killed" for a time. When this happens, "the people of the world" (Rev 11:10) will be glad and exchange gifts. Thus, at the end of this woe, the Beast who ascends from out of the Abyss will kill the Two Witnesses; but after 3½ days they will be resurrected and carried to heaven in great glory.

This event has to do with the temporary fall of both religions, though Revelation says *"the temple and altar"* will remain standing. The temple and the altar are the core foundations of both religions, which will never fall.

7th Trumpet: Third Woe
Announcement of the Ark (Rev. 11:19)

*And the temple of God was opened in heaven, and there was seen in his temple **the ark** of his testament: and there were lightnings, and voices, and thunderings, and an earthquake, and great hail.*

In this trumpet, as we shall see, we see the arrival of the hour of the Woman who is the New Ark.

PHASE 1:
The Great
Tribulation Has Begun!
(Began end of 2012)

ℭℨ

The revelation of Jesus Christ, which God gave to Him,
to show His servants what must happen soon.
He made it known by sending His angel to His servant John,
who gives witness to the word of God
and to the testimony of Jesus Christ by reporting what he saw.
Blessed is the one who reads aloud
and **blessed are those who listen to this prophetic message**
and heed what is written in it,
for the appointed time is near.
Revelation 1:1-4

The Great Tribulation (see Matt. 24:21) has begun and will last 3½ years (2013-2016). Toward the end of this period, the Antichrist will rise to power. Jesus announced this through Maria Divine Mercy (MDM), saying:

The Great Tribulation will commence, as I have said, before the end of 2012.

Jesus has stated that the tribulation spoken of in Matthew 24 has begun, and that the Great Tribulation will began the end of 2012:

*Time is short now. **Everything is going to happen quickly**...*
*You are now, My children, in the middle of what is called the Tribulation as foretold in My Holy Book. **The second part, the Great Tribulation will commence as I have said before the end of 2012**. This is not meant to instill fear in you... but to make you aware of the urgency for My children to pray for My help.[21]*

*For those intellectual experts who proclaim to be able to analyze My teachings and then go as far as attempting to predict a date for when I will come again I say this. If you try to assume that you have been able to discern the year for My return then you are sadly mistaken. No one will be given this date not even the angels in Heaven or My Beloved Mother. But this I can reveal. The Tribulation started some time ago. **The Great Tribulation will begin at the end of 2012.** This terrible period is being mitigated through the prayers of My dearly beloved followers. It will also be diluted through the conversion achieved after The Warning (author's note: this is discussed in an upcoming chapter) takes place. This event is good news My Children. It is to help eradicate the slavery by man to The Evil One.[22]*

YOU, the reader, have a choice:

Turn your back in disbelief, bury your head in the sand,

Or

Believe in faith, take courage, and respond with an open heart...

Then ask: Is God really trying to warn us? Could these heavenly warnings really be based on authentic divine communications? If it is, then what do I need to do?

If you decide to respond, then:

1. Listen and accept the truth of your future options.

2. Decide what path you wish to take.

3. Pray then for your soul and those of your loved ones.

God is sending the world signs and messages to help guide you… *to prepare you so that when all the events occur you will be kept safe*. And this is His final communication!

The Angels of the Great Tribulation – Gabriel, Raphael, and Michael

The Bible speaks of the three great archangels who assist humanity in times of need. One locutionist reveals their mission to us in our time:

*[Gabriel, Raphael, and Michael] are **the Angels of your time**. They are **the Angels of the final time of the purification and the great tribulation**.*

*They are the Angels of your time. To them is entrusted a special task during the period of **the trial and the great chastisement**. To them befalls the task of saving the people of God, of gathering, from every part of the earth, those who are being called to form part of the little remnant which will remain faithful, **in the safe refuge of my Immaculate Heart**.*

*They are the Angels of your time. Above all, they are **the Angels who reveal to you the final events described in the sealed Book**.*

*To the **Archangel Michael** is entrusted the task of leading the cohorts of the angels and of my faithful children into the battle against the trained and well equipped armies of Satan, of evil, of the satanic and masonic forces, now organized on a worldwide scale into a single* *great force, in order to set themselves against God and against his Christ.*

Saint Michael will above all intervene to fight against the ancient enemy, Lucifer, who in the final hour will appear with all the dark power of **the Antichrist***. His is the task of fighting against him and of conquering him, of driving him out into his reign of darkness and fire, offering to your heavenly Mother the chain with which she will bind him, and the key with which to lock the door of the abyss, from which he will no longer be able to come out to harm the world.*

To the **Archangel Raphael** *is entrusted the mission of taking part as a heavenly physician in the great struggle, in order to help you and to heal those who are stricken and wounded.*

As he restored sight to Tobit, so too will he give vision to millions of my poor children, who have been made blind by sins, by errors and by the great darkness of your days, so that they may once again believe and contemplate the divine splendor of the truth.

To the **Archangel Gabriel** *is entrusted the great mission of announcing the return of Jesus in glory, to restore his reign in the world.*

As the heavenly announcement of the first coming of my Son into the world came through him, so once again will he be the bright messenger of the **second coming** *of Jesus in glory. This* **second coming** *will take place in the power and the light, with* **Jesus who will appear upon the clouds of heaven, in the splendor of his divinity, to subject all things to Himself***. And thus the divine power of my Son Jesus* **will be made manifest to the entire created universe***.*

To the Archangel, who is called 'Power of God,' is given the task of announcing to all the closely approaching return of Christ, with the force of his divine power.

For this reason, I invite you today to honor, to pray, and to invoke the protection of these three Archangels, called to carry out such a great mission **in the conclusive time of the great tribulation and to bring you into the heart of the final events***, through which you are now being called to live with confidence and with great hope.*[23]

Chapter Five

The Three Waves of Disruption

CB

The first events of the Great Tribulation will entail three waves of disruptions, as follows:

1) The first entity to cause disruption is the persecution that will be caused by **global political, banking, and so called Human Rights Organizations**. Their goal is power and control.
2) The second entity to cause disruption is the One World Order taking control of **the Middle East**.
3) The third entity to cause disruption will be **Russia and China**. Many countries are now secretly giving over their control to the One World Government. These sinister groups and their political forces will try to dictate how you live.

According to the messages of Maria Divine Mercy:

They will force the people to receive a special identification, known as the Mark of the Beast. **Your money will be worthless.** *Your access to food and other necessities will only be possible through the Mark... Do not take it, as it will be idolatry.*

*The New One World currency, which will be presented to an incredulous community, is designed to control you. Then once that happens they will try to deprive you of food. This New World Order is led by Masonic forces... This will be **worse than what happened to the Jews under the reign of Satan's disciple, Hitler**.*

The Tribulation will be seen clearly in Israel. The Jews will be treated terribly, and wars will spread. Nations will introduce new laws that amount to communism. As one source relates:

Events leading up The WARNING and how communism will have seemed to take over most of the world:
We now apparently are getting closer to this great SUPERNATURAL event. Remember, [today] people rarely use the term 'communism,' but one needs to look at the goals of this political and economic system. One of the goals is the use of art, music, education and media to condition people to accept the essential elements of Marxism without identifying them as such. After a few generations of this conditioning, Marxism becomes the new reality without a violent revolution.

*As Pat Buchanan stated, 'The United States has undergone a cultural, moral, and religious revolution...We are two countries now. We are two countries morally, culturally, socially, and theologically. Cultural wars do not lend themselves to peaceful co-existence. One side prevails or the other side prevails. The truth is that, while we won the Cold War with political and economic Communism, **we lost the war with cultural Marxism, which is now dominant**. Those of us who are traditionalist, we are the counterculture.*'[24]

Afterwards, the antichrist, as the man of peace, will arrange the peace treaty in the Middle East and with Israel, and thus he enter the world stage. **Russia and China will soon control the whole world. But, many people will not see or know this because their workings will be hidden.** They will work to wipe out all traces of God. Then, finally, God's hand of justice will strike.

During this time, **the European Union will crush all traces of God**, and abolish Christianity. The European Union will applaud the false prophet as the rising leader of the new church. He will rule from the city of Rome and proceed to tamper with the true teachings of the Church. **The Church shall remain infallible**, but not through the false prophet and his lies. Through the work of the antichrist and the false prophet, a false sense of peace will be created. **Many will have no idea that the end times are unfolding as they unfold!**

Our Lady makes it clear that we are not to blame God, but realize that what is coming is the result of free will and manmade destruction. And she tells us not to respond to the violence with violence:

*These will be the actions of **man against man**. In this way, no one can blame Almighty God. The destructive fires will not come from heaven but from hell, through the decisions of those whom Satan controls. They will be **large and violent events**, not like those that the world has gotten used to in recent years. There will be **many events because nations will respond**. No one will act sanely or rationally.*

*Anger will pour out and lead to **unheard of violence and destruction**. No one will be spared who lies in its path. All will be touched – good and bad. Now I explain why I speak.*

When all of this happens, I do not want my children to act like the world. I want them to stand apart and not get caught up in the violence. Satan wants you to be in his army. He wants anger to flow from your hearts, just as it will flow so freely from the hearts of your neighbors. He wants to entrap you. He wants you to take up arms. He wants you to strike back. He wants you to yield to his fires of violence. See this for what it is. Everything will be Satanic. The fires will burn in the hearts of the good and the evil person. Satan does not care who fires the bullets, as long as others are harmed and suffer.

*I say this at the top of my voice to everyone who is my child. **When the events begin, you are to hurt no one.** You are not to take up weapons.*

*You are to **flee all violence**, especially the violence that you yourself might cause. If you heed my words, I will save you. If you do not, then you are no better than the rest. These are words that most will reject, but I speak them so some will listen and be saved.*[25]

The war will come in stages and spread quickly; first with Israel, then with Europe, and finally with America. Our Lady says that the radical Muslims *"want to control the world and they will use violence to gain their goal."*[26]

Chapter Six

First Wave:
Economic Turmoil & Collapse

ଔ

The United States is sinking further and further into debt. It is crippled in a great morass, a cesspool of inaction. It is becoming weakened by its severe economic problems. **Europe** continues to battle its debt crisis with inadequate reforms, drawing ever closer to the point when economic collapse seems inevitable. Meanwhile, **China** gains greater global power, having designs to conquer the world. With America's economic debt, China feels it now has the upper hand. One locutionist gives detail as follows:

*This **first round of evil** will begin with **scarcity**, but the greater evil will result from the **selfish response to scarcity**. When nations and groups see themselves as threatened, they will begin to **horde** for the future, setting aside much greater resources than they really need. This creates even greater scarcities because they do not think of others and they **overestimate the problems**. The unity that has been forged in what is called "the global economy" will be tested, stretched out, and, in some cases, broken. Even in the greatest of all unities, **the United***

States, the scarcities will begin to affect life. America was built upon abundance and, with abundance, the belief that all should share. Scarcity will be a new experience for modern Americans. I say that it is not too late for America but people must pray for new leadership.[27]

Our Lady points out that economic collapse is coming:

*The entire (American) system is weighed down and is about to **collapse**. The money will not be there to support the system. Federal and state governments are in debt. No one can shake out the system and rejuvenate it. How long can Washington continue in this way before everything collapses? The warning signs are everywhere, but people think that things will go on as usual.*

*So, I say this clearly, Washington, you are much, much closer to **financial collapse** than you can possibly imagine. It is right around the corner. Yet, you do nothing – deficit after deficit, always making the building higher and paying no attention to the foundation that can no longer sustain your debt.*[28]

*So much will be blown away. So many financial institutions that once stood strong will be swept away in the flood of debt, victims of selfishness and greed... I will call the perpetrators into my courtroom of justice for all to see. I will call elected officials before the people and expose their hearts. I will call owners before the public. When all is revealed, they will call it **scandalous**. So, when scandals abound, when the secrets are made public, when greed and avarice are uncovered, know that I am trying to provide an atmosphere that is clearly **a help to the economy** and can be put in place. Unfortunately, **scandals are needed to correct greed**.*[29]

The Shaking, the Panic, the Calm, and Then the Collapse

American Locutionist continues:

*The world will begin to **shake**. What was thought secure and certain will be seen as toppling and collapsing. This will cause **panic**. It will be followed by a short period of **calm**, when things seem to settle down. Do not be fooled. The original tremors are a warning signal calling people to turn back to their faith. The time of calm is given so decisions can be made and the faith relationship can be restored.*

*I must insist this time of calm is not to be wasted. Otherwise, the final chance will be squandered. After the calm, comes the **collapse**. Every institution not built on solid rock will go under. All of the weaknesses built into the **economic** system will become evident. Trust will vanish. People will say, "Why didn't I see this coming?" **Despair and fear** will grip many. Earth is all they have and their earth is collapsing.*

A Regained Faith

*But those who used the time of calm to strengthen their faith, those who again sought the blessings of the Church and returned with their families to regular worship, these will find the light and strength that they need. Their **newly-regained faith will be their light in the darkness**. I cannot be any clearer.*[30]

When everything begins, there will be many surprises. *Those who were thought to be strong, will fall quickly, while those who seemed to be weak will persevere because of their faith. How will people handle this adversity? First, let me describe what will happen so that those who read my words, can prepare. I will lead them but they must not wait.*

*The **relationships of faith must be made strong**. This is **the way to survive**. People must strengthen their ties to others, the bonds of their faith. When the tragedy first hits, people will be shocked. How could this ever happen? There will be great turmoil and the leaders will be scrambling to come up with answers. But those who have placed themselves in my heart will not give way to useless anxiety. They will have a firmness of heart. They will know my words. This is my promise, "I will provide. I will take care of you". As a mother says to all of her* *children in any crisis, "Stay together. Stay close to me. Do not wander. The road is too dangerous."*

*The great problems will not be in the beginning. In the beginning, there will be shock and wonderment. There will be anger. "How could they allow this to happen?" I am talking about the **economic woes that will come upon the West, and even to America**. Who will survive these drastic changes? Not those with resources (for these will whittle away) but those who bond together in faith and who seek ways to help each other.*

*This will be a time of great sacrifice. **The individualism of America**, sparked by the decades of affluence, will be reversed. People will need each other to survive. Families will be reunited by the need to put together their incomes. New forms of helping others will emerge. Where the churches are vital and alive, the people will coalesce and the church will again become a focal point for the community.*[31]

*The holes are opening up in **the American economy**, gigantic gaps that no amount of money can fill in. American life is spiraling downward and out of control. No one can see **how fast all of this will transpire**. There is still an aura of unreality, as if this could never happen in America.*

O America, you will tumble and tumble, wondering when this downturn will bottom out...

*This is my promise. **If** you place first what I place first and elect officials who hold my values, **then your economy will turn around**. However, if you continue to elect those who are unworthy but promise you economic blessings, your economy will continue to tumble.*[32]

How Far Will the American Economic Collapse Go?

American Locutionist continues:

You see the shaking of the American economic system and the default crisis. **There will be no default.** *At the last minute an* **extraordinary emergency measure** *will rescue America from this problem. However, the economic system will be weakened, especially in the eyes of the world.*

This will send forth waves of uncertainty. Money supplies will tighten, as will credit advances. The effects of this will be felt in all the nations. There will be greater pressures and higher expectancies. The result will be felt most in those countries that are already weak and already have trouble in keeping up with the others... In these countries there will be major economic disasters. (Jesus) [33]

Chapter Seven

Second Wave:
Israel Is the Target

☙

Jesus said to His disciples:
When you see Jerusalem surrounded by armies,
know that its desolation is at hand...
for these days are the time of punishment
when all the Scriptures are fulfilled.
Luke 21:20-22

For a terrible calamity will come upon the earth
and a wrathful judgment upon this people.
They will fall by the edge of the sword
and be taken as captives to all the Gentiles;
and Jerusalem will be trampled underfoot by the Gentiles
until the times of the Gentiles are fulfilled.
Luke 21:23-24

The Great Tribulation will commence with the surrounding of
Jerusalem. Our Lady speaks to us through the American Locutionist

about the convulsions to the great battle, and which will begin in the Middle East:

*This is what faces mankind... **the convulsions of war, economic collapse and massive destructions**. These are **inevitable unless man listens to me**. I say this now so that as the convulsions continue people will remember my word and will gain a measure of hope. They will say, "Our heavenly Mother foresaw all of this. She warned us that this would happen. We must go to her and find refuge **in her Immaculate Heart**".*

*The convulsions **will begin in the Middle East**. The uprisings have removed the obstacles to Satan's plan. The forces of Muslim radicalism can now be joined even more. They will begin to claim control of countries where they had been suppressed. They will have access to more money and to a more open communication. As the American influence lessens, they need not fear any military might coming against them.*[34]

Our Lady says that the shift of power is taking place to set up the beginning of the apocalyptic event:

*[The forces of evil] have moved to control **Egypt** and will do the same in **Iraq**, **Pakistan** and **Afghanistan**. The whole face of that region will change very quickly. Dark clouds will surround **Israel**, which is **their primary target**.*[35]

*Iran will move against its neighbor, **Iraq**, and will control as much as possible. Iraq will suffer much from all the internal struggles and the external incursions. I weep over Iraq to see it dismembered and helpless.*

***Afghanistan** will not stand. Everything will fall. The regime will be toppled and chaos will exist. The Taliban will grow strong and feel that they have no one to oppose them now that America has withdrawn.*

***Pakistan** will become **the biggest problem**. Its borders will be porous and evil will flow freely, back and forth. The military will assume more* control. Civilian leadership will be very weakened and ready to collapse. Al-Qaeda will be waiting in the wings. This will be its **greatest prize – to control nuclear arms**. The stage is set for such a scenario.[36]

The Clash of Nations

Anyone who keeps up with the news can see that the Middle East is realigning itself and its developing outcome is two opposing forces:

*You do not need a keen intellect to see what is ahead, **the clash of nations**. Right now, internal strifes are consuming the energies of many nations in the Middle East. When this process is over and Satan has in place those whom he wants to serve him, he will move into the next phase of his plan.*
*This will take place especially in **Afghanistan** and, most importantly, in **Pakistan**... the whole area will become the easy prey of the terrorists. They will quickly claim everything. No one will oppose them and both countries will fall under their control. This will pose enormous new problems, coupled with the growing nuclear program in Iran. The rise of the Muslim brotherhood in **Egypt** and the new direction of **Turkey**.*
*The nations are in turmoil but God is not just in his heavens. He would help man and he wants the survival of **Israel**. He wants to establish in Israel the great "Light to the Nations", my son, Jesus Christ. This is the battle behind the scenes.[37]*

Not the Muslims as a People

It is important to note that we are not opposed the Muslims as a people, but must be on guard against the extreme radical Muslims. It is they who will bring about the Arab winter of desolation and destruction. One source discusses the dangers:

In these Mideast disruptions, the radical darkness of the Muslim world is hidden but when the current leaders are toppled, they will use this opportunity to diminish the number of the other Muslims, to increase their own converts and to assume leadership in these countries.

Arab Winter of Desolation and Destruction

*These deceptions **will not bring about an Arab spring but an Arab winter of desolation and destruction**. They will not bring about the kingdom of God. They will only enhance the powers of darkness which oppose the kingdom.*[38]

The purpose of these fires was to weaken all the protection, all the buffers around Israel. This is what is happening but this is not meant to be Satan's final attack. (Jesus)[39] *The protection around **Israel** is being stripped away. The natural protections are being removed. A time will come when Israel will have no natural way of protecting itself. At that moment, **I will save Israel** and then the Covenant of my Blood will become the central act. The Church will be enriched by Israel, and all will see that the Catholic Church is the true Church, **when Israel and the Catholic Church are one**. Satan sees the importance of Jerusalem. His eyes are on Jerusalem to destroy it. My heart is on Jerusalem to protect it. (Jesus)*[40]

*There is a small group, tightly knit, which stays hidden. They gather money and resources and plot against **Israel**. Someday, they will inflict damage upon Israel as they did against the Israeli embassy in Egypt (on September 10, 2011). As they draw closer, Israel will have no power to push them back because the buffers of protection have been taken away. It is a difficult and perilous time for Israel. Few know how close the destructive forces are to breaking through the Israeli defenses. (Jesus)*[41]

Nuclear Threat Rises in the Middle East: Watch Out for Iran & Pakistan

The Middle East is preparing itself by the attaining of nuclear weapons:

*There will be a growing power of **Iran** and of **Pakistan**, two countries who have or will have **nuclear arms**. So, the situation is quite grave and their influence will spread. This influence will be evil and destructive, and will totally change the region into a hotbed of potential violence, that will not go away and which cannot be dealt with...*

*Can you not see, O West? You are helpless before these enemies. Your technology and weapons have not conquered because the evil is so deep. When the troops pull out, the next chapter will be written, far worse than this present chapter. Let the reality set in, a reality that my words have tried to express so often. **The battle is between heaven and hell and because you do not seek heavenly help, hell is destroying the world.** Seek heaven's help. Return to faith and belief. Invoke me and I will help you.*[42]

*__Pakistan__ will be a **source of great problems**. The support of the United States and its ties to Pakistan have been weakened by the killing of Bin Laden. The present government, weak as it is, is the only fence standing between the rebels and the **nuclear arms**. When the government is toppled, America will try to secure the arms, but its military might will not be enough. The rebels are too large and too firmly implanted – too extensive among the people.*

Even if the people do not belong to the rebels, they feel no enmity to the group. That is why the government is so weak in its fight against the terrorist group. It does not want to offend a large segment of its people and must make some political responses against the United States. (Jesus)[43]

__The grave danger lies in Pakistan with the weakness of the government, the power of the terrorists and the possession of nuclear weapons.__ This is an explosive mix. Order will unravel quickly, presenting unforeseen problems of an enormous magnitude.

*In all of this, the West just sleeps, tied up in economic problems that seem more important. World leadership slips from the hands of **America** which has no clear identity on the world stage.*

*Satan thinks globally. One event follows another. All are linked together. He knows where the pipelines go and those countries that are so dependent on oil. He wants to attack and destroy that system so the West is thrown into confusion. **Nowhere is the West so vulnerable as in their need for Mideast oil.**[44]* The message is clear: all of this will affect **America** because of its need for oil.

Nuclear arms threaten Israel: *The **nuclear arms** are being moved into place. Soon they will be **aimed at Israel**... **Iran** is not arming itself for self-defense. Satan owns their hearts. From the very beginning, they had **their target, Israel**.[45]*

Orchestrated Wars

*All of the wars you see taking place in the Middle East and beyond have been orchestrated. They are **not a coincidence**. Understand that so many countries at once did not rise up on their own. They were helped by the Evil Group in all Governments. Those Governments who control the World. These leaders in the Middle East are now being removed to make way for the liberators, those who will proclaim justice and peaceful means to help My Children. But that is not their intention. Their intention is to control My beloved people The Jews who are under threat now on all sides.[46]*

The Unfolding of Satan's Drama
& The Point of No Return

The heavenly messages to the American Locutionist reveal that the final preparations for the apocalyptic events have passed a point of no return:

*With the **Egyptian** uprising (in January 2011), the events of darkness have **passed the point of no return**. The **great confrontation** between the devil and the Woman **has begun**. People do not grasp that **events have entered a new stage**. They think these are just a new level of the* *old problems.* **January 2011** *was* **the point of no return** *because Satan decided to begin his drama.*

The Egyptian uprising has meant that Israel has lost some layers of protection. Israel knows that it is endangered more than before. So, **the drama has begun.** *Satan has sent out the first actors in front of the curtain to begin the show. Soon the curtain will pull back and everything will begin in its fullness. (Jesus)*[47]

The significance of the Egyptian uprising, which began in 2011, cannot be underestimated. It is the beginning of what will lead to the ultimate confrontation:

The forces of evil have passed the point of no return. *The ultimate clash between good and evil is* **inevitable.** *Many view the uprising in Egypt in a positive way. They see that a dictator has been removed. However, you must see it in another way, that* **a war has broken out.** *Many see the uprising as good but this is the way Satan acts. He gets people to do his work by making them think that they are pursuing their own goals. Later, when they have done his work, he reveals himself. Then it is too late to do anything. See this clearly.* **Egypt is the first step towards the ultimate confrontation.**[48]

The Center of the Demonic Forces is in Egypt

Our Lady reveals where the center of the evil is:

So, what will happen in **Egypt***? The radical Muslims, with their tight knit unity and their Sha'riah law, will make gains, step by step, because they have a clear goal. They know what they want and they have wanted this for decades. They will not change, especially now that the great prize is closer to their grasps. They will unite even more. They will harden their positions. They will demand concessions far beyond their numbers. When they gain what they ask for, they will begin to ask for even more. This is your state, O Egypt. You thought you were gaining your freedom. Instead, you have only gained a* *different dictator (author wonders if this refers to Morsi??) who will impose greater burdens upon you.*[49]

Cairo (Egypt) is **the center of the demonic forces**. *From there, the disturbances will continue to spread. There is no peace in Cairo and there will never be peace. Satan has set up his stronghold. He owns so many people – the military, the Muslim brotherhood, and by the spread of violence, even those who oppose the military. He holds all in his power, some directly and others indirectly. The city has entered into a darkness that no human efforts can lift...*

As I said before, he fulfills his plans secretly and only when they are in place does he reveal himself. Now, through the army, he is gradually revealing the full depth of his plan. **He has chosen Cairo as his center**. *He has a firm hold. There will never be peace. He does not want it. There will never be reconciliation among all the groups. He ferments only hatred and division.*[50]

A Leader Will Arise Uniting the Middle East

Israel's power will be taken and the only solution will be to sign a treaty where they will become slaves to the antichrist. Our Lord reveals more about what is to come:

All of **these events will tilt the power to the Muslim world** *and many Muslims will rejoice to see that they are gaining the upper hand much more quickly than they thought possible.*

The most important issue has been overlooked. Up to now, the Muslim world has been divided because of the various dictators. Now, these have been or will be soon toppled. There is a new possibility of Muslim **unity brought about by radical Muslims**.

This sudden possibility of some union of **Muslim nations under a religious leader** *will lead many to believe that they can be that leader. Important people will begin to move toward Muslim unity along religious lines. These men will not succeed but they will move the process along.*

*Then, **one will arise** who will take advantage of all of these forces **and will somewhat unite the Muslim world for his purposes**. (Jesus)*[51]

The War Spreads to Europe

Europe is on the verge of economic collapse. It will also suffer from the spreading of war:

Italy will be instrumental in the fall out which will trigger the involvement of global powers in a war – all these events are inevitable but prayer can ease suffering. Pray, My daughter, that people will turn to Me and ask Me for help and guidance through these times of turmoil.
I do not want to see My children suffer. But suffer they will until the truth is revealed during The Warning. Pray now for those misguided dictators who kill innocent souls.[52]

Chapter Eight

Third Wave:

Communist Russia Will Rise Again...

Aligned with China

ॐ

The visionaries of the reported apparitions of Garabandal said in 1965 that all of these apocalyptic-like events would come to pass *"when Communism comes again."* They said:

In the Great Tribulation, there will be a *"sudden and unexpected tribulation of Communism, led by Russia... Russia will rule the world... The Church will be on the point of perishing and will pass through a terrible trial, that of Communism... it will be very hard to practice religion... priests will have to go into hiding... the Pope will not be able to be in Rome either. He was being persecuted too... when Communism comes again, everything will happen (said in 1965,*

Communism fell in 1989)... These difficult events will take place before the Warning because the Warning itself will take place when the situation will be at its worst."

The problem is Russia. *She is **the mother of iniquity**. She loves neither America nor Israel. That is why my mother asked that Russia be consecrated to her Immaculate Heart. When Russia is consecrated all will be drawn together. For now she spreads her iniquity. All the other evil is nourished by her, for she still wants to be the first among the nations. She uses others for her goals, finding partners in evils. (Jesus)*[53]

*The wars that are ahead will be much different. There will be **no clear lines, nor any taking of land**. They will be **wars of destruction, like the world has never seen**, fought quickly but then lingering on, with no clear winner. This is Satan's goal...*

*It is endless and will remain so **until Russia is consecrated to my Immaculate Heart**. Then the heavenly Father will give peace to the world.*

Many will say that Russia is not the problem but I see the truth. I see what happens behind the scenes. Why does anyone trust that leader whose heart is so ambitious to have Russia regain its military and diplomatic powers? He saw these taken away and he wants to regroup them. He is already acting, trying to draw the neighboring nations into a unity which he will use for his demonic plans. Who confronts him? Who opposes him? He acts without any opposition. He is no longer seen as the sinister force. He has changed his costume, but not his heart. Keep your eye on Russia. Do not allow him to expand his influence.

*The West is relaxing. They are saying "Russia is our friend. Russia is no longer a problem". How foolish can you be? **The heart of Russia's leaders still belongs to Satan.** Do not be fooled by the seeming lack of resources. Satan possesses his heart and he can arm him in a second. What do you think Satan is doing in **Iran**? Does not **Russia** delight? Does he not participate? Russia is not on the sidelines. They are active* *participants.* **Wake up!** *I want Russia consecrated to my Immaculate Heart before it is too late. It is already very late.*[54]

To Russia

You beat down your people and tried to build an atheistic system on their backs. You took whatever was in your grasp, deceiving the West and making gains at the bargaining tables, destroying the rights of people who were not your own. This is your twentieth century legacy to the world... Turn back. Your **flirtation with the Middle East** *will not gain your goals. What are you seeking? A new role? A new identity? A return to greatness? If you had been truly great I would not have humbled you by breaking your system. I indeed have humbled you but you did not repent.*

You just sought another road. "I will return to my former greatness", you say in your heart. "I will find new friends with whom to conspire. I will make new arrangements in the Muslim world. With these, I will rise to power again". **You fool!** *They are plotting your destruction, just as they are plotting the destruction of the West.*[55]

Consecration and Conversion of Russia

If the evil is worldwide, then the purging of hearts must also be worldwide. Let the message be clear. First, hearts must be purged, then the evil can be cast out. How ready I am to bring about this worldwide purging but the heart of the world must be prepared. That is why I want a Year of Fatima proclaimed by the Holy Father to prepare for the **Consecration of Russia** *to my Immaculate Heart. Let him not delay!*[56]

In the midst of strife, you must say "The Evil One is at work", but even more, you must say, **"I will invite Mary, the Woman***, the sworn enemy of Satan. She will defeat him." Yes, just ask me to come, whenever there is strife. I will come and the sting of Satan will have no power. The issues can be resolved in light and the solutions will be lasting ones.*

*This is why I ask that **Russia** be consecrated to me. I am waiting and waiting to be invited. I wait in the wings waiting for my cue to come onto the world stage. When I come, I will overcome the Evil One.*

Why do I wait for the whole church to invite me? Why do I want the Pope and the bishops to do this publicly? When a couple invites me, I come on the family stage. So, when the whole Church invites me, I come on to the world stage. By this public worldwide invitation, all will know, "Mary has been invited". When invited, I will release all my powers and the fires of hell will be quenched. Then, man can solve his disputes according to right reason.[57]

When all the world knows that it is calling on God, he will act so the world will see the connection and will know who brought about his rescue. This is why the Consecration of Russia to my Immaculate Heart must be done publicly, for all the world to know. Then, when the whole course of human history is changed, all will recognize that it has come from heaven.[58]

The Two Consecrations (of Russia) – One Done, One Still Needed

Our Lady responded favorably to the Marian Year (1987) that was declared by Bl. John Paul II:

*Do not be afraid to pierce the mysteries because these are mysteries of life, which will bring eternal life to those who follow my words. Now, there are towers of death, powerful and seemingly invincible. These will collapse like the Communist system. My son, Pope John Paul II, **consecrated a year to me** (1987) and look at what happened during that year. The wall came down and Communism was toppled, without a single shot being fired and without war being declared. All of this happened before the eyes of all, on the 2000 anniversary of my birth, deliberately highlighted by the pope from behind the Iron Curtain. It was for him that I did this.*

*Now, **I will raise up another person who will do a greater consecration, the one I have asked for at Fatima**. All the world will* *know that this has been done, completed with all the bishops and with the world looking on…*

*What will happen when the pope consecrates Russia to my Immaculate Heart? My armies will go forth. I will call all the little ones. They will know that my great request has been fulfilled. They will say, "We are at a new moment in history. It has taken us **almost 100 years** (since 1917) but at last, the request has been fulfilled." There will be a new hope and a new spirit. All those who worked so hard to bring this about, will experience unbelievable joy. They will have a new power. They will know that their Queen has finally been proclaimed and that I finally am placed on the lampstand. This will not just be a mental reality. I will send my presence all over the world. My army will experience that I am with them. Then, they will march.*[59]

The New Rise of Russia and Why the 1984 Consecration Was Accepted but Not Enough

*The popes made numerous dedications and whenever a dedication was made, I showed my response by great blessings. Yet, **my request for the Consecration of Russia to my Immaculate Heart to be made by the pope in union with all the world's bishops has not been made**. The evil has not been attacked as I directed, so it still resides in the heart of this country which is so expansive…*

*Now, the stage is set. Russia is clawing its way back into prominence. The goals are clear, the same goals they have always had – **to destroy other nations** and to co-op other nations by circumstances so that they become **a world power**.*

Of itself, Russia does not have the resources to dominate the world, but if they entrap other nations (as they did with the Iron Curtain), then they can lift themselves to prominence…

*What would connect nations (today)? The answer is selfish interests that look to the destruction of other nations. Evil has a great power to unite. When **evil interests are shared by nations that are looking to rise to power**, then the bonds become very strong even though the nations themselves seem very different. This is what is happening behind the scenes. So, **open your eyes to Russia**.*[60]

*There will be no lasting peace until every atomic weapon is destroyed and man returns to the simplicity of the pre-atomic age. Can this ever happen? It is **the only solution**. These arms cannot continue to be in man's power and never be used. Can man return to that moment when these weapons of war never existed? **I hold that grace in my Immaculate Heart and I await the consecration of Russia**.*[61]

*So, I must stress this again. I want the Holy Father to consecrate **Russia**, in union with all the bishops of the world, to my Immaculate Heart. Then Russia will be truly mine and I will begin to work signs and wonders. Both the West and the East will see what I am doing. Everything will go forth and all will begin. **This will be the first act in the new drama**.*[62]

The Pope Must Proclaim a Year of Fatima

*I wait for the Consecration of Russia to be done by the Holy Father. He must move quickly before it is too late. The world events must convince him that no other force exists that can turn back **the satanic destruction of the world and of the Church that is taking place**. Mankind will be helpless and the Church will be helpless. (There will be scandal after scandal.)*

Everything is going in reverse. Power is slipping away, both from world leaders and Church leaders. The bonds of stability that held the world together are loosening. The world does not know what to do but the Church knows and the Pope knows. The Pope must cut away those who tell him to stay away from Fatima. They are the voices of Satan and need to be silenced.

***The Pope must draw near to Fatima**. He must study Fatima. He must encircle himself with advisers who both know and love Fatima. He must preach on Fatima. He must instruct the whole Church. He must tell the bishops that they are to fully embrace the message and teaching of Fatima... I will bring the people back to the sacraments. This will quickly prepare for the Consecration of Russia. Fervor will return. Hearts will see the great mistakes they have made. There will be a gigantic "turning back". However, the effort must be "all-out". A* *letter will not suffice. A homily, here or there, won't even be noticed. Even to speak of me in a general way, will gain no attention.*

So, I speak to my son, my beloved Pope. Place the light of Fatima in your own heart. Let that light grow. Let that light diminish all the other lights, even the brilliant light of your human plans. The world, at this point, does not need your theological teachings, (as brilliant as they are). They need my simple teachings that I gave to the three children, especially to Lucy. She is a light placed under a bushel basket and it is time for you to put her on the lampstand.[63]

Go to Fatima Now

Command to the Holy Father

What can I say to you? How much must I warn you? Go to Fatima! Take all the believers with you. Go to Fatima as quickly as possible! All that you need lies in my Immaculate Heart at Fatima. Do not listen to those in high places who caution prudence or who tell you to wait. Holy Father, lead my Church to Fatima. Why are you waiting? What is the delay? If I had not spoken, if I had not appeared, if I had not placed the treasures there, then I could excuse you. Things would not be so clear. Clear away your desk. Set aside the other issues. Proclaim a year of Fatima. Be very specific. Get people to read my messages. Get them to understand the great blessings that remain unopened. People need concrete advice on how to walk. This is a clear path. Before the destruction begins, I want my whole Church to go to Fatima. I will be there.

Let no one ask in the middle of all that will happen, "Where is Mary?" I have told you where I am. Those who go there, in body or in spirit, will be kept safe.[64]

The Woman Asks for the Fatima Secret to Be Published in Full

Mankind, this is where you are. How foolish you are to think that Satan can possess nuclear arms and never use them. They will be used. How far and how great the destruction depends on your turning to me, *on how many **listen to my words and come into my Immaculate Heart**. Let the Church proclaim these words. The Church can reveal the full secret of Fatima. I have already spoken. The Church need only say, "This is what the Virgin of Fatima has said".*

Why are my words held back? Whose so-called prudence is covering over my Wisdom? If I have spoken these words (and were they not given to the most faithful of my messengers – the three children of Fatima), then why are they not published? If they are not published, I will remove those who are covering them over and replace them with my true servants who will release the full light of Fatima.[65]

Our Lady reportedly says through the American Locutionist that she has now waited long enough for the world to respond:

*I have waited ninety-five years (1917 to 2012) for mankind to respond and share with me in this glory. I will begin to intervene, not because mankind has heeded my messages, but because **I cannot wait**. Those who are with me will get the glory. **I will intervene unilaterally**, without the cooperation of mankind which has delayed ninety five years. I intervene unilaterally because, if I wait any longer, the world would destroy itself. So, let us begin. Know that **my heavenly intervention has now started**.*[66]

HOW China & Russia Are Going To Take Control

Jesus reportedly discusses through MDM how China (the Red Dragon) and Russia (the Bear) will take control so easily:

Each nation will be taken over by another. They will fight amongst each other for power. Many nations will begin to introduce laws, which amount to communism.

Then there will come a time when the Red Dragon and the Bear will control all, but many people will not realize this because much of this dictatorship will be hidden from public eyes.

Know this. When attempts to wipe out the Name of God take root, and you become slaves to lies, then the Hand of My Father will strike.

One third of the world will be wiped out and Divine Intervention will continue until the last day. To mitigate the evil laws, which will be introduced into your countries, where the Truth will be hidden from you, you must recite this Crusade Prayer (87) to protect nations from evil.

Crusade Prayer (87) Protect our Nation from Evil

O Father, on behalf of Your Son save us from communism.
Save us from dictatorship.
Protect our nation against paganism.
Save our children from harm.
Help us to see the Light of God.
Open our hearts to the Teachings of Your Son.
Help all Churches to remain true to the Word of God.
We beg You to keep our nations safe from persecution.
Dearest Lord look upon us with Mercy
no matter how we offend You.
Jesus, Son of Man, cover us with Your Precious Blood.
Save us from the snares of the evil one.
We implore You, dear God, to intervene and stop evil from engulfing
the world at this time. Amen.

MDM continues:

Pray, pray, pray for the Heart of My Father is broken at the speed in which sinful laws are being brought before every nation on earth at this time on earth. Hope, pray and trust in Me so that this devastation can be diluted.

Pray that we as many of God's children will keep their eyes open at all times and they remain loyal to the Truth of the My Teachings.[67]

Our Lady adds:

*Soon, **divisions will be forced** upon Christians. This is why united you will become a strong army worthy to proclaim the Word of God. Divided, you will be sucked into a vacuum where **pagan laws will be forced upon your Church**. When you cause division there can be no unity. Only those strong of faith, united within the Heart of my Son, will forge ahead in my Son's army.*[68]

Chapter Nine

The Importance of Medjugorje

CB

If you follow Mary you wind up with Jesus.
I don't mean be a follower of – I'm just saying what happens if you
follow her… If you follow a drunk you wind up at a liquor store.
If you follow a nun from Mother Teresa's order you wind up in the
company of Jesus in his distressing disguise of poverty.
These are just things that happen.
If you follow Mary, from the beginning of the story right through to the
end, you wind up with Jesus.
There is NO other reason to follow Mary. Don't let anyone trick you
into thinking Catholics believe differently.
Words of a street evangelist

Do whatever He tells you!
Mary's last words in the Bible (John 2:5)

Our Lady has been reportedly appearing and giving messages in
Medjugorje since 1981. In our times, another heavenly apparition of

major significance is *Medjugorje*. It is the greatest reported Marian apparition in history, and it will be the final of her apparitions given *in this way* until the end of time. Unprecedented in history, Our Lady Queen of Peace has been visiting with visionaries *daily* for over a quarter century, so as to form us in her School of Prayer and Holiness, just as she did her Son in His daily life in Nazareth. The Church confirms that the faithful may meditate on the messages, spread them and that **private pilgrimages to Medjugorje are permitted**. There have been many significant supporters of this still-ongoing apparition.

Blessed John Paul II wrote in his own hand, *"I thank Sophia (a friend) for everything concerning Medjugorje. I, too, go there everyday as a pilgrim in my prayers."* He also said: *"Medjugorje is the hope for the entire world, the spiritual heart of the world."*

Blessed Mother Teresa, again in her own hand, wrote: *"We are all praying one Hail Mary before Holy Mass to Our Lady of Medjugorje!"*

Hundreds of cardinals and bishops have visited Medjugorje as pilgrims (or have expressed their support for what is happening there), along with tens of thousands of priests and tens of millions of lay pilgrims.

The Ten Secrets

As I reported in my book, *The Secrets, Chastisement, & Triumph*, just as at Fatima in 1917 when Our Lady had given the visionaries three secrets, so too, at Medjugorje, Mary is reportedly giving the visionaries **ten secrets** of worldwide significance. The first three secrets of Medjugorje have to do with warnings. According to visionary, Mirjana, ***"The first two secrets** (the first of which is 'not good' and will 'shake us up') come as advance **warnings** for the whole world and as proof the Blessed Virgin Mary is here in Medjugorje,"* while **the third secret concerns a *"permanent, indestructible and beautiful"* Sign** that will appear in Medjugorje on the hill of the first apparitions, which will remain until the end of time. Our Lady has promised to leave a supernatural, indestructible, and visible sign on the mountain where she first appeared. Our Lady said: *"This sign will be given for the atheists. You faithful already have signs and you have become the sign for the atheists. You faithful must not wait for the sign before you convert; convert soon. This time is a time of grace for you. You can never thank God enough for His grace. The time is for deepening your faith and for your conversion. When the sign comes, it will be too late for many."* The sign is to bring many to reconciliation and conversion. The Sign that will appear in Medjugorje will bring great joy to many. But, pertaining to this Sign, Mirjana said: *"After the visible Sign those who are alive will have little time for conversion."* It seems that many will see the miracle and believe – there will be many conversions – but that others may at this point see the miracle and still not believe or convert. Mary speaks to us today, saying: ***"Hurry to be converted. I need your prayers and your penance."*** In this regard, she also said: *"Return to prayer! Nothing is more needed than prayer."* When the Sign comes, then we will know that the world's punishment is near.

The final secrets are very serious. Our Lady has said that the eighth secret is worse than the other seven. The ninth secret is even worse. The tenth secret is utterly dire and cannot be lessened whatsoever, she said. The ninth and tenth secrets are grave matters. They are a chastisement for the sins of the world. The punishment is inevitable because we cannot expect the conversion of the entire world. The chastisement can be lessened by prayers and penance, but it can not be suppressed entirely. Visionary Mirjana says that Mary asks us to prepare spiritually and not to panic, but to convert now. Mirjana says that God is love, only love, and that cruelty and evil come from Satan. Those who freely choose Satan and disobey God's Commandments will perish. Punishments come for the sins of the world. When all the secrets have been given to all six of the visionaries, then the apparitions will cease on a daily basis, and the secrets will begin to occur, some of which will be announced to the world (what, how, and where) three days before each occurs by the spiritual director of the visionaries (Mirjana has chosen Fr. Petar Ljubicic, O.F.M.).

The secrets are conditional. An evil which threatened the world as part of the seventh secret has been eliminated through prayer and fasting. For that reason the Blessed Virgin continues to ask for prayer and fasting. The invitation to prayer and penance is destined to ward off evil and war and above all to save souls. Our Lady says: *"You have forgotten that with prayer and fasting you can ward off wars, suspend natural laws."[69]*

Through the American Locutionist, Our Lady says:

*These are my clear words. You are on the brink of **nuclear war**. You are helpless. Your rational approaches cannot defeat the evil that is being unleashed. Your treaties are useless. Your diplomatic approaches have failed, one after another.*
*I wait for you. I can lead you away from **the coming catastrophes**. These catastrophes I have revealed to the children of **Medjugorje**. They already know them. They are my **ten secrets**. Yet, I gave them a **message of hope**, but their words are muted. Many have not heard. The Church must proclaim them with full voice. How long must the visionaries persevere until the Church sees their words as so vital? Why not bring the story to the center? Why not bring the visionaries into the limelight? No longer keep them in the shadows. The validity of these apparitions is attested to on every side.[70]*

Fatima and Medjugorje – Preparing for a Greater Light

Relating the messages and Miracle of the Sun that occurred at Fatima (1917) with the messages and great Miracle that will occur at Medjugorje (and also at Garabandal), Our Lady told locutionist Fr. Gobbi:

*You will see very soon the extraordinary signs which I will give, in order that you may **prepare yourselves for the very great miracle***

*which is at this time about to be accomplished. The miracle of the sun, which took place during my last apparition (at Fatima), was only a prophetic sign to indicate to you that you should all **look at the Book which is still sealed** (Revelation). **Today I am being sent by God to open this Book**, in order that the secrets may be revealed to you.* "[71]
God is sending Mary to open the Book of the Apocalypse, and to reveal its mystery, in our times.

Through the American Locutionist, Our Lady says:

Today, I pour out the deepest words of my Immaculate Heart...
*At an important moment, as the New World was just beginning to open up to the European explorers, I appeared to St. Juan Diego at **Guadalupe**. There began the greatest moment of conversions to Jesus in all of history, a power that continues until this day.*
*Can this not happen again? Cannot the Father again send me as his heavenly messenger. It has already happened. The sun itself was shaken at **Fatima**. The visions continue each day at **Medjugorje**. Both of these will come into a full brilliance. Their light has not been spent. These two sites are preparing hearts but the full brilliance of my Son is still to come – soon, so very soon. Prepare the way of the Lord.*[72]
*'**Go to Medjugorje'**. I am not speaking physically (although that benefits everyone). I am speaking spiritually.*[73]

The Hope of Medjugorje

Our Lady is revealing the future of the World at Medjugorje:

*What lies ahead is hidden from man's view, but revealed by God to those whom he loves, so that these events will be a sign to all the world of the power of God, and of the care of God. These events I have revealed to the visionaries of Medjugorje and I will continue to reveal them until the revelations come to their fullness. Then all will be ready for the "unveiling of **the secrets**"...*
I will continue to appear until all of them have the ten secrets. Then, the stage will be set for the gradual revealing of the secrets followed

by their fulfillment. Learn about this little village. Learn about my apparitions. So many graces are contained in these revelations.[74]

The Secrets of Medjugorje, which will be pre-announced publicly 3 days prior to their occurrence, are indications of future events and how the Providence of God is in control of all things. American Locutionist discusses as follows:

I speak to the nations, but they do not listen. I speak to the Church. Even the Church does not listen. So, I speak to my chosen ones. My voice is clear and I do not mince my words or hide truths with high-sounding language. The issues are too important.

When the Clash Comes
*When everything comes to a head, when the powers of good and evil clash, the following will take place and the power of evil will become so evident. All will see that the world is being permanently changed. The power of good will seem to be absent. "Where is God?" they will cry out?" This is **the beginning stage**. It seems that only evil has power and that it will conquer all. This is like the early days of World War II when Hitler's armies moved so quickly. Seemingly, no force was present to oppose him.*
*The good people **must not despair**. The heavenly Father has not abandoned them. They must remember that he saw these events before they happened and that I even arranged through the children of **Medjugorje** that **the great events will be announced to the world three days before they happen**. I did this to give **hope**. People will say, "Our mother knew about these events. She will be with us".*

Learn About Medjugorje
*That is what you should learn from Medjugorje. **I know the future events**. I have revealed them already to the visionaries and they will reveal them to the world. I have done all of this to give hope in the middle of the darkness. Learn about my special actions to these visionaries. Read the stories. They will bring you to faith.*[75]

The Greatness of Medjugorje

I will open up doors that have been closed from all eternity, special doors of saving graces that have never been seen before. At first, many will not believe. They will question, "Can these graces really be from heaven?" This has already begun at **Medjugorje** *but many still question. How can I appear every day for years and still the world does not believe or listen to my messages?...*

Now, let me continue. **Medjugorje is my light, a light set on the mountain for all to see.** *From there will come forth a saving stream. Yes, let all eyes and ears be upon that little village because from it will come those words that are important for all the world to hear. Let the village become even more known and loved. The streams of grace which I have planted there are deep and only the beginning waters of grace have, as yet, gone forth. Do not say "We have tasted of the waters of Medjugorje and they have not provided all that we need." Go back to those waters, read my messages. Pray and repent. Above all, prepare. Soon, so very soon, Medjugorje will no longer be just a stream. It will be* **a mighty ocean covering the world with a knowledge of God and of events which come from his hands**. *Do not wait. If you prepare your hearts, you will receive much. If you do not prepare, you will have broken cisterns that hold no water.*[76]

PHASE 2: The Great Apostasy

☙

Meanwhile, the Church will continue to suffer interior division and apostasy, which will become more defined and blatant. Our Lady announces what's coming through Fr. Gobbi:

The times which were foretold to you by the prophet Zechariah have now come –

***I will strike the shepherd**, and the sheep will be completely scattered; and then I will turn my hand against the little ones.*

*In all the land, **two thirds of them will be cut off and perish**; and one third shall be left.*

***I will pass this third through fire**; I will refine it as silver is refined, test it as gold is tested.*

It will call upon my Name, and I will hear it; I will say: "This is my people." And it will say: "The Lord is my God." (Zech. 13:7-9)[77]

Chapter Ten

A False Christ &

A False Church

CB

Let's summarize what the Bible and prophecy says about the false Christ and the false church:

- The Scriptures say that all the leaders of the world will commit adultery with Antichrist.

- He will be the false christ leading the world.

- He shall make an agreement with the many for a 7-year period.

- But, half way through, he will abolish the Mass (the sacrifice and oblation). He will set up the horrible abomination (see

Daniel 9:27, 12:11). This abomination will make everything desolate.

- When this occurs, Jesus says that the faithful are to flee to the mountains (Mt. 24:16, Mk. 13:14, Lk. 21:21). In Luke, Jesus further says that we will know the time has arrived when we see armies surrounding Jerusalem.

- He will be given a mouth to utter proud words and blasphemy against God, to blaspheme His Name, and His tabernacle, and them that dwell in heaven (the Saints), and to exercise his authority for forty-two months (Revelation 13:5).

- This shall go on for 1,290 days. It shall be a time unsurpassed in distress since nations began.

- Finally, 45 days later (total of 1, 335 days), the power of the destroyer of the holy people will be brought to an end (Daniel 12:7-12).

As Our Lady discusses through Fr. Gobbi:

The beast with the two horns like a lamb indicates Freemasonry infiltrated into the interior of the Church, *that is to say,* *ecclesiastical Masonry*, *which has spread especially among the members of the hierarchy. This Masonic infiltration, in the interior of the Church, was already foretold to you by me at Fatima, when I announced to you that Satan would enter in even to the summit of the Church... The task of ecclesiastical Masonry is that of destroying Christ and His Church, building a new idol, namely a false christ and a false church...*

Ecclesiastical Masonry goes as far as even *building a statue in honor of the beast and forces all to adore this statue...* *they substitute for God a strong, powerful and dominating idol.* *An idol so powerful that it puts to death all who do not adore the statue of the beast*. *An idol so strong and dominating as to cause all, small and great, rich and* *poor, freeman and slaves, **to receive a mark** on the right hand and on the forehead, and that no one can buy or sell without having this mark, that is to say, the **name of the beast or the number of its name.** **This great idol**, built to be served by all, as I have already revealed to you in the preceding message, **is a false church and a false christ.**[78]*

*Freemasonry, assisted by its ecclesiastical form, will succeed in its great design: that of setting up an idol to put in the place of Christ and of his Church. **A false christ and a false church.** Consequently, **the statue built in honor of the first beast**, to be adored by all the inhabitants of the earth and which **will seal with its mark** all those who want to buy or sell, is that of the Antichrist. You have thus arrived at the peak of the purification, of the great tribulation and of the apostasy. The apostasy will be, as of then, generalized because **almost all will follow the false christ and the false church.** Then the door will be open for the appearance of the man or of the very **person of the Antichrist!***

Chapter Eleven

How the False Prophet Will Take Control

from Within the Church

☙

St. Hildegard, who is the newest (35th) Doctor of the Church, explains about the rise of the Antichrist, saying:

When the great ruler exterminates the Turks almost entirely, one of the remaining Mohammadans will be converted, become a priest, bishop and cardinal, and when the new pope is elected (immediately before Antichrist) this cardinal will kill the (newly elected) pope before he is crowned, through jealousy, wishing to be pope himself; then when the other cardinals elect the next pope this cardinal will proclaim himself Anti-pope, and two-thirds of the Christians will go with him.

The Church-approved apparitions of Our Lady of Akita offer more details as follows:

*With the Rosary, pray for the Pope, the bishops and the priests. The work of **the devil will infiltrate even into the Church** in such a way that one will see cardinals opposing cardinals, and bishops against other bishops. The priests who venerate me will be scorned and opposed by their Confreres. The churches and altars will be sacked. The Church will be full of those who accept compromises and the demon will press many priests and consecrated souls to leave the service of the Lord. The demon will rage especially against souls consecrated to God.* (Our Lady of Akita)

Chapter Twelve

The True Pope: Peter the Roman

❧

The pope will have much to suffer.
Fatima

There have been many prophecies about the apostasy that has already begun within the Church. **St. Malachy** was a twelfth century Saint prophesied **concerning** the final true Pope of our time, **the Pope who will reign after Pope Benedict XVI**, stating about him:

*In **the final persecution** of the Holy Roman Church there will reign **Peter the Roman**, who will feed his flock amid **many tribulations**, after which **the seven-hilled city (Rome) will be destroyed** and the dreadful Judge will judge the people.*

Also, Joachim of Fiore prophesied:

Antichrist will overthrow the pope and usurp his see.

John of Vitiguerro (13th century) added:

*The pope will change his residence and the Church will not be defended for twenty-five months or more because, during all that time there will be **no Pope in Rome**... [But] after many tribulations, a Pope shall be elected out of those who survived the persecutions.*

About what will happen to the Pope as he flees Rome, St. Pius X, early in the twentieth century revealed some detail, saying:

*I saw one of my successors taking to flight over the bodies of his brethren. He will take refuge in disguise somewhere; and after a short retirement **he will die a cruel death**. The present wickedness of the world is only the beginning of the sorrows which must take place before the end of the world.[79]*

John of the Cleft Rock (14th Century) also prophesied:

*Towards the end of the world, tyrants and hostile mobs will rob the Church and the clergy of all their possessions and will afflict and martyr them. Those who heap the most abuse upon them will be held in high esteem... At that time, the Pope with his cardinals will have to flee Rome in tragic circumstances to a place where they will be unknown. **The Pope will die a cruel death** in his exile. The sufferings of the Church will be much greater than at any previous time in her history.[80]*

He also said:

*It is said that twenty centuries after the Incarnation of the Word, the Beast in its turn shall become man. About the year 2000 A.D., **Antichrist** will reveal himself to the world.[81]*

And as Our Lady of Fatima famously warned:

*Russia will spread her errors in every country, raising up wars and persecution against the Church; many will be martyred. **The Holy Father will have much to suffer**, and many nations will be destroyed.*

The Church, the Mystical Body of Christ, is about to undergo her final persecution and crucifixion, before entering into her glorious resurrection into the era of peace.

Pope Will Flee Rome Before the Warning

Jesus reportedly speaks through locutionist MDM, stating:

*My Holy Vicar **Pope Benedict needs your prayers**. Pray for him daily for he needs protection on every level to take him through the torment that lies ahead. It is important that My followers keep alert to **any new Pope that may come forward for he will not be from God**...*
*The **Church of Peter is My church**. But when the keys are handed back to God the Father, which they will be now, **the church becomes part of My Kingdom. I am the truth. Follow the truth at all times.***

*Pray to Me now for the graces required to ensure you will rise above the deceit of Satan in time. Otherwise, **the False Prophet** will ensnare My beloved children through his charismatic, charmful ways. The ways of The Deceiver with whom he is entangled. **Satan will not win over My Church** if My servants are alert to the deceit and see it for what it is. A diabolical lie from which, if you become involved and swear allegiance to this **new abomination**, there will be no return! I love you all and yearn for your support during **these End Times**.*[82]

*Pray for My beloved **Pope Benedict**. He is surrounded by very powerful enemies of God. Gluttons for power and control of My Church. Prayer can help delay his imminent departure when he **will be forced to leave The Vatican as foretold**. Pray, pray, pray for this period in time for it will be the darkest ever to befall my sacred servants, Bishops, Cardinals and all true followers of Mine. The keys of Rome will now be handed back to God, the Almighty Father.*
***The time has come for the [great] battle** against Satan and his evil followers. Their attempts to sabotage mankind will be dealt with most severely for they will endure great suffering for their evil acts.*

*Rise now, My children. Place all your trust, confidence and devotion to Me as a priority. **Daily prayer, Mass and The Eucharist** will help Me, and My Father, stamp out this evil.[83]*

*My beloved Vicar's days are now numbered. He will have **left the Vatican before The Warning** takes place. Trust in Me. Obey Me. You are now progressing well. But never take your eyes away from Me. Do not, however, be afraid to **live your life as you would normally** as long as prayer and devotion to Me is an integral and important part. [84]*

When the Pope Goes to Israel

According to American Locutionist, the Pope will go to Israel in an act of peace:

*I will call a son from the West and he will go to the Middle East. He will bring no armaments of war, no secular powers, no large bureaucracy. He will come because I have given him my word. He already knows to come. To come and to lay down his life and to plant afresh the seed of God's word. He will be **my Pope**. With him, will come others, not to conquer any land or to claim any kingdom. They will come only because I said to them, "Go to where I lived. Go to where my Son preached". All of them will go in faith and when they come, they will do only what I tell them to do. There will be only a short time, just as my Son preached only a short time. They will find disciples and they will carry on the word.[85]*

Mary's Gift to **Israel** will be her Message & the Pope. She advises Israel as follows:

*Now you have other enemies, with even greater weapons. They, too, surround you on every side. Your future is no longer in your hands. Do not trust your weapons and your armies. Your forefathers did that with the Romans and failed. Your Messiah came to save you and you rejected him. Now, I come, a true daughter of Israel. **I come with my words to save you**. Listen to these messages and I will lead you by a* *safe path.* **Then, I will send my son, the Pope**, *who will bring the gift of peace.*[86]

*Just as when God raised up Cyrus and set his seal upon him to allow the exiles to return, so I will raise up someone according to my own heart. He, too, will act in a surprising way. You will know who it is. Like Cyrus, he will be known to the nations. When he acts, you will also know that he is acting totally on your behalf. He will do this unselfishly because he is not an Israeli. He will come because I have sent him. His heart will be gentle and kind. You will ask him, "Why did you come to save us?" He will respond, "**The woman clothed with the sun sent me.** She is from you. She is one of you. She has not forgotten you even though you have rejected her Son".*

A New Beginning
Then, Israel, we will begin again. The former rejections will be set aside. The old will be swept away. I will take you to myself. Like the nations, you, too, will call me "Mother".[87] Jesus adds: **Jerusalem is at the center** *of My Heart because* **there I will gather the nations for world peace.** *(Jesus)*[88]

To the Church in the Middle East
How dark it is for my Church in **the Middle East**. *Satan is uprooting the Church that has been planted for centuries, but I will place a new vineyard there.*
The strife will continue and believers will be caught in the crossfire of constant turmoil. The Church will be severely damaged. I will weep and I will wait for my son, the pope, to come and place a new vine in the old vineyard. Many will see it as small, but it will be young and vibrant, freed from the past divisions, a new Church, a free Church, **an Israel Church**, *planted in the right soil.*[89]

The Pope's Death in Jerusalem
Although I do not reveal the exact time and dates (for this is not yet needed), I point to **the signs of the times** *which all can read. When the exact moments come closer, I can be more specific because all can*

understand. Before the culminating events, other moments will happen which will lead up to it. It will not come as a surprise to anyone who listens to my words. This is why I speak, to prepare you so that when all the events occur you will be kept safe. Your house will be built upon rock and will not collapse…

Pushing back the time of these events is just a delay, not a postponement. The clash must come. *This is the only way to dispel these forces of evil. They have claimed too many hearts and the message of repentance does not reach these hearts. They **are intent on a holy war and on the destruction of Israel**. They will not turn back. They believe that their cause is a holy one and that they will quickly dominate the world. This force has been building for centuries, consolidating its powers, suffering losses at some moments, but always moving forward, convinced that its cause is true and will inevitably conquer.*

*What can I do with such an evil force, which uses the sword to gain its goals? My Son told his followers to put away the sword and to lay down their lives for each other. This will be **the turning point, when my son, the pope, will lay down his life**. Then, the Spirit of Jesus will be poured forth upon a world in shock, a world made ready to weep and repent. Before that, much must take place.*[90]

***Jerusalem is the world's center stage**, where two dramas are played out. The first was 2000 years ago. The second will be in modern times. Jerusalem is the world stage where the kingdoms of good and evil clash.*

There will be efforts to gain peace for Israel but these will fail. These efforts are good but the world leaders do not see the depth of the problem, or the deeper clash that only faith reveals…

*There will also be a modern drama. At just the right moment in the Father's plan, **the Pope will go to Jerusalem**. Again, there will be anger and hatred. He will go **as a man of peace**. The **enemies** will use violence, as they have so often used terrorism. Their hatred against Israel will spill over. **Their weapons will kill the Pope**. Yet, he will be the victor. By his death, the weapons of violence will be seen for what they are – weapons that would strike down my Vicar, the great man of* *peace, who came to Jerusalem in my name.* **His death will usher in the gift of peace for the whole world, especially for Jerusalem.** *(Jesus)...*

[The Pope] will enter the city like Jesus, a messenger of God's peace... There will be the Pope's death, but I will temper the sufferings and remove the unnecessary torments. Death will come suddenly and quickly.[91]

Rome and Jerusalem

Great vision is needed because **the devil believes that he is finally able to destroy the Church.** *He has almost all of his people in place to attack the Church of Rome. However, the heart of my church is not in Rome, but in Jerusalem. The church was transplanted to Rome because Jerusalem would not survive. So, the move of Peter and Paul to Rome was my will.*

Rome is not Jerusalem. All the churches see the uniqueness of Jerusalem. **After the Pope is killed, there will be a question. Will the papacy stay in Jerusalem or return to Rome?** *The deceased pope will have instructed his followers clearly. Some people will remember the splendor of Rome and will want to return. They will return but those who are faithful will elect a new pope and the world will know that* **the soul of the church is in Jerusalem.** *This small seed will grow strong in Jerusalem and the gift will take root. (Jesus)*[92]

The Churches Will Unite

As we approach the era of peace, the Church and Israel will unite, and all other Christians will come to be united with the Church.

Churches will see what they have never seen and do what they thought they would never do. Seeing **the union of Israel and the Catholic Church,** *they will say, "We must be one". All the barriers to unity, put up over the many centuries, will be swept away in one breath of the Spirit.*

There will be the ingathering prophesied by Isaiah. All the riches of the nations will come to Israel. This will be true wealth, the spiritual wealth of **all the Churches gathering as one in Jerusalem with Israel** *and the Catholic Church. My prayer will be fulfilled, that all would be one as the Father and I are one.*

*Also, the world will see something quite different, what they have never seen. They will see the **Churches united and all the Churches united with Israel**. The world will experience a powerful call to come out of darkness. **The Church and Israel will be a light to all nations**. The light will not be lessened or covered over by divisions of the Churches or divisions between the Churches and Israel. The world will not be able to escape the invitation. The unity will stand before them inviting them to accept Me as Lord. (Jesus)*[93]

The Valley of Decision

*After the events of Jerusalem and the unifying of the Church with Israel, I will call all the nations into the **Valley of Decision**. It does not need to be a physical valley because all the nations are already linked by communications. This Valley of Decisions will be a special moment in history.*

Just as Israel was in the moment of distress, so the world itself will be in a moment of complete helplessness. But I will gather the nations and there will be a new breath in the air, a new opportunity, when all the nations will be united into the light. Some nations will leave the Valley and return to darkness, but most will stay in the light. Armaments will be limited. Money will be spent on food. There will be international cooperation that has been sought by many but never brought about.

*I will give these blessings to all the nations in the Valley of Decision as a free gift from my hands. There will be **peace and a new springtime**. (Jesus)*[94]

A New Pope & the Age of Mary

In the midst of these events, an extraordinary election of the new pope will occur:

*Now I will come to the central point so there will be no mistake. The Cardinals will meet **to elect a pope** but an extraordinary intervention* *of God will occur that will alert the whole world to the special nature of this office. They will seek to discern this intervention, to grasp what is the will of God, but everything will not be clear at first. Some, however, will speak in divine wisdom and the search will begin to find the one whom God wants to raise up. He will not come forward at first, even though he knows that he is chosen by God. He will wait until the discussion is concluded and the Cardinals are settled. Then new manifestations will occur which will signal clearly the one whom the heavenly Father wants as his Pope. This will be a complete surprise to the world and to the Church but not to the one upon whom the mantle falls. This is my chosen son, the one whom I have picked. I want all of this to happen in a startling manner so the world and the Church know that this one was chosen by heaven, by God and not by men. He will be prepared because I will have prepared him. **He will be the pope of Fatima and bring to fruition all of the gifts of Fatima, just in time to prepare the Church and the world for the Satanic onslaught.***[95]

A Pope Son

*So, I will stand at the side of another son, a human son, whom I will lift up to the papacy. No one will doubt who it is. I will not let him stay in the shadows (even though at present he is covered with the greatest of shadows and is hidden in my heart). I will bring him forth for all to see. He will acknowledge completely that I alone have lifted him up to the papacy. I will put my seal upon him. He will act only in my name. He will have **a Marian papacy**, rooted totally in my promises, especially in the words that I spoke at Fatima. With this pope, **the Age of Mary** will come to its total height and will forever be upon the lampstand until the end of time.*

Hidden But Promised

When this is accomplished, all the light and power which I have placed in the hearts of many come to fulfillment. When I fulfill this promise, those who have pushed aside my devotions will see their foolishness. I say to all, "Pray for this pope son of mine. He is hidden deeply in my heart because I want nothing to harm him. Pray that all the startling events take place so that he is raised aloft. In him the nations will rejoice".[96]

The Consecration of Russia and the Jerusalem Papacy

Jesus discusses the election and short reign of the future pope and the restoration of Jerusalem as the great city of peace for the whole world:

*When all is put in place and all the events are about to occur, **I will raise up a son to be the pope.** He will be well instructed in My ways and he will not fail Me. I will have instructed him for years and then, **through the most extraordinary of events**, I will lift him to where no one thought he would ever attain.*
He will be a man of faith and will walk only in My ways and in My light. All will be clear to him because I will have revealed everything ahead of time. There will be no doubt and no hesitancy.

The Two Goals of a Short Papacy
*Because of the confusion of the world, he will set aside many of the usual tasks, and **will focus on the tasks that I had revealed to him ahead of time – the consecration of Russia to the Immaculate Heart and the moving of the papacy from Rome to Jerusalem.** These are the two important goals of **his short papacy.***
*My Church will be positioned again, just as I positioned the Church when I placed Peter and Paul in Rome and led them to their martyrdom. This planted My Church in Rome, where it has been for all these centuries. Now it is time to root it again in the soil of Israel and in the Middle East. It is **in Jerusalem that all will find peace.** No longer will My death and resurrection be set aside. All will see that **Jerusalem is the holy city.** Because of that holiness, peace will come to the world.*
*All will tell the story, the fathers to their children. They will tell the story of what I accomplished in Jerusalem and why **Jerusalem is the center of the world.** Yes, I say, the center of the world. Other cities will exist and have their own importance but it is to Jerusalem that*

they will look for their wisdom. Presidents and kings, men and women with political power, will submit to the wisdom of Jerusalem and all the nations will walk again by My light. See all the events in this light. It will not be accomplished in one step or two steps.

How can I shake the present order? How much that now exists must be set aside? I will use many to accomplish My plan, even the strategies and the powers of the Evil One will unwittingly bring it about. Step by step. All will proceed until all the nations see what I have done to exalt the mountain of Zion.[97]

It seems from this message that the future Pope will focus on the two goals of consecrating Russia to the Immaculate Heart and moving the papacy to Jerusalem. And as Our Lady of Fatima famously warned:

If my requests are granted, Russia will be converted and there will be peace.

*If not, Russia will spread her errors in every country, raising up wars and persecution against the Church; many will be martyred. **The Holy Father will have much to suffer**, and many nations will be destroyed.*

To date, Russia has not been converted. Thus, it now seems clearer than ever that these conditional warnings are about to unfold.

There are two other recognized prophecies of our time that indicate the coming martyrdom of the Pope. The famous dream of St. John Bosco shows the Mother Church, the Bark of Peter, with the Pope at the helm, moving through the storm and battle to anchor the Mother Ship of the Church to the pillars of the Eucharist and Our Lady. In his vision, St. Bosco sees the martyrdom of the Pope. The Third Secret of Fatima, given by Our Lady in 1917 to the visionaries of Fatima, and revealed publicly by John Paul II in 2000 (the first two secrets having already been revealed and fulfilled), also reveals more heavenly prophecy about the sufferings of the pope and the faithful in these times, as follows:

*At the left of Our Lady and a little above, we saw **an Angel with a flaming sword** in his left hand; flashing, it gave out flames that looked as though they would set the world on fire; **but** they died out in contact with the splendor that **Our Lady radiated towards him** from her right hand: pointing to the earth with his right hand, the Angel cried out in a loud voice: **'Penance, Penance, Penance!'** And we saw in an immense light that is God: 'something similar to how people appear in a mirror when they pass in front of it' **a Bishop dressed in White** 'we had the impression that it was the Holy Father'. Other Bishops, Priests, men and women Religious going up a steep mountain, at the top of which there was a big Cross of rough-hewn trunks as of a cork-tree with the bark; before reaching there **the Holy Father passed through a big city half in ruins and half trembling with halting step, afflicted with pain and sorrow, he prayed for the souls of the corpses he met on his way; having reached the top of the mountain, on his knees at the foot of the big Cross he was killed** by a group of soldiers who fired bullets and arrows at him, and in the same way there died one after another the other Bishops, Priests, men and women Religious, and various lay people of different ranks and positions. Beneath the two arms of the Cross there were **two Angels** each with a crystal aspersorium in his hand, in which they **gathered up the blood of the Martyrs and with it sprinkled the souls** that were making their way to God.[98]*

Cardinal Ratzinger stated, *"the vision speaks of dangers and how we might be saved from them."* He is reminding us that all prophecy has a conditional element, and we can respond to the prophecy by prayer, conversion, and penance, so as to change its course. Let us respond, respond now, and move forward with hope.

Chapter Thirteen

Russia Will Raise Her Flag Over St. Peter's Dome

CB

Soon, global powers will be involved in a war in Europe. The fallout of the banking system and the escalation of wars in the Middle East will trigger it. Forces will overcome Europe and introduce Communism. China will gain a strong foothold as well. MDM

Sr. Elena Aiello was declared Blessed on September 14, 2011, Feast of the Exultation of the Holy Cross, by Pope Benedict XVI. Blessed Elena was a Mystic, Stigmatist, Victim Soul, Prophetess, and Foundress of the Minim Tertiaries of the Passion of Our Lord Jesus Christ. She died in the 1960s. Her prophecy includes the following:

*Russia will march upon all the nations of Europe, particularly Italy, and **will raise her flag over the Dome of St. Peter's**. Italy will be severely tired by a great revolution, and Rome will be purified in*

blood for its many sins, especially those of impurity! The flock is about to be dispersed and the Pope must suffer greatly!...

*If the people do not recognize in these scourges the warnings of Divine Mercy, and do not return to God with truly Christian living, ANOTHER TERRIBLE WAR WILL COME FROM THE EAST TO THE WEST. **RUSSIA WITH HER SECRET ARMIES WILL BATTLE AMERICA; WILL OVERRUN EUROPE**...*

Oh, what a horrible vision I see! A great revolution is going on in Rome! They are entering the Vatican. The Pope is all alone; he is praying. They are holding the Pope. They take him by force.

Will Berlusconi be killed, as one locutionist privately reports?

What does the Bible say about Russia (the Bear) in Revelation 13:

*And I saw a beast rising out of the sea, with ten horns and seven heads, with ten diadems upon its horns and a blasphemous name upon its heads. And the beast that I saw was like a leopard, its feet were **like a bear's**, and its mouth was like a lion's mouth. And to it the dragon gave his power and his throne and great authority. One of its heads seemed to have a mortal wound, but **its mortal wound was healed**, and the whole earth followed the beast with wonder. Men worshiped the dragon, for he had given his authority to the beast, and they worshiped the beast, saying, "Who is like the beast, and who can fight against it?" And the beast was given a mouth uttering haughty and blasphemous words, and it was allowed to exercise authority for forty-two months; it opened its mouth to utter blasphemies against God, blaspheming his name and his dwelling, that is, those who dwell in heaven. Also it was allowed to make war on the saints and to conquer them. And authority was given it over every tribe and people and tongue and nation, and all who dwell on earth will worship it, every one whose name has not been written before the foundation of the world in the book of life of the Lamb that was slain.*

Interestingly, Communist Russia looked like it had a mortal wound in the 1990s when it collapsed. But, it was only wounded, and it is rising again. Men will worship the dragon (China) who will give his authority to the beast (Russia) which will reign over the earth for 42 months. During this time, the great persecution will take place, whereby Russia will make war on the faithful of God and martyr them.

At the Church-approved apparition of **La Salette**, Our Lady spoke about a temporary period of peace, saying it will last 25 years, as an interim in the context of two series of events – between the two periods of Russian Communism. Our Lady summarizes the three stages of the events of the Apocalypse, saying:

The righteous will suffer greatly. Their prayers, their penances and their tears will rise up to Heaven and all of God's people will beg for forgiveness and mercy and will plead for my help and intercession. And then Jesus Christ, in an act of His justice and His great mercy will command His angels to have all His enemies put to death. ***Suddenly, the persecutors of the Church of Jesus Christ and all those given over to sin will perish and the earth will become desert-like. And then peace will be made, and man will be reconciled with God.*** *Jesus Christ will be served, worshipped, and glorified. Charity will flourish everywhere.* ***The new kings will be the right arm of the holy Church,*** *which will be strong, humble, pious, poor but fervent in the imitation of the virtues of Jesus Christ. The Gospel will be preached everywhere and mankind will make great progress in its faith, for there will be unity among the workers of Jesus Christ and man will live in fear of God.*

This peace among men will be short-lived. Twenty-five years of plentiful harvests will make them forget that the sins of men are the cause of all the troubles on this earth. *A forerunner of the Antichrist, with his troops gathered from several nations, will fight against the true Christ, the only Savior of the world. He will shed much blood and will want to annihilate the worship of God to make himself be looked upon as a God.*

This prophecy seems to prophecy the two stages of Communism, as mentioned by the Garabandal visionaries. The first stage ended beginning in 1989 with the fall of the Berlin Wall and was completed by 1991 in the USSR. So 25 years of temporary peace has ensued, as the La Salette prophecy indicated, which will end thus in 2014-2016. Then, will commence the second stage of the prophecy, when the wars will usher in the time of the antichrist. And so will unfold the apocalyptic battle that has already begun.

The prophecy of La Salette speaks about the Antichrist, saying:

Lastly, hell will reign on earth…
*The **seasons will be changed**, the earth will produce only bad fruits, the stars will lose their regular movements, the moon will reflect only a feeble reddish light; water and fire will give to the globe of the earth convulsive movements and horrible earthquakes which will cause to be engulfed mountains, cities..*
Rome will lose the faith and become the seat of the antichrist.
*The demons of the air with the antichrist will perform great wonders on the earth and in the air, and **men will corrupt themselves more and more**. God will have care of His faithful servants and men of good will; the Gospel will be preached everywhere, all peoples and all nations will have knowledge of the truth!*
***The Church will be eclipsed**, the world will be in consternation [the Church will be eclipsed in this sense, that **1) one will not know which is the true pope; 2) for a time: the holy Sacrifice will cease to be offered in churches,** and also in houses: so there will be no more public worship. But she saw that yet the holy Sacrifice would not cease: it would be offered in caves, in tunnels, in barns and in alcoves.]*
*Woe to the inhabitants of the earth! There will be **bloody wars and famines**; pestilences and contagious diseases… **all the universe will be struck with terror, and many will let themselves be misled** because they have not adored the true Christ living among them. It is time; the sun darkens; faith alone will live.*

Behold the time; the abyss opens. Behold the king of kings of darkness. Behold the beast with his subjects, calling himself the savior of the world. He will raise himself up with pride into the air in order to go even up to heaven.[99]

Bl. John Paul II also spoke of La Salette and its connection to other Marian prophecies, saying:

If victory comes it will be brought by Mary. *Christ will conquer through her, because He wants the Church's victories now and in the future to be linked to her... I could see... **that there was a certain continuity among La Salette, Lourdes, and Fatima**.*

St. Hildegard, the newest Doctor of the Church, prophesied about the antichrist as follows:

The son of perdition (the Antichrist), who will reign very few of times, will come at the end day of the duration of the world, at the times corresponding to the moment just before the sun disappears from the horizon...

After having passed a licentious youth among very perverted men, and in a desert, she being conducted by a demon disguised as an angel of light, the mother of the son of perdition will conceive and give birth without knowing the father. In another land, she will make men believe that her birth was some miraculous thing, seeing that she had not appointed a spouse, and she will ignore that, she will say, how the infant she had brought into the world had been formed in her womb, and the people will regard it as a saint and qualified to the title.

The son of perdition is this very wicked beast who will put to death those who refuse to believe in him; who will associate with kings, priests, the great and the rich; who will mistake the humility and will esteem pride; who will finally subjugate the entire universe by his diabolic means.

He will gain over many people and tell them: "You are allowed to do all that you please; renounce the fasts; it suffices that you love me; I who am your God."

He will show them treasures and riches, and he will permit them to riot in all sorts of festivities, as they please. He will oblige them to practice circumcision and other Judaic observances, and he will tell them: "Those who believe in me will receive pardon of their sins and will live with me eternally."

He will reject baptism and evangelism, and he will reject in derision all the precepts the Spirit has given to men of my part.

Then he will say to his partisans, "Strike me with a sword, and place my corpse in a proper shroud until the day of my resurrection." They will believe him to have really given over to death, and from his mortal wound he will make a striking semblance of resuscitation.

After which, he will compose himself a certain cipher, which he will say is to be a pledge of salute; he will give it to all his servitors like the sign of our faith in heaven, and he will command them to adore it. Concerning those who, for the love of my name, will refuse to render this sacrilegious adoration to the son of perdition, he will put them to death amidst the cruelest torments.

But I will defend my two Witnesses, Enoch and Elias, whom I have reserved for those times. Their mission will be to combat the man of evil and reprimand him in the sight of the faithful whom he has seduced. They will have the virtue of operating the most brilliant miracles, in all the places where the son of perdition has spread his evil doctrines. In the meanwhile, I will permit this evildoer to put them to death; but I will give them in heaven the recompense of their travails.

Later, however, after the coming of Enoch and Elias, the Antichrist will be destroyed, and the Church will sing forth with unprecedented glory, and the victims of the great error will throng to return to the fold.

St. Hildegard elaborated on the life of Antichrist in her book - Heptachronon:

The Man of Sin will be born of an ungodly woman who, from her infancy, will have been initiated into occult sciences and the wiles of the demon. She will live in the desert with perverse men, and abandon herself to crime with so much the greater ardor, as she will think she is authorized thereby to by the revelations of an angel. And thus, in the fire of burning concupiscence she will conceive the Son of Perdition, without knowing by what father. Then she will teach that fornication is permitted, declaring herself holy and honored as a saint.

But Lucifer, the old and cunning serpent, will find the fruit of her womb with his infernal spirit and entirely possess the fruit of sin.

Now when he shall have attained the age of manhood, he will set himself up as a new master and teach perverse doctrine. Soon he will revolt against the saints; and he will acquire such great power that in the madness of his pride he would raise himself above the clouds; and as in the beginning Satan said: "I will be like unto the most high," and fell; so in those days, he will fall when he will say in the person of his son, "I am the Savior of the World!"

He will ally himself with the kings, the princes and the powerful ones of the earth; he will condemn humility and will extol all the doctrines of pride. His magic art will feign the most astonishing prodigies; he will disturb the atmosphere, command thunder and tempest, produce hail and horrible lightning. He will move mountains, dry up streams, reanimate the withered verdure of forests. His arts will be practiced upon the elements, but chiefly upon man will he exhaust his infernal power. He will seem to take away health and restore it. How so? By sending some possessed soul into a dead body, to move it for a time. But these resurrections will be of short duration.

At the sight of these things, many will be terrified and will believe in him; and some, preserving their primitive faith, will nevertheless court the favor of the Man of Sin or fear his displeasure. And so many will be led astray among those who, shutting the interior eye of their soul, will live habitually in exterior things...

After the Antichrist has ascended a high mountain and been destroyed by Christ, many erring souls will return to truth, and men will make rapid progress in the ways of holiness.

St. Hildegard gave more details about the Antichrist in her Vision X:

Nothing good will enter into him nor be able to be in him. For he will be nourished in diverse and secret places, lest he should be known by men, and he will be imbued with all diabolical arts, and he will be hidden until he is of full age, nor will he show the perversities which will be in him, until he knows himself to be full and superabundant in all iniquities.

He will appear to agitate the air, to make fire descend from heaven, to produce rainbows, lightning, thunder and hail, to tumble mountains, dry up streams, to strip the verdure of trees, of forests, and to restore them again. He will also appear to be able to make men sick or well at will, to chase out demons, and at times even to resuscitate the dead, making a cadaver move like it was alive. But this kind of resurrection will never endure beyond a little time, for the glory of God will not suffer it...

*From the beginning of his course **many battles** and many things contrary to the lawful dispensation will arise, and **charity will be extinguished in men**. In them also will arise bitterness and harshness and there will be **so many heresies** that heretics will preach their errors openly and certainly; and there shall be so much doubt and incertitude in the Catholic faith of Christians that men shall be in doubt of what God they invoke, and many signs shall appear in the sun and moon, and in the stars and in the waters, and in other elements and creatures, so that, as it were in a picture, future events shall be foretold in their portents.*

*Then **so much sadness** shall occupy men at that time, that they shall be led to die as if for nothing. But those who are perfect in the Catholic faith will await in great contrition what God wills to ordain. And these great tribulations shall proceed in this way, while the Son of Perdition shall open his mouth in the words of falsehood and his deceptions, heaven and earth shall tremble together. But after the fall of the Antichrist the glory of the Son of God shall be increased.*

As soon as he is born, he will have teeth and pronounce blasphemies; in short, he will be a born devil. He will emit fearful cries, work miracles, and wallow in luxury and vice. He will have brothers who are also demons incarnate, and at the age of twelve, they will distinguish themselves in brilliant achievements. They will command an armed force, which will be supported by the infernal legions.

After the Son of Perdition has accomplished all of his evil designs, he will call together all of his believers and tell them that he wishes to ascend into heaven.

At the moment of his ascension, a thunderbolt will strike him to the ground, and he will die.

The mountain where he was established for the operation of his ascension, in an instant will be covered with a thick cloud which emits an unbearable odor of truly infernal corruption... At the sight of his body, the eyes of great number of persons will open and they will be made to see their miserable error.

After the sorrowful defeat of the Son of Perdition, the spouse of my Son, who is the Church, will shine with a glory without equal, and the victims of the error will be impressed to reenter the sheepfold.

As to the day, after the fall of Antichrist, when the world will end, man must not seek to know, for he can never learn it. That secret the Father has reserved for Himself.

Chapter Fourteen

China Is the Red Dragon

❦

*Then another sign appeared in the sky; it was **a huge red dragon**, with seven heads and ten horns, and on its heads were seven diadems. Its tail swept away a third of the stars in the sky and hurled them down to the earth. Then the dragon stood before the woman about to give birth, to devour her child when she gave birth.*

Revelation 12:3-4

Babylon (the European Union), the Bear (Russia), and the Red Dragon (China)

The Red Dragon – China

Through Fr. Gobbi, Our Lady reveals the buildup to the Apocalypse, especially regarding the Red Dragon, which is Communism and epitomized by China:

*The huge Red Dragon is **atheistic communism** which has spread everywhere the error of the denial and obstinate rejection of God. The huge Red Dragon is **Marxist atheism**, which appears with **ten horns**, namely the power of its means of communication, in order to lead humanity to disobey the Ten Commandments of God, and with **seven heads**, upon each of which is a crown, signs of authority and royalty (see Revelation 17). The crowned heads indicate the nations in which atheistic communism is established and rules with the force of its ideological, political and military power. It is "red" because it uses wars and blood to gain conquests.*

*The huge Red Dragon has succeeded during these years in conquering humanity with the error of its **theoretical and practical atheism, which has now seduced all nations of the earth**. It has thus succeeded in building up for itself **a new civilization without God**, materialistic, egoistic, hedonistic, arid and cold, which carries within itself the seeds of corruption and of death.*[100] *The Red Dragon works to bring all humanity to do without God, to **the denial of God**, and therefore spreads the error of atheism.*[101]

*Now you are living in that period of time when the Red Dragon, that is to say Marxist atheism, is spreading throughout the whole world and is increasingly bringing about the ruin of souls. **He is indeed succeeding in seducing and casting down a third of the stars of heaven. These stars, in the firmament of the Church, are the pastors (priests).***[102]

About atheistic communism, Pius XI states:

*Today we see something that world history has never seen before: The waving of the flag of Satan in the battle against God and religion, against all peoples, and in all parts of the world; a phenomenon that outdoes all that happened before. **Atheistic Communism surpasses all previous persecutions in the Church**, even that of Nero and Diocletian, not only in its extent, but also in its violence.*

The Persecution by the Red Dragon

*While Satan will rise through his poor misguided followers... this will be for just a short period. It will, I must warn you though, be **a frightening period of persecution headed by the Red Dragon** and those political entities, not of God. Through **prayer and the sacraments** you will find the strength to persevere during these trials. All of these events have been foretold and must come to pass so that evil can be finally stamped out in the world. It is necessary, therefore, that this **purification** and series of **chastisements** take place. Because **only then will the world be ready for the New Paradise on earth.**[103]*

In the Book of Revelation, the destruction of 'Babylon', a city that seems to be a symbol of every kind of evil, is foretold. Elsewhere in the Book of Revelation, Babylon is the name of a whore who rules over the kings of the earth and rides upon a seven-headed beast. In one of the Bible's most famous cases of numerology, the beast is assigned the identifying number 666 (the mark of the Beast).

***The two allies Russia and China will join forces.** This will happen as the beast with the ten horns rises to dominate their long-suffering innocent people.*
The beast with the ten horns is the European Union, My daughter, referred to as Babylon in the Book of Revelation.
*Babylon (Europe) will fall and be dominated by the **big Red Dragon, China and its ally the Bear, Russia.***
*When this happens **communism will rule** and woe to anyone seen to practice their religion in their presence.*
All religions will be banned but Christians will suffer the biggest persecution.
***Roman Catholics will not be tolerated at all and they will have to hold masses in secret.**[104]*

*Know this, though, the **Red Dragon (China) you were told about some time ago has now risen** his head coyly but with a deadly intent of devouring Christians all over the world.*

Patient for so long in waiting he will now swoop down and, with fire from his mouth, destroy everything that represents homage to Me, God of the Most High and My beloved Son, Jesus Christ.

Europe will be his first target and then the United States of America. Communism will be introduced *and woe to those who oppose the reign of the Red Dragon.*

My daughter I realize that the recent divine messages given to you are distracting but the truth must be revealed.

It is only through the prophecies made known that faith will be restored. This is the reason why prophecies are being given to My children now so that they will recognize the truth of My teachings.

All prophecies given to My prophets Daniel and John will unfold layer by layer. (God the Father)[105]

The Downfall of the European Union (Babylon)

The European Union is *"Babylon the Great, the Mother of Prostitutes and Abominations of the Earth."* She has seven heads and ten horns (Revelation 17:3). In the case of this beast, Revelation states that the seven heads are seven hills (Rome has seven hills) and the ten horns are ten "kings" or political leaders. Thus, the European Union's apocalyptic downfall is prophesied to take place at the hands of the beast with seven heads and ten horns (Russia and/or China). Both the Red Dragon (China) and the Beast like a bear (Russia) have seven heads and ten horns:

"And another sign appeared in heaven, behold, a great, fiery red dragon having seven heads and ten horns, and seven diadems on his heads." Revelation 12:3

This is China.

"And I saw a beast rising up out of the sea, having seven heads and ten horns, and on his horns ten crowns, and on his heads a blasphemous name." Revelation 13:1

This is Russia.

The beast has 7 heads and 10 horns, just like the dragon has 7 heads and 10 horns. Thus, China and Russia will cause the downfall of Europe. While Europe (Babylon) claims to be a queen, she is widowed. (Revelation 18:7) She is widowed because she has abandoned her spouse, the Church.

Chapter Fifteen

The European Union Is Babylon Fal

l

i

n

g

ઝ

One of the seven angels said to John:
Come here. I will show you the judgment on the great harlot who lives near the many waters. The kings of the earth have had intercourse with her, and the inhabitants of the earth became drunk on the wine of her harlotry...
I saw a woman seated on a scarlet beast that was covered with blasphemous names, with **seven heads and ten horns**... She held in her hand a gold cup that was filled with the abominable and sordid deeds of her harlotry. On her forehead was written a name, which is a mystery, *"**Babylon the great, the mother of harlots and of the abominations of the earth**"*... [she] was drunk on the blood of the holy ones and on the blood of the witnesses to Jesus... Then he said to me,

The waters that you saw where the harlot lives represent large
numbers of peoples, nations, and tongues. The ten horns that you saw
and the beast will hate the harlot; they will leave her desolate and
naked; they will eat her flesh and consume her with fire.
Revelation 17:1-16

I, John, saw another angel coming down from heaven,
having great authority,
and the earth became illumined by his splendor.
He cried out in a mighty voice:
*"Fallen, **fallen is Babylon the great**...*
a cage for every unclean and disgusting beast."
A mighty angel picked up a stone like a huge millstone
and threw it into the sea and said:
"With such force will Babylon the great city be thrown down,
and will never be found again...
Because your merchants were the great ones of the world,
all nations were led astray by your magic potion."
Revelation 18:1-23

We learn some of the details of how the European Union will
fall, as Jesus reportedly speaks through Maria Divine Mercy, saying:

In the Book of Revelation, the destruction of 'Babylon', a city that
seems to be a symbol of every kind of evil, is foretold. Elsewhere in the
Book of Revelation, Babylon is the name of a whore who rules over the
kings of the earth and rides upon a seven-headed beast. In one of the
Bible's most famous cases of numerology, the beast is assigned the
identifying number 666 (the mark of the Beast).

The two allies Russia and China will join forces. *This will happen as*
the beast with the ten horns rises to dominate their long-suffering
innocent people.

The beast with the ten horns is the European Union, My daughter, referred to as Babylon in the Book of Revelation.

Babylon (Europe) will fall and [then] be dominated by the **big Red Dragon, China and its ally the Bear, Russia.**

When this happens **communism will rule** *and woe to anyone seen to practice their religion in their presence.*

All religions will be banned but Christians will suffer the biggest persecution.

Roman Catholics will not be tolerated at all and they will have to hold masses in secret.

Europe will be his first target and then the United States of America.

Communism will be introduced *and woe to those who oppose the reign of the Red Dragon.* (MDM)

While Europe (Babylon) claims to be a queen, she is widowed (Revelation 18:7). She is widowed because she has abandoned her spouse, the Church.

Promoting the Anti-Commandments and Anti-Virtues

> *He shall speak against the Most High*
> *and wear down the holy ones of the Most High,*
> *intending to* **change the feast days and the law**.
> *They shall be handed over to him*
> *for a time, two times, and half a time.*
> Daniel 7:25

The "ten horns" and "seven heads" of Babylon are related to the moral law, which the European Union has replaced with the anti-laws and anti-virtues, as Our Lady discusses through Fr. Gobbi:

The Ten Horns – The Ten Sins of Lawlessness

*The Lord has communicated His law with **the ten commandments**, Freemasonry spreads everywhere, through the power of its **ten horns**, a law which is **completely opposed to that of God**...*

*Human events are constantly getting worse and worse. **Men have forgotten God; many obstinately deny Him**. How many there are now who ignore Him in practice!*

*This poor, poor generation whose sorry lot it is to be so polluted and corrupted by the Evil Spirit, who has risen up against God to repeat again his challenge: 'Non serviam: I will not serve; **I will not acknowledge God!**'*[106]

To this effect, the anti-commandments that are promoted today are:

I. TO THE FIRST COMMANDMENT: You shall not have any other God but Me.
- Promotes the worship of **false idols, such as materialism, hedonism, and practical atheism, as well as New Age spiritism and superstition.**

II. TO THE SECOND COMMANDMENT: You shall not take the Name of God in vain.
- Promotes **blaspheming God and Christ, in many subtle and diabolical ways.**

III. TO THE THIRD COMMANDMENT: Remember to keep holy the Sabbath Days.
- Promotes **transforming Sunday into a weekend, into a day of sports, of competitions and of entertainments.**

IV. TO THE FOURTH COMMANDMENT: Honor your father and your mother.
- Promotes a **new model of family based on cohabitation, even between homosexuals.**

V. TO THE FIFTH COMMANDMENT: You shall not kill.
- Promotes **making abortion legal everywhere**, in **making euthanasia acceptable**, and in **causing respect due to the value of human life to all but disappear**.

VI. TO THE SIXTH COMMANDMENT: You shall not commit impure acts.
- Justifies, exalts, and propagates **every form of impurity**, even to the justification of acts against nature.

VII. TO THE SEVENTH COMMANDMENT: You shall not steal.
- Promotes **theft, violence, kidnapping, and robbery, which spread more and more**.

VIII. TO THE EIGHTH COMMANDMENT: You shall not bear false witness.
- Promotes **the law of deceit, lying, and duplicity, which becomes more and more propagated**.

IX. and X. TO THE NINTH AND TENTH COMMANDMENT: You shall not covet the goods and the wife of another.
- Works to **corrupt the depths of the conscience**, betraying the mind and the heart of man.

*In this way souls become driven along **the perverse and wicked road of disobedience** to the laws of the Lord, become submerged in sin and are thus prevented from receiving the gift of grace and the life of God.*[107]

The evils of our day are magnified because humanity has been led to no longer see evil as evil or to repent of evil after committing it. Today, instead society has been led into a great crisis of faith, such that, they have been duped into believing that:

1. There is no devil
2. There is no sin
3. Sin is good

Thus, today, each person commits sin and engages in evil, and does so without ever repenting. Oh, how many souls are being lost, and without anyone mourning them, including themselves, until it is too late!

The Seven Heads – The Seven Capital Vices

*To the **seven theological and cardinal virtues**, which are the fruit of living in the grace of God, Freemasonry counters with the diffusion of **the seven capital vices**, which are the fruit of living habitually in the state of sin. To faith it opposes pride; to hope, lust; to charity, avarice; to prudence, anger; to fortitude, sloth; to justice, envy; to temperance, gluttony.*

***Whoever becomes a victim of the seven capital vices is gradually led to take away the worship that is due to God alone**, in order to give it to false divinities, who are the very personification of all these vices. **And in this consists the greatest and most horrible blasphemy**. This is why on **every head of the beast** there is written a blasphemous name. Each Masonic lodge has the task of making a different divinity adored.*

The first three capital sins are of particular threat. We must combat against the first three capital sins by living the theological virtues (faith, hope, and love) and embracing the spirit of the evangelical counsels (poverty, chastity, and obedience) to help us fight the three temptations of the spiritual life (the world, the flesh, and the devil):

1. FAITH (and obedience): replaced by pride
   - leads one to offer worship to **the god of human reason and haughtiness, of technology and progress (to the demonic spirit)**.

2. HOPE (and chastity): replaced by lust
   - brings one to offer worship to **the god of sexuality and impurity (to the fleshly spirit)**.

3. CHARITY (and voluntary poverty of spirit): replaced by greed
   - spreads everywhere the worship of **the god of money (and the worldly spirit)**.

4. PRUDENCE: replaced by anger
   - leads one to offer worship to **the god of discord and division**.

5. FORTITUDE: replaced by laziness
   - disseminates the worship of **the idol of fear of public opinion and exploitation**.

6. JUSTICE: replaced by envy
   - leads one to offer worship to **the idol of violence and war**.

7. TEMPERANCE: replaced by gluttony
   - leads one to offer worship to the so highly extolled **idol of hedonism, of materialism, and of pleasure**.

*The task of the Masonic lodges is that of working today, with great astuteness, **to bring humanity everywhere to disdain the holy law of God, to work in opposition to the ten commandments, and to take away the worship due to God alone in order to offer it to certain false idols** which become extolled and adored by an ever increasing number of people: **reason, flesh, money, discord, domination, violence, pleasure. Thus souls are precipitated into the dark slavery of evil, of vice and of sin and, at the moment of death and of the judgment of God, into the pool of eternal fire which is hell...***

*For this reason **I am training all my children to observe the ten commandments of God; to live the Gospel to the letter; to make frequent use of the sacraments, especially those of penance and***

Eucharistic communion, *as necessary helps in order to remain in the* ***grace of God; to practice the virtues vigorously, to walk always along the path of goodness, of love, of purity and of holiness.***[108]

Babylon Will Fall: Warning to Europe

This superpower influences the world through its military, economic, and political strength. However, the European Union will ultimately be destroyed by what appears to be a conspiracy. The destruction of Babylon will pave the way for the Antichrist to rise to world dominance. He will use foreign help to accomplish this, as Daniel states:

He will attack the mightiest fortresses *with the help of a foreign god and will greatly honor those who acknowledge him. He will make them rulers over many people and will distribute the land at a price* (Daniel 11:36-39).

When Babylon is taken over by the Antichrist and False Prophet, then the world will surely say: *"Who is like the beast? Who can make war against him?"*

Jesus reportedly warns through the American Locutionist, saying:

*Turn back to me or **your European Union will collapse** like the paper building that it is. Do not say, "Our economies are flourishing. Our way of life is succeeding". You have forgotten your Mother, the Church... Your hearts are joined in money and in your economic system but not in the Catholic faith.*
*If you exalt my Pope, I will exalt you. If you listen to his wisdom, I will lead you along a path of survival. **Otherwise, your destruction is near** at hand because your union is a union of convenience, not of faith.*[109]

PHASE 3: The Great Havoc of War & Disaster...

Including in America

 CB

Death and Hades were given authority over a quarter of the earth, to kill with sword, famine and plague, and by means of the beasts of the earth.
Revelation 6

There will be famines and earthquakes in various places.
All this is only the beginning of the birth pangs.
Matthew 24

Then He said to them,
Nation will rise against nation, and kingdom against kingdom.
There will be powerful earthquakes, famines, and plagues
from place to place.
Luke 21:9-11

Jesus gives warning about the disasters to come through Maria Divine Mercy:

*Tell the world that the **ecological disasters foretold will now strike the earth**. All will commence now. So many. So quickly. And all due to the blind eyes turned on the word of God the Father by sinners wrapped up in their dens of iniquity.*

*The time has come for **the [great] battle** to rid the world of evil and the rule of Satan. God the Father is now about to unleash many **earthquakes, tsunamis** and **floods** in an effort to make you wake up. [The] plots to overthrow world leaders, those in power of Religious groups, and to introduce control measures including a **one-world currency** will not be ignored.*

America's Relationship with Mary stems from the days of its founding. America has one last chance to decide. Our Lady calls the United States to lead the world to peace:

*I hold America in my heart. It is so special and **formally dedicated to my Immaculate Conception**. It is built upon religious principles which are now covered over. What has happened to America? It is awash in material goods that it cannot afford, drowning in a debt that it cannot pay and killing its young before they are born.*

*What has happened to the light set upon the mountain? To the city set on the hill? America's foundations have been shaken. **Slavery** began the problem. Human beings were reduced to cattle. Then, blood was shed in the Civil War. A seed of evil was sown and not recognized – the seed of violence, brother killing brother...*

***Money**. Money is your false god, America, and money will be your downfall. You will drown in the very money which you print so plentifully. It **will not be worth what it says it is**. It will become the laughing stock of the nations. The mighty dollar will be like a sick man who has no strength... In your years of good fortune, you brought back to life those nations who were broken. Never will I forget your generosity. But **if you do not repent**, I cannot restore you. If I do not restore you, many will have nowhere else to turn.*[110]

*America will go to the (2012 presidential) election and make a choice, a choice between light and darkness. Their issue will be the economy but the economy is not my issue. My issue is life and the protection of **the unborn**. My issue is truth and the protection of **marriage**. My issue is holiness and the keeping of **the commandments**. If America votes for my issues, then I will care for its economy. However, if America votes in a selfish way, electing those who will not protect life, who will not protect marriage and who will not protect my commandments, **then I cannot and will not save America**.*

*It will enter into a **total darkness**, without any hope. People will wring their hands and ask, "What can be done?" It is too late. They have made their choice and they scorned my issues.*

Let the word go forth and let all see clearly before it is too late...

***The problems for the West will come from the West**. Your eyes are looking to foreign borders, to cultures not your own. However, the Evil One has, for a long time, gained the hearts of your own – your own leaders, your own statesmen, your own bankers. They are like Judases, ready to sell you out, ready to betray you for their own interests. They placed their trust in you when they saw you as strong. Now, they realize that you are weak. "America is not the place to invest. Let us take our money elsewhere". This is what will happen. **Your own sons will abandon you**. They will not stand by you in the time of trial. Your weaknesses will be magnified by their departure. O America, when will you turn to me?*[111]

America used to be a generous country. It would make many sacrifices to gain what was true and good for others. Now, it is a selfish country, where everyone looks to their own interests.

*How can I save you, **America**, a country so close to my heart? There is only one path. Return to the generosity and sacrifice that made you great. Return to the truth that guided you.*[112]

*Listen to me, **America**... America, I have raised you up to feed the world... I have raised you up so you could export your medicines, not your weapons. I have raised you up to eradicate disease and to bless the poor. Instead, you send forth your soldiers; not your doctors, your* *weapons not your food... Do not listen to your bankers. Listen to the cries of the poor and the hungry in other nations. **If you care for them, I will care for you**. If you let them grow hungry, I will let your children also **taste the evil of famine**.*

***America**... You are dying from within, unable to reverse the tide that has been unleashed by your turning to the secular. Your roots were religious, based upon the strength of the Churches and the high morality of your people, in the sanctity of life and the holiness of marriage. You guarded your young against pornography. All was in order. You flourished in the discipline of your life and in the discipline of your spending... I want to draw you back to where you belong and where you will thrive again. I would draw you to a nation under God, but you will not come. You want your freedoms, even those which violate God's will. You do not want to be a nation under God. You cry out, "Do not speak to us, O God. We do not want to know your will. We do not want to ask, "What is God's will?" When voices are raised about God's will, you say, "We have separation of Church and State." Shall we go our separate ways? Do you want to form your secular state? Is this what you want? Are you asking for a divorce? A divorce from the woman who gave birth to a nation?*

Think it over again. Ask yourself, "What course am I choosing? Do I really want to follow the road of Europe? Or, should I go back to the Churches? Should I ask them to teach me again? Should I say to the Churches, "Teach my children for they no longer know right from wrong. I have taught them what works. I have given them skills. But, they have never learned who created them or the way of true life. Here, take my children and teach them the ways of the Lord".

***It is not too late, America**, but our separation must be ended. You have listened to the wrong voices and have cast out the mother of your children...*

I must raise up a new army and once more stir the consciences of the world. These peacemakers will be gunned down, as were the others who preached non-violence...

*You have wandered down the wrong road, **America**, taking to yourself prerogatives that you do not have. Return to the heart of the republic.*

Let the voices of peace be raised. They have not been heard from in a long time.[113]

The world is exploding – Syria, Afghanistan, Egypt, Iraq, Iran and so many other places. Where is America? I look to America and it refuses to take its proper place, a place for which I designed it and the reason that I raised it to power... There was a time when it would pay any price, bear any burden, fight any foe. America did not seek to dominate but to liberate, not to control people but to free them. Now, it slinks back into the shadows, unwilling to commit its strength to what is true and good.
When will America say, "We must do the right thing?"...
Where is America as the fires explode and feed one another? I will tell you where it is. It is looking out for its own interests. It no longer leads. It follows. It no longer says, "This is the right path of goodness and truth"...
America, you have rejected my Son, the light of the world. Your leaders no longer look to him for light. What can I do? I must look for someone for whom my Son, Jesus, is still the light of the world. I must raise him up and scatter all the others. It will happen before your very eyes.[114]

Our Lady of America and Her Prophecy of War

Sr. Mary Ephram was told by Our Lady of America: *"America, the United States in particular, is being given the tremendous, yet privileged opportunity to lead all nations in a spiritual renewal never before so necessary, so important, so vital."* Mary said that she was coming to America now as a last resort. Sr. Mary Ephram wrote that Mary *"promised that **greater miracles than those granted at Lourdes and Fatima** would be granted here in America, the United States in particular, if we would do as she desires."* Mary promised *"miracles of the soul."*

Our Lady says: *"I am Our Lady of America. **I desire that my children honor me, especially by the purity of their lives.**"*

The American Locutionist also speaks about the restoration of purity:

*I will again clad **America** in the modesty that used to protect its young people, and in the innocence that used to prevail in its entertainments. Oh, how far these have eroded; how far out of sight are the standards that used to guide the filmmakers. This was the Age of Innocence for America, when censorship was not a dirty word and individual expression was limited for the good of the community.*[115]

She speaks of the pivotal role of the United States -- for good or for evil – in our times, saying:

***It is the United States that is to lead the world to peace**, the peace of Christ, the peace that He brought with Him from heaven... **Dear children, unless the United States accepts and carries out faithfully the mandate given to it by heaven to lead the world to peace, there will come upon it and all nations a great havoc of war and incredible suffering**. If, however, the United States is faithful to this mandate from heaven and yet fails in the pursuit of peace because the rest of the world will not accept or cooperate, then the United States will not be burdened with the punishment about to fall.*
Weep, then, dear children, weep with your mother over the sins of men... Intercede with me before the throne of mercy, for sin is overwhelming the world and punishment is not far away.
***It is the darkest hour**, but if men will come to me, my Immaculate Heart will make it bright again with the mercy which my Son will rain down through my hands. **Help me save those who will not save themselves.** Help me bring once again the sunshine of God's peace upon the world.*
*If my desires are not fulfilled much suffering will come to this land. **My faithful one, if my warnings are taken seriously and enough of my children strive constantly and faithfully to renew and reform themselves in their inward and outward lives, then there will be no nuclear war.** What happens to the world*

*depends upon those who live in it. There must be much more good than evil prevailing in order to prevent the holocaust that is so near approaching. Yet I tell you, my daughter, even should such a destruction happen because there were not enough souls who took my warning seriously, **there will remain a remnant, untouched by the chaos who, having been faithful in following me and spreading my warnings**, will gradually inhabit the earth again with their dedicated and holy lives.* [116]

Our Lady of America is calling the United States to lead the world, to establish peace, to restore the virtue of purity, and to protect the family.

America Will Be Attacked Starting with New York

American Locutionist warns that America will soon suffer terrorist attacks, beginning with New York City:

Evil works in hiding, so that the effects cannot be prepared for and the greatest possible damage is inflicted. This is the pattern – sudden surprises, catching people off guard...
*After 9/11, America said, "We will rebuild and we will kill those who killed us". It did not say, "We must repent because we ourselves have killed millions of our unborn citizens". When destruction happens again I want you to say, "Let us cleanse our nation of the death of **abortion**". Otherwise, it needs to happen a third time until you finally get the message. **You are the greatest murderers of your own citizens**. New York was the first site and **New York** will be the second site. **Then it will spread** to other cities, more quickly than anyone could imagine, until many of the largest cities are struck. The **focus will be the trains and subways**. There great confusion happens immediately and people quickly panic.*
*After these series of strikes, many will live in **fear** and normal life will be greatly disrupted, out of all proportion to the power of the terrorists who have maximized the damage they inflicted. With a small number of people and a small amount of explosives, they will manage **to cripple much of American life.***

What will be America's response? The political leaders will know what to say to enhance their importance. Civil leaders will respond to try to restore a normal routine. But will anyone cry out – "Do you not see? **Because we kill the unborn, God has lifted his protecting hand from a country that used to keep his laws.** *"*[117]

Through Maria Divine Mercy, God the Father said:

My hand is being withheld from punishing man for the sins he commits through the power of prayer. **I will cast down a severe chastisement** *if man does not turn away from the sin of* **murder and abortion**. *Already you, My children, have seen My anger through earthquakes, floods, tsunamis and other ecological turmoil. I must chastise you children* **for you cannot avoid punishment** *for your offenses against your fellow man.*

The sins of **abortion** *will be punished when* **My hand will fall with force on those nations which condone this abomination**. *You will not be allowed to murder my helpless creation and should your Governments continue to pass laws, condoning this cowardly practice, you will see* **My anger descend with such force that you will beg for the mercy of life**...

My punishment on countries guilty of legalizing abortion will wipe out nations. *Your countries will divide into little pieces and fall into the ocean. Your vile clinics and hospitals where you carry out these practices will close and you, the guilty among you, will* **be cast into the fires of Hell for your heinous crimes.**

I come to give you this Warning now. **Never condone abortion.** *Put your foot down in your countries and fight to prevent this* **global genocide** *from continuing. If your Governments continue to inflict their act of horror on My creation you will be dealt a powerful reprimand.*

Heed now this, one of My most urgent warnings to the Human Race. **Take the life of My unborn and I will take yours.** *Pray hard children for the faith of all My children as they continue to ignore the teachings given to you since the beginning of time.*[118]

Our Lady tells us that she needs to bring America into the desert so that it can be purified of its empty culture:

The human family is drained of its rich traditions and society is robbed of the moral code that kept it functioning so well.
Now, nothing is left. All has been poured out. It is too late. Attempts to restore what has been lost are fruitless...
***America**, you have become a desolate culture, stripped naked of your values. You are a shell that holds no substance and a skeleton with no flesh on your bones. Whatever is good, you mocked. Whatever is true, you distort. You are a cloud that carries no water and a box that carries no treasure. You are empty, totally empty. You are dead and think you are alive.*
***If I send preachers to you, you mock them. If I send people who speak the truth, you attack them.** Only the wise and the clever get a hearing. Only those whom you want to hear gain a say.*
*What can I do? **I will lead you into the desert...** When you are ready to hear my words, I will speak to you. Right now, your hearts are broken wineskins which cannot hold my word.*[119]

Jesus discusses the evils of our culture through Maria Divine Mercy:

*My children who are guilty of hateful sin enjoy the fact that their evil behavior is applauded for its entertainment value. **Pornography seeps into so many homes** around the world by **TV channels who present these evil atrocities as harmless humorous fun**. These same channels who refuse to speak My name. **Violence also is glamorized** not only on TV but in games making them so acceptable that people now consider the act of violence a natural thing...*
Those guilty of sexual deviant behavior and those who flaunt their bodies in an obscene immoral way will suffer excruciating pain for eternity...
***Sins of the flesh are abhorrent to Me. So many souls are perishing in Hell because of the sin of pornography and sexually deviant acts.** Let them know what their fate will be unless they show remorse.*[120]

Evil Is Presented As Being Good While Good As Evil

When man questions his faith he needs to think. If he is in doubt then he must ask Me to open his eyes. If he is finding it difficult to pray he must ask Me to open his mouth. But if he won't listen to the truth then he needs the prayer of others.

*My children I am deeply concerned at the way in which evil is presented as being good while good is being presented as evil. **Everything in your world is back to front.** For those of you without a deep devotion to Me you will be none the wiser.*

Actions are now being perpetrated in the world at every level of government, church and state in your name and you are oblivious to this.

***Bad laws are being introduced** and presented to mankind as being in their best interests. This includes **new regimes, medicine, foreign aid, vaccination** and the preaching **of new religions** and **other doctrines**. Never has there been so much confusion amongst My children.*[121]

A Philosopher's Perspective of America Today

Dr. Peter Kreeft speaks about the issues of America's demise in his article: **The Winning Strategy (for winning the Culture Wars)**:

***If the God of life does not respond to this culture of death with judgment, God is not God.** If God does not honor the blood of the hundreds of millions of innocent victims then the God of the Bible, the God of Israel, the God of orphans and widows, the Defender of the defenseless, is a man-made myth, a fairy tale.*

Where is the culture of death coming from? Here. America is the center of the culture of death. America is the world's one and only cultural superpower. If I haven't shocked you yet, I will now. Do you know what Muslims call us? They call us "The Great Satan." And do you know what I call them? I call them right.

But America has the most just, and moral, and wise, and biblical historical and constitutional foundation in all the world. America is one of the most religious countries in the world. The Church is big and rich and free in America.

*Yes. Just like ancient Israel. And **if God still loves his Church in America, he will soon make it small and poor and persecuted**, as he did to ancient Israel, so that he can keep it alive. If he loves us, he will prune us, and we will bleed, and the blood of the martyrs will be the seed of the Church again, and a second spring will come—but not without blood. It never happens without blood, sacrifice, and suffering. The continuation of Christ's work—if it is really Christ's work and not a comfortable counterfeit—can never happen without the Cross.*

*I don't mean merely that Western civilization will die. That's a piece of trivia. I mean eternal souls will die. Billions of Ramons and Vladamirs and Janes and Tiffanies will go to Hell. That's what's at stake in this war: not just whether America will become a banana republic, or whether we'll forget Shakespeare, or even whether some nuclear terrorist will incinerate half of humanity, but whether our children and our children's children will see God forever. That's what's at stake in "Hollywood versus America." That's why **we must wake up and smell the rotting souls**.*

Dr. Kreeft says there are two enemies – Satan and sin:

Our enemies are demons. *Fallen angels. Evil spirits [and servants of Satan].*

So says Jesus Christ: "Do not fear those who can kill the body and then has no more power over you. I will tell you whom to fear. Fear him who has power to destroy both body and soul in Hell."

So says St. Peter, the first pope: "The Devil, like a roaring lion, is going through the world seeking the ruin of souls. Resist him, steadfast in the faith."

So says St. Paul: "We wrestle not against flesh and blood, but against principalities and powers of wickedness in high places."

*So said **Pope Leo the XIII, who received a vision of the 20th century** that history has proved terrifyingly true. He saw Satan, at the beginning of time, allowed one century in which to do his worst work,* *and he chose the 20th. This pope with the name and heart of a lion was so overcome by the terror of this vision that he fell into a trance. When he awoke, he composed a prayer (see below) for the whole Church to use to get it through the 20th century. The prayer was widely known and prayed after every Mass—until the '60s: exactly when the Church was struck with that incomparably swift disaster that we have not yet named (but which future historians will), the disaster that has destroyed a third of our priests, two-thirds of our nuns, and nine-tenths of our children's theological knowledge; the disaster that has turned the faith of our fathers into the doubts of our dissenters, the wine of the Gospel into the water of psychobabble.*

Mary's Call to the United States

Through the American Locutionist, Our Lady reportedly says:

Another movement must stir. New voices must be raised, *"We will not turn our backs on God. We will not renounce our Christian roots. We will not have our identity changed. We began as a Christian nation. We prospered as a Christian nation. We will only continue to exist if we remain a Christian nation."*
Stop holding back. Come out of hiding. Speak up. Confront this erasing of Christian identity. You are the majority. Your voice should be strong. Look at your numbers. All you need is a voice, my voice, saying to you, "Take back your nation. Reclaim your house, before it is too late! I will help you."[122]

*The forces of destruction will continue to multiply as **atomic weapons** proliferate and fall into the hands of terrorists who are committed **to the destruction of the West and the rise of the Muslim faith**. This will present new and more dangerous situations. The resources of **the West** will be stretched thin, easily able to be penetrated. So, what can be done in the face of these mounting problems?... There is no need for mankind to go **down the road of nuclear war** but the time is short and people must realize the urgency. Do not wait! Do not wait! **Gather*** *now in intercession. Begin in the home. Move to the parish and then spread everywhere. Hands must be lifted in intercession.*[123]

*Who will be the first to renounce violence and choose the way to peace? These will be **the peacemakers of the New Age.** This was the path which my Son chose when he told Peter to put away his sword (Mt.26:52). This has been the path of everyone who truly followed my Son. They always closed the door of death, even if it meant their own death.*

*The world will cry out, "We cannot do this. There is violence everywhere". Begin where there is no violence. Is the child within the womb violent? Does he attack anyone? Why is the door of death so open to him? Close that door first and a new gentleness will settle upon **America**.*[124]

Warning of Radical Muslim Threat and Invitation to Respond

If only we would do what Our Lady asks. Why not do it and see what happens? She explains what happened when one country did what she is asking and when one historical battle turned everything around because of Our Lady's intervention:

*When will people learn? There are solutions to worldwide problems but they lie in my Immaculate Heart. But what people turn to me and invoke me? **Look at the Philippines**! They invoked me and I ridded them of their dictator without any bloodshed. **Contrast the two, the Philippines and the Middle East** and you will see two, quite different models. Dictators can be removed without plunging a nation into a furnace of suffering.*[125]

*Let me take you back in history to the famous Battle of **Lepanto** (1571) when Europe could have been overwhelmed by the Muslims. So many in secular Europe forget their history. They do not realize how only those with faith saved the Western civilization from being totally wiped out by the Muslim attacks. Only the papacy continued to rally the forces of good. Many others, caught up as usual in their selfish* *interests, would not cooperate and would not turn their eyes to the threat. Only the pope and those whom he could stir were interested in this vital battle.*

Although outmanned and really no match for the Muslim fleet, the papal forces won the victory and the West was saved. This naval battle was reinforced by the many who recited the rosary, and so this feast was established, (by Pope Pius V), as an annual reminder of the power of the rosary.

O reader, learn the true history that has been taken from you. ***The Muslim threat is again at your door.*** *This time, new methods are used, very effective and powerful. You, on the other hand, are asleep.* ***You do not realize how soon will be the day when America will be attacked****, an America that is so unprepared to respond, an America that is willing to compromise the truth. The Muslims have no desire to compromise. They seek only conquest.* ***Do you want your children and your grandchildren to live under Muslim rule? Then wake up. Take the rosary in your hands and begin to pray it, today and every day.***[126]

However, if America does not seek me, if it continues to turn its back, then nothing can be done. Pray, ***America****. Fall to your knees. Your own efforts are worthless against this darkness which you have chosen.*[127]

America, the Economy, Abortion, and War

We know why God will bring His justice upon us:

Yes, ***America****, that is what you have done. You are becoming like Europe. You are removing the title* religious *and substituting* secular*. Like Samson, you have fallen into the hands of Delilah and she is taking away your strength. Wake up before she cuts off all you hair and delivers you over to your most hated enemies. That is exactly what will happen. Your enemies look on. They watch and wait. It is not yet the moment. You still have some strength but soon, yes very soon, you will be their prey.*

Wake up. Wake up. *The word* <u>religious</u> *is fading. When it is totally erased, you will fall. This does not have to happen.*[128]

O America, how could this have happened to you whom I have blessed from the beginning? You took my title away from your largest river. (The Mississippi was originally called the River of the Immaculate Conception.) Now, you further strip yourself of your religious clothing. Well, continue. Continue your secular course and I will have you stand naked before the nations, an economic laughing stock. You have put aside your traditions... **It will all be taken away from you by your creditors.** *They will close your doors and shut down your excesses. Must it come to this? Is there no solution? I can offer you solutions, but you will not listen. I can point out a road, but you will not follow. Still, I must try. I cannot give up on America, the nation I have taken as my own.*[129]

I told you that **America** *chose the darkness. In the bible, when Israel went against the voices of the prophets, they chose their path of darkness. I let them walk their path until they repented and turned back to me. The same thing is happening in America. The economic scourge is like the Babylonian invasion of Jerusalem, the result of their sins... The* **economic weakness** *results from their choosing the darkness of* **abortion.**[130]

I will pick out one sin, the most heinous of sins, the one that most arouses the anger of God. I will preach against that sin. My message will be easily understood and this is my promise. "If the world repents of this one sin, I will hold back the chastisements of God and there will be a springtime without a winter. Otherwise, **the deadliest of winters will settle upon the earth.***

The sin that stirs the anger of the Father is the **killing of the unborn.** *Repent of this sin and turn back to life. I will protect you, if you protect these little ones.*[131]

America, *your debt crisis is rooted in your divisions and your divisions are rooted in your Supreme Court abortion decision.*[132]

I give you another chance because you have been generous in the past. This is also your future hope. To save your economy, turn your eyes abroad. See the starving of the world and feed them as you have never fed them before. As your food enters the stomachs of the world's hungry, then my economic blessings will flow into your financial systems. That is my promise. **The hungry of the world are the doors to your economic recovery.**[133]

"All of a sudden", that is all that I need to say. "All of a sudden" **the events...** *will sweep across the world, as no other year in history. So, my words become more urgent, "Watch and pray". Can you not find time to pray? Cannot the family gather in prayer? Can you not find a few minutes for your rosary? All of these seem so small but they are beginning steps leading to far greater favors.*
I can only say, "All of a sudden". When events happen "all of a sudden", there is no more time to prepare. Do not wait. "All of a sudden" the events will pour out so quickly.[134]

A new army will come forth *for which* **the West** *is not prepared. They do not realize that Satan has not revealed all of his strengths. The West thinks they are prepared... They are not facing a human intellect but an angelic intellect (Satan) that is far greater than theirs... He probes, not just from the outside but from the inside. He knows people in high places whom he can corrupt. He has them in his back pocket. They lead sinful lives and are open to blackmail and extortion... They are given to vices that they must keep secret. Satan has a hidden army. They do not even know that they belong to him. However, when he needs them to fail in their duties, they will not be free to resist. They are compromised men and women, yet they hold sensitive positions and are entrusted with important secrets. This is what I call* **"Satan's Hidden Army".**[135]

When the Woman Spoke to George Washington

American Locutionist continues:

*There are unimaginable problems ahead. The world has seen only a few, the previews of what is to come. There will be a **great shift of power** away from those nations that used to call upon me. Yes, I must say it, "that used to call upon me". Long ago, they left the Church. They left the side of my Son. They adopted different values and put on a different garment. Now, they are Christian in name only. Their building still stands but they have no foundation. Their people are not united in faith. They have nothing holding them together. The secular spirit only responds in prosperity and abundance. It dissolves when faced with catastrophe. "Every man for himself". This is the cry of the secular man. "How can I preserve what is mine?" are the thoughts of his heart. Where does that leave a nation in the time of crisis? To whom can they turn, when all are seeking their own interests?*

***America** still breathes. It still has life. It still remains **my hope**. If only I can cure it of its sickness, it will regain its strength. Even more, it will regain its purpose, the noble purpose for which I brought it forth. Let me define the purpose of America.*

George Washington

*O America, **I appeared to your first president when he was still a general at Valley Forge**. I told him of **three moments in the history of the republic** – the present moment in which he found himself, a future moment when brother would kill brother, and a moment yet to come. Go back and read those words. They are recorded by your historians. See what I said about the first two moments that have already happened. Then, you will believe my words about **the third moment which is about to happen**. More important, you will understand that this republic came about through my hands and that **your nation has always been in my hands**. Then, you will turn to me.*[136]

The account of Washington's vision appeared in a newspaper article first published in the National Tribune in 1859 and reprinted in 1880. Later reprinted in The Stars and Stripes newspaper owned by the National Tribune, in 1931 and the latest printing on December 21, 1950. The vision was related to a reporter named Wesley Bradshaw by an officer who served under General Washington at Valley Forge, named Anthony Sherman. In the vision, Washington sees three great trials that America would face. These were the Revolutionary War, the Civil War, and the greatest threat, a war fought on the soil of the United States as the final conflict near the time of Jesus' return to reign on the earth.

Here is an excerpt from the vision:

*And again I heard the mysterious voice saying, 'Son of the Republic, look and learn.' At this the dark, shadowy angel placed a trumpet to his mouth, and blew three distinct blasts; and taking water from the ocean, he sprinkled it upon Europe, Asia and Africa. Then my eyes beheld a fearful scene: from each of these countries arose thick, black clouds that were soon joined into one. Throughout this mass there gleamed a dark red light by which I saw hordes of armed men, who, moving with the cloud, marched by land and sailed by sea to **America**. Our country was enveloped in this volume of cloud, and 1 saw these **vast armies devastate the whole country** and burn the villages, towns and cities that I beheld springing up. As my ears listened to the thundering of the cannon, clashing of swords, and the shouts and cries of **millions in mortal combat**, I heard again the mysterious voice saying, 'Son of the Republic, look and learn.' When the voice had ceased, the dark shadowy angel placed his trumpet once more to his mouth, and blew a long and fearful blast.*

*Instantly **a light as of a thousand suns** shone down from above me, and pierced and broke into fragments the dark cloud which enveloped America. At the same moment **the angel** upon whose head still shone the word 'Union,' and who bore our national flag in one hand and a sword in the other, descended from the heavens attended by legions of white spirits. These immediately joined the inhabitants of America, who I perceived were well nigh overcome, but who immediately **taking courage again**, closed up their broken ranks and renewed the battle. Again, amid the fearful noise of the conflict, I heard the mysterious voice saying, 'Son of the Republic, look and learn.' As the voice ceased, the shadowy angel for the last time dipped water from the* *ocean and sprinkled it upon America. Instantly the dark cloud rolled back, together with the armies it had brought, leaving* **the inhabitants of the land victorious***!*

Then once more I beheld the villages, towns and cities springing up where I had seen them before, while the bright angel, planting the azure standard he had brought in the midst of them, cried with a loud voice: 'While the stars remain, and the heavens send down dew upon the earth, so long shall the Union last.' And taking from his brow the crown on which blazoned the word 'Union,' he placed it upon the National Standard while the people, kneeling down, said, 'Amen.'

The scene instantly began to fade and dissolve, and I at last saw nothing but the rising, curling vapor I at first beheld. This also disappearing, I found myself once more gazing upon the mysterious visitor, who, in the same voice I had heard before, said, 'Son of the Republic, what you have seen is thus interpreted: Three great perils will come upon the Republic. The most fearful is the third, but in this greatest conflict the whole world united shall not prevail against her. Let every child of the Republic learn to live for his God, his land and the Union.' With these words the vision vanished, and I started from my seat and felt that I had seen a vision wherein had been shown to me the birth, progress, and destiny of the United States.

America Belongs to Our Lady

American Locutionist continues:

I am the one who led Christopher Columbus and my name was on his ship. I am the one who sent the missionaries and people of good will to these new lands, bringing the faith and the civilization of Europe. I am the one who has kept at bay the atomic power unleashed for the first time so many years ago, but never used since. I am the one who has limited natural disasters. I am the one standing between the Father and the Divine Chastisements.[137]

Our Lady to Nancy Fowler – America at War with Russia and China

Georgia visionary Nancy Fowler reportedly received apparitions and locutions in the 1990s about the times we are living in. Her messages offer a summary of all we have been discussing in this book, and a good overview of the apocalyptic events of our times. Jesus reportedly said:

Beware of the Orient. [138]
The Chinese woman was crying because her family was going off to war. [139]
A great war is coming. Unless My children wholeheartedly turn back to Me, I will not stop the war. [140]
China is a real enemy. **From China will come a great war.** *Do not trust China. Do not trust China. Do not trust China. I will say no more.* [141]
The United States will be at war. I tell you now that many nations will be wiped off the face of the earth. Man will destroy man. In your sinfulness, you shall perish. Unceasingly pray and beg for My mercy. Time is running out. I tell you, more signs will I give. Man will not be able to ignore Me. I will bring My presence into the world as a great act of mercy as I have never done before. [142]
Do not trust Russia. I tell you, do not be fooled by false peace. [143]
Do not think that communism is dead. I tell you, it is on the rise. As you have chosen to follow the master of deception, then so shall you be deceived. [144]
Fire will fall from Heaven... Woe to this sinful generation. China, Russia and Korea will be involved in a major war. [145]
Korea, China and Russia are a deadly trio. [146]
America will be a slave state unless you return to Me and make reparation for your grievous crimes. [147]

Nancy said, *"I keep seeing these soldiers and think they are on our soil."* Our Lord responded: *"It is a true vision.* **The day will come when soldiers will be on your soil unless you turn back to Me.**"

Our Blessed Mother reportedly spoke to Nancy, saying:

Please, little children, amend your lives. Ask God's forgiveness and offer sacrifices daily. Please, children, you must not offend God any longer. I come with a serious warning. A great war will come upon this world, greater than man has ever known. Pray, children, pray. Amend your ways. Please. I invite you to pray the Rosary for peace.[148]

A New Pentecost

I am the Immaculate Conception. I am the spouse of the Holy Spirit. Behold a new Pentecost is coming. A new heaven and a new earth is dawning but first the old will be destroyed.
Fire will fall down from Heaven. Lightning will flash from one end of the sky to the other and the earth will plunge into a darkness it has never seen. The world has chosen these punishments.[149]

The Warning

The time will come when all mankind will see their sins. This is a time of grace. It is a great grace from God. Some of my children will experience intense heat. It is a healing.[150]

Natural Disasters

Jesus said to Nancy:

My children, you have ignored God long enough. Woe be to the inhabitants of the earth. With a mighty blow I will pound the earth, earthquake after earthquake, volcanoes will erupt, tidal waves, famine. The water will become polluted in many places. Diseases, every kind of affliction awaits this sinful generation.
You choose to sin of your own free will, then with your own free will you will suffer.[151]
There will be many new diseases coming.[152]

The clock continues to tick. The hour is rapidly approaching when one disaster after another will befall you. There will be fighting everywhere. There will be famine and polluted water in many places.

Great waves will crash upon your shores and you will experience cold when you should experience warmth. Flood waters will increase in many places. Fire will be upon the earth. You will think that the heavens and the earth have rebelled against you. The clock continues to tick.
Darkness will fall over the whole world and stars will fall.[153]

Remedy of the Coming Events

Know that all that I have told you and more will come to pass. Repent. Repent. Repent. If you have ears, open them. If you have eyes, open them and come back to me. Please, dear children.[154]

The New Era to Come

Our Blessed Mother said to Nancy:

Little ones, be prepared for the kingdom of God in your midst, for the reign of the Immaculate Heart.[155]

PHASE 4: The Great Warning...
of God's Mercy

ᘓ

Jesus said to his disciples:
Awesome sights and mighty signs will come from the sky...   There will
be signs in the sun, the moon, and the stars,
and on earth nations will be in dismay,
perplexed by the roaring of the sea and the waves.
People will die of fright
in anticipation of what is coming upon the world,
for the powers of the heavens will be shaken.
Luke 21:11, 25-26

The Great Warning seems to correspond with the 6th and 7th seals of the Book of Revelation, which comes after the opening of the previous seals of apostasy, wars, and natural disasters. The Warning has two parts:

1. An event like 2 comets colliding and a red cross in the sky above the earth

2. An interior mini-judgment, like a revelation of our sins; how we stand in the light of God's justice. It will be a correction of the conscience of the world.   (Garabandal)

There will be given to mankind a great sign in the heavens of this sort: all the light of the heavens will be totally extinguished... There will be **a great darkness** *over the whole earth. Then* **a great sign of the cross will appear** *in the sky. From the openings from where the hands and feet of the savior were nailed will come forth great lights which will light up the earth for a period of time. This will happen before the very final days. It is the sign for the end of the world.* **After it will come the days of justice!...** (Jesus to St. Faustina)

The Warning will shock everyone. They will see **great signs in the skies** before The Warning takes place. Stars will clash with such impact that man will confuse the **spectacle they see in the sky as being catastrophic**. As these comets infuse **a great red sky will result** and the **sign of my cross will be seen all over the world** by everyone. Many will be frightened. But I say rejoice for you will see, for the first time in your lives, a truly Divine Sign that represents **great news of God's mercy for sinners everywhere...** *Do not be fearful of The Warning. Await it with joy.* (MDM)

When the Warning occurs, great conversion will occur throughout the world. Then, the people will be hungry for this message and the truth contained in the unsealed book, promised to the world for these the end times.

Your soul will be illuminated and you will see what good deeds, and bad deeds, you conducted throughout your lives. At that stage, many of you will embrace the Love of God. Sadly, many will be too stubborn to accept their wrongdoing. They will be cast away and will suffer terribly. (MDM)

The Warning

The world is about to experience the greatest act of God's mercy in history, since the time of Christ's death. Every man, woman, and child over the age of reason will be shown His mercy to bring humanity to conversion. **The Warning will purify God's children in preparation for the Second Coming.** Through it, many people will seek forgiveness for their sins who would not otherwise have done so.

Jesus tells us what we must expect during The Warning:

*Give them details in advance so that when they see **the red sky flare up**, a reflection of My Great Mercy, they will know that there is nothing to fear. Instead they must rejoice for here, at last for many of My children around the world, will be the proof they have been seeking all their lives.*

*Great rejoicing amongst My children is what I yearn for, not tears of sadness. When you see **My cross** you will all know then the passion of My love for all of you.*

Many will weep tears of great joy for they will know I have come to flood their souls with the grace of redemption. For others who don't know Me they will be frightened for then the true realization of the graveness of their sins will become apparent.

*Followers of mine everywhere I call on you to show great courage by telling My children that they must not fear when they witness this **divine spectacular display of My Great Mercy** for mankind.* [156]

The skies will open up during the Warning. There is nothing to fear about The Warning. In the mercy of God, man will find peace!

A Dramatic Event

*Be prepared, all of you, for soon you will witness the Power of God and His Divine Intervention in the world, when He will stop all that is, **for a period of fifteen minutes**.* [157]

*It will shock many people in the world as it will be a dramatic event where **the skies will open and the flames of Mercy will shoot up*** *across the world. For many people will not understand what is happening. So shocked will they be they will mistakenly think that they are witnessing the end of the world. Tell them to **rejoice** when they witness My Glory for this, if you are properly prepared for it, will be the most spectacular example of My Mercy since the day of My Crucifixion. This, My children, will be your saving grace and will prevent those who would otherwise have been condemned from entering the depths of Hell.*

*All My children everywhere must **warn lost souls as to what to expect**. Urge them to seek reconciliation by confessing their sins now. It is important that as many people as possible are in a state of grace beforehand as they may not survive this event due to shock. Far better to witness this Divine Spectacular event first, rather than being unprepared at the final day of Judgment...*
Go now in peace. Do not be fearful. Just pray for those souls with no faith so they do not die in mortal sin.[158]

Related Prophecies from Saint Hildegard, Newest Doctor of the Church

*Before **the comet** comes, many nations, the good excepted, will be scourged by want and famine. The great nation in the ocean that is inhabited by people of different tribes and descent will be devastated by earthquake, storm, and tidal wave. It will be divided and, in great part, submerged. That nation will also have many misfortunes at sea and lose its colonies.*

[After the] great Comet, the great nation will be devastated by earthquakes, storms, and great waves of water, causing much want and plagues. The ocean will also flood many other countries, so that all coastal cities will live in fear, with many destroyed.

All seacoast cities will be fearful, and many of them will be destroyed by tidal waves, and most living creatures will be killed, and even those who escape will die from a horrible disease. For in none of those cities does a person live according to the Laws of God.

A powerful wind will rise in the North, carrying heavy fog and the densest dust, and it will fill their throats and eyes so that they will cease their butchery and be stricken with a great fear.

Another locutionist offers more details:

Two comets will collide, My cross will appear in a red sky

*My dearly beloved daughter time is near. The Warning is close now. It is with great sorrow that I must tell you that many souls will not heed these messages about The Warning. **My word falls on deaf ears.** Why won't they listen? I am not only giving them My great gift of Mercy when I will shower My graces over the whole world, I am also **trying to prepare them** for this event. Many **millions of sinners will rejoice** when they are shown My great mercy. Others won't get a chance to redeem themselves in time because they **will die of shock.***

*My daughter, you must do everything you can to **warn the world.** Because **this great event will shock everyon**e. They will see **great signs in the skies** before The Warning takes place. Stars will clash with such impact that man will confuse the **spectacle they see in the sky as being catastrophic.** As these **comets** infuse **a great red sky will result** and the **sign of my cross will be seen all over the world** by everyone. Many will be frightened. But I say **rejoice** for you will see, for the first time in your lives, a truly Divine Sign that represents **great news for sinners everywhere.***

*See My cross then and you will know that My great mercy is being given to each of you, My precious children. For it was with the deep abiding love that I held for you that I died, willingly, on the cross to save you. When you see **the crosses in the sky** during The Warning, you will know that this is **a sign of My love** for you.*

*Pray My beloved followers that your brothers and sisters can rejoice when they, too, are shown **the proof of My existence.** Pray that they will accept that this is their chance to redeem themselves in My eyes. That this great act of Mercy will save their souls, if they will allow Me to help them.*

You will be shown what it is like to die in mortal sin

*The Warning will be **a purifying experience** for all of you. It may be **unpleasant in part** especially for those in grave sin. Because, for the first time ever, you will be shown what it feels like when the light of God disappears from your life. Your souls will feel the abandonment felt by those who die in mortal sin. These **poor souls who left it too late** to ask God to forgive them their sins. Remember it is important that I allow all of you to feel this emptiness of soul. For only then will you finally understand that, without the light of God in your souls, you cease to feel. Your soul and body would be just empty vessels. Even sinners feel the light of God because He is present in every one of His children on earth. But when you die in mortal sin, this light no longer exists.*

Prepare now for this great event. Save your souls while you can. For it will only be when the light of God leaves you that you will finally realize the empty, barren and darkness that Satan offers which is full of anguish and terror.

Replenish your souls. Rejoice now for The Warning will save you and bring you closer to My Sacred Heart.

Welcome the Warning. For then you will be given the proof of Eternal Life and know how important it is.[159]

The Swords of Justice will fall on those who fail to prepare adequately for The Warning.

*My flames of Divine Mercy, presented to the world to give each of you a taste of what the Final Day of Judgment will be like, is going to be misinterpreted by so many of you. This great day of **The Warning** draws closer by the month so you must now put aside the time in preparing for My Divine Mercy.*

*Many, many souls will find it difficult to understand what this event really means. **So many will, as a result, die of shock which saddens Me.** Because, for those who do not survive, it will be because of the sorry state of their souls.*

*Catholics everywhere **seek confession now** if you want to benefit from My great act of love and mercy. Christians and other faiths speak in* *silence and tell God how remorseful you are, how much you regret your transgressions and then ask Him to forgive you for your sins.*

*Only those who are strong of heart in their love for Me and God, the Almighty Father, will be prepared adequately. Others, because of their strength in mind and character **will finally understand the truth and accept Me with love in their hearts.***

***As for others, so harsh will the shock be, that when their souls are revealed to them in their darkness they will drop dead.** By then it will be too late to seek forgiveness. There will be no hope for them. Pray, pray all of you so that as many souls as possible will survive great act of Mercy.*[160]

*I must share with you the feelings I am enduring now. The first is one of happiness because I am to bring so much mercy to My children during the Illumination of Conscience which is close. And then there are my tears of great sadness for those oblivious to this event and who are unprepared. My children will need to tell as many of their friends and family of this great event in order to save their souls. No matter if they smile and ridicule your claims for, afterwards, they will thank you. **Tell them the truth.** Ask them to open their minds. They should be made aware of what they will witness because when they see **My cross in the sky** they will be prepared. That is all they need to understand. Then they will accept the discomfort they will endure when their past lives are played out before their eyes. **Tell them to review their life** and remind them of the harm that they may have inflicted on their fellow brothers and sisters.*[161]

A Great Sign in the Sky

The Lord spoke to St. Faustina about **a great darkness and a great sign**, explaining what would accompany it, saying:

Before I come as a just judge, I am coming first as 'King of Mercy!' *Let all men now approach the throne of my mercy with absolute confidence! Some time before the last days of final justice arrive, there will be given to mankind a great sign in the heavens of this sort: all the light of the heavens will be totally extinguished...*

*There will be **a great darkness** over the whole earth. Then **a great sign of the cross will appear** in the sky. From the openings from where the hands and feet of the savior were nailed will come forth great lights which will light up the earth for a period of time. This will happen before the very final days. It is the sign for the end of the world. **After it will come the days of justice!** Let souls have recourse to the fount of my mercy while there is still time! Woe to him who does not recognize the time of my visitation...*

*In the Old Covenant I sent prophets wielding thunderbolts to My people. **Today I am sending you with My mercy to the people of the whole world.** I do not want to punish aching mankind, but I desire to heal it, pressing it to My merciful Heart. I use punishment when they themselves force Me to do so; My hand is reluctant to take hold of the sword of justice. **Before the Day of Justice, I am sending the Day of Mercy.**[162]*

People Will Respond In Different Ways

The Fire of the Holy Spirit will be felt in the hearts of everyone.

1) For those who are in a state of grace, it will be a feeling of joy, love and compassion for Me, your Jesus.

2) For those in a state of venial sin, you will feel the pain of Purgatory, but you will soon be purified and then you will feel a deep peace and love within your hearts for Me.

3) For those of you in mortal sin, you will experience the wretchedness and pain as if you have been plunged into the fires of Hell. Some of you, in this state of sin, will beg for My forgiveness and favor to stop your internal suffering. This I will grant to you if you can find true remorse in your heart and accept that your sins cause Me grievous hurt and pain for they insult God.

4) Then there will be those poor unfortunate souls who will spit at Me, fight with Me and then turn their backs. The terror, they will feel, will be because their souls are infested by Satan. They will not be able to stand the pain when they witness My Light and they will run into the embrace of the evil one whose darkness brings them comfort.

5) Finally there will be those who will die instantly because of the shock they will experience. Please pray for these souls every day, for your prayers will gain for them entrance to My Kingdom.

This is one of the greatest miracles ever accorded to God's children.

My Revelation to you, during this event, will wake you up to the fact that My Promise, to come back to save the human race so they can inherit the Glorious Life ahead, will soon be realized.[163]

Spread My Word After the Warning

*My children, as soon as The Warning happens and when conversion takes place move quickly to **spread My most Holy Word**. There is an urgency to this because this will be a crucial period. That is when, through the work of My beloved followers everywhere, that My children will stay on the right path. It will be the time when **prayer and conversion can dilute the impact of the havoc** which will come about through the **reign of both the Anti-Christ and the False Prophet.***
*Accept the truth now for what it is. **Do not fear** the truth. Embrace it. For when you do you will be set free and your confidence in Me will enable you to defend My word properly. Fear will hold you back My precious children. **Courage** will win souls... I will, with the help of God, the Eternal Father, lead you so you can march with all My children towards the New Paradise which awaits you all.*[164]

The time for The Warning is now close and it will happen quickly in the blink of an eye. All will be stopped in their tracks as they witness My Great Mercy. Pray for all those in mortal sin as a priority. They need your prayers for many of them will drop stone dead from shock when they see the horror, as seen through My eyes, of the sinful atrocities they have committed.[165]

*This is what I am preparing for, a gift come down from heaven that will touch every heart, a **divine illumination**, in the interior part of every human being.*

*But that event must be prepared for. The Church must be aware. The people must be told. But who will tell them? What preacher is adequate for this task? That is why it has become my task to prepare the world through these teachings... there will be a **period of signs and wonders**. This should alert people to the coming manifestation. Unfortunately, the world will remain in darkness. However, because of worldwide communications, individuals will have access, both to my words and to the news about these manifestations (which have already begun, especially at Medjugorje). At least, part of the world will be prepared. Even some secular media will note these events, not from a religious purpose but merely because they are newsworthy. This, too, will further my purposes.*[166]

*This great Warning is the manifestation of My Divine Mercy given to Sister Faustina. This great act of My Mercy was foretold and it will be during The Warning that My Great Mercy will envelop the whole world. My blood and water will gush forth so that you will all know the truth at last. Tell those who do not believe in Me, or My Eternal Father, that this event will happen. Then when it does they will be able to withstand the shock of My Mercy, which will **save millions** of souls during The Warning from the grasp of Satan. The truth, when revealed, will save so many from the fires of Hell.*

The Holy Spirit thereafter present in My children everywhere will help defeat the works of The Evil One. All of you must spread the word about how mankind needs to prepare their souls in advance. For even believers must understand that they too will find it emotionally disturbing to view their own past sinful behavior as it appears to Me.

*I call on all of you now to **seek confession**. For those other Christians you must kneel down and pray for redemption. For those who are unsure of this prophecy please keep your hearts open for when you witness this ecological but supernatural event it is important that you understand that this is the greatest miracle you will ever see and that it is My great gift to you all. Consider this. **This is how the Final Day*** *of Judgment will unfold only this time you will not be condemned. You will be given a new lease of life when your soul will be saved to enable you to restore to the level I desire of it.[167]*

They, My beloved children, need to know that when I come soon they will come face to face with Me. How I long to show them that I really do exist and how I await the joy on their faces when they witness My love and mercy.

For many of My children will fall down and **cry tears of relief.** *Tears of joy and happiness. Tears of wonder and love. For, at last, it will be possible to live a new life thereafter where all can follow the truth of My teachings.*

My children will not realize the significance of this **Great Act of Mercy,** *the greatest gift ever bestowed on mankind since My Crucifixion. For it will be through this gift of The Warning that* **man's eyes will be finally opened to the truth of their entire existence on this earth and beyond.**

Those who are alive in this world today must understand how privileged they are to be given the proof of the existence of God, the Eternal Father and I, His beloved Son, although this is beyond your comprehension.

After the Warning do not turn back to your old ways

I urge all of you that when you have seen My presence and shown how sin, not only offends me but propels you down the pathway to Hell that you must not turn back to your old ways.

The period after the Warning is crucial for world peace *and your salvation. Do not reject this gift. Grasp it with both arms. Let The Warning bring you as one in Me. When you do this and pray for guidance you will be rewarded with the New Paradise on Earth where you will want for nothing.[168]*

Tell those souls who refuse to pray to push aside their pride and distaste and turn to Me now to ask for forgiveness. Be clear that **many, many souls will not survive this imminent event***...*

*Tell the world this event is going to save them. Many will repent during this mystical experience. They will feel **a burning sensation**, not unlike that experienced by souls in purgatory. This will give them an insight as to what souls, who are not fully clean, have to go through before they can see the glorious light of Heaven. By **simply accepting** that this event may take place they can survive it. Turn to me and say "Please guide me towards the light and goodness of your great mercy and forgive me for my sins" and **I will pardon you instantly**. Then after The Warning you will experience a **deep peace and joy** in your soul.*[169]

My children must understand that The Warning, while a great act of Mercy, is only the first phase in what will be a very difficult and challenging time for all My children. For after that those hardened sinners and followers of Satan will deny My existence.
Atheists will say it was a global illusion. Scientists will look for a logical explanation but there wont be one. Meanwhile My followers will be torn in two. Many millions will have converted but they will be confused by the lies spread by the Evil Group, the One World deadly organization whose goal is to destroy the little people for their own financial gain.
*Children if enough people cannot stay on the true path then **it will not be possible to avert the impact of the Chastisement**. For this is when God the Father will move to stop sinners from destroying His creation and His children. He will unleash earthquakes on a magnitude never experienced before, volcanoes in the most unlikely places and the earth will be tossed like a ship in rough waters with no anchor to hold it in one place.*[170]

Do not be fearful of The Warning await it with joy
*My dearly beloved daughter, tell My precious children that they **must not be fearful of The Warning**. Many will feel frightened and this is understandable. But they must listen carefully to Me. I will come to each of you. You will see Me and feel Me in your heart and soul. My presence will flood your souls with the purest of love and compassion*

so you should be joyful. At last you will see Me and your soul will be enveloped with love and excitement.

For sinners and unbelievers, *most of them will simply be relieved that I exist. For their witness of My Holy Presence will be the blood that is needed to flood their souls with the nourishment missing for so long. Many will suffer the torment, as I endure, when they see their sins unroll before them. Heartbroken when they see how they have offended Me they will beg Me to forgive them.*

Children over the age of reason *will also see how they, too, offend me through sin. In many instances those children who deny My existence, although they are aware of the truth, will run to Me. They will ask Me to embrace them and will not want Me to let them go.*

*Even the most hardened sinners will fail not to be affected by this supernatural event. Children you must ignore rumor. Ignore stories which are sensational. There is nothing to fear. **The Warning must be awaited with pure joy in your hearts**.*

I await the time with so much love in My heart when I will pour out My Divine Mercy over each of you everywhere throughout the world. This is the moment when, afterwards, you will realize how fortunate you, of this generation, are. How can you not recognize the mercy that will be shown to mankind? In the past so many souls died in grievous sin. Now, all sinners will finally understand the truth at last.

It is not easy for My children to acknowledge the existence of Me or My Eternal Father. Without proof of a material kind many do not want to get to know Me. Many have no interest or belief in the divine realm. This event will open their eyes to the simple fact that life does not end on earth. It continues for eternity. That is the reason why they must prepare their souls.

The warning will show them what they must do to rectify this. Remember children I am your savior. I love you all in a way that is beyond your comprehension. Await My arrival with love and calmness. Fear not the dramatic spectacle in the sky and the color of the rays which will be spread everywhere to herald My arrival. This will prepare you for the moment.

Please pray that all mankind will feel joy in their hearts for this event will mean salvation for mankind on a magnitude that will save so many souls and enable them to enter the new paradise on earth.[171]

Fear of The Warning is not something I encourage.
Pray now for your own and other souls through the act of redemption and before your face to face encounter with Me your beloved Savior.
I smile with joy and happiness when I think of the moment when this great Gift of My Mercy is revealed to My children. **It is a homecoming the likes of which cannot be described.** *For this will be when your hearts will be filled with My divine love. Your souls will be enlightened finally in preparation for the New Paradise on earth. I will then bring you the comfort missing in your lives up to now when you will become in union with Me.*[172]

Children do not become discouraged by rumor or tales of despair facing mankind. Instead look to Me now and confide in Me your fears. Mankind will be given such a wonderful gift. Not only will man encounter Me face to face but they will be overjoyed to learn and see the truth presented before their very eyes.
This is to be **a great day in history** *when hope and love will be shown to all of you. Even hardened sinners will fall down and weep tears of remorse. This is good news, children, for all can be saved if they abandon their pride and ego. All, through their own free will, are to be united to allow Me to enter their hearts so that they can be guided towards the light.*
For many sinners in mortal sin this light will burn their eyes and their soul. It will be painful. If they can only endure the fright of seeing how they offend Me they will become strong and will convert.[173]

Please Welcome the Warning
My Warning, the Great Act of Mercy is such a great gift of love so **please welcome it for it will result in much conversion.** *Conversion will be so widespread that it will create a great sense of love and peace when My children have been humbled by this great event.* **Then there will be strength in their numbers.** *The more people who believe*

in The Truth the weaker then will be the impact of the New World Group. Prayer and much of it can avert much of the damage they will attempt to inflict. So please never forget to **pray the Holy Rosary and the Divine Mercy [Chaplet]** *for both combined will help wipe out much of this pending evil. Go now do not fear. Look with enthusiasm for a new beginning, a new peace where evil will be stamped out for good.*[174]

When you see My light, the **flames of My love, materialize in the skies shortly, let you not be in doubt.** *This will not be an illusion. It will be a reality and you must humble yourselves to open your eyes to the truth. Do not turn your eyes away or cower in fear. You must greet my presence as your last chance for salvation. It is I who come to envelop you in My arms…*

When you see My flames of glory in the skies be joyful. Any doubts you ever had about the existence of God the Father will disappear. To benefit from the graces that The Warning will bring to your soul so that you can be saved, **you must appear little in My eyes and ask Me to forgive you** *for your sins. My love will then flood your soul and you will come back to Me and your rightful home.*

Resist My mercy out of arrogance or intellectual reasoning and you will be lost.

Await now My mercy with joy and enthusiasm for you will become whole again. You will be reborn.[175]

While many will come face to face with Me during The Warning, I will not come the second time until Judgment Day.[176]

What The Warning Will Offer

According to Fr. Philip Bebie, in his book, *The Warning*, there will be several characteristics of the Warning as follows:

1. It will be like the conversion of Saul/St. Paul
2. It will make us aware of God
3. It will show us our sins, convict the world of its sins

4. It will be a taste of eternity
5. It will be the work of God's Mercy
6. It will be a sign of the future, a sign of the times
7. It will be the direct intervention of God
8. It will call us to choose
9. It calls us to prepare for the Great Miracle
10. It will be two-part, together with the Great Miracle[177]

After the Warning

The period after The Warning will change the way man will look at the world. No more will material pleasures and excesses excite. No more will people treat, as gods, the idols they make of celebrities and wealth. No more will they be so quick to condemn or treat their neighbor cruelly.

The new world, after The Warning, will be a place where love for Me and God the Father will be revered with respect. Many leaders in countries, not of the Christian faith, will pay homage to My Father. Those in places of power who control people's finances will repent in their droves. Many more will peel back their layers of power and share with their brothers and sisters the bread that comes from God the Father. For this bread is for all and is meant to be shared equally.

Many good things will evolve as a result of the Warning. However many souls will not be strong enough in their faith. They, sadly, will go back to their old ways. Seduced by the promises of power, wealth, control and love of self, they will reject God the Father. They will know the truth yet it will still not be enough for them. These poor weak sinners will be a thorn in your side children. Without your prayers their sins will cause havoc in a world which will have been recouped during its new purification.

Prayer, My children is so important. You must ask God the Father to accept your request to quash the persecution which is being planned by these people. Enough prayer can, and will, avert much of the horror these sinners will try to inflict on the world. So many of you are blind to the plan which is being plotted behind your backs. The signs are bring revealed consistently but you fail to recognize them.[178] *Heed this. You will not have to fend for yourselves much longer for very soon now, after The Warning, there will be a more positive feeling of light and love in the world. All is not lost, My daughter.*

Pray for those who convert during The Warning that they will stay on the path of truth. Pray that love for Me and My Eternal Father will become stronger among those followers who already know the truth.

As long as My children embrace the gift of The Warning then there is nothing to fear.

*For those who do not stay on the path and who turn back to sinful ways they have much to fear. My Father will not allow them to infest others through their wayward and wicked ways. **They will be stopped**. Sadly, many will turn away from the truth and try to continue to inflict power and control over the rest of My children.*

***Pray that the Chastisement will be diluted**. Your prayers will help to convert and avert such situations. **This is now the time of waiting**. Praying. Preparing and ensuring that as many people as possible know what to expect.*[179]

*My great gift of Mercy will bring **huge relief to believers** and create **a vast sense of euphoria among those non-believers who will convert**. When they discover the truth they will be **light of heart** and they will be **filled with love for God**, the Eternal Father and Me, your Divine Savior. Even non-Christians will understand the truth of My existence. Finally, this will create **a great sense of joy and love in the world**.*

The Warning Must Be Followed by Prayer

*It is important, however, to remember **one important lesson** regarding The Warning. This great event, when all of you will see not only your sins as I see them but will understand the truth about the next life, **must be followed by prayer**.*

*Sadly, **many will fall back into sin afterwards**. Now is the time to prepare to avoid this situation by **praying My Divine Mercy chaplet*** *every day of your lives.* *By getting into the habit of praying this powerful prayer you will* **retain the level of conversion and faith** *which will sweep the world thereafter.*

Rejoice, pray and thank Me, your Divine Savior for this great mercy. Kneel and give praise to God, the Father, for the gift of My sacrifice. **Prayer** *will help dilute the impact of the persecution by the New World global alliance which will follow. If enough of you remain loyal to me, My teachings and continue to* **pray** *as well as* **receive the sacraments** *you can change the course of events which would follow.*

How powerful My Divine Mercy is. So many of you still do not understand the significance of it. Many, sadly have never heard of it before...

Create Divine Mercy prayer groups all over the world and use this prayer for every person known to you who may be dying for **I will** **guarantee their salvation** *if you do... Pray as you have never prayed before and then more souls will be saved. Then you will all become part of* **the new world I promised you when Heaven and Earth merge as one**. *This glorious future is for all of you. Rather than fear this great change, open your minds, hearts and souls to the great joy ahead. By merging as one great powerful group all over the world, in each country, in every family, in every Church and in every community you will make a great difference.*

Your prayers will help prevent much of the persecution *which will happen as foretold. So out of deference to Me, your ever Loving Savior, follow me now.*

I live in each on each of you. I know what is contained in your hearts and souls. By giving Me your pledge of Mercy for your brothers and sisters you **will receive special graces**.[180]

Chapter Sixteen

The Great Miracle...

of God's Love

ૹ

Mary has reportedly revealed that the Great Miracle and Permanent Sign will occur in Garabandal within one year after the Warning. Our Lady has also promised a miracle permanent sign will appear in Medjugorje and in Cuenca. The three signs will remain there until the end of time.

These three reported Marian apparitions sites (Garabandal, Medjugorje, and Cuenca) purport that a Miracle will be granted with a Sign to remain where the apparitions took place, for the whole world to believe.

A similar miracle took place with the Aztecs in the New World when Our Lady granted the Sign of the Guadalupe image. Read on to learn more about this fascinating miracle and how it relates to the Great Miracle about to occur in our time.

Our Lady is revealing the future of the world to the visionaries of Medjugorje, who are receiving 10 secrets from Heaven. These events will be a sign to all the world of the power of God, and of the care of God, and concerning **the coming catastrophes**. The ten Medjugorje secrets will be gradually revealed, and each will be publicly announced 3 days before their fulfillment.

It is important for the reader to learn about Medjugorje! There are so many graces contained in these heavenly messages. We must remember that Christ saw these events before they happened and that Our Lady even arranged through the children of **Medjugorje** that **the great events will be announced to the world three days before they happen**. She is being sent by God to give us **hope**.

Very soon after this manifestation of the Lord's Mercy in the Great Warning, the Lord will manifest a Great Miracle in Garabandal. The message is summarized as follows:

A miracle is to occur in Garabandal within 12 months after the Warning... It will be on a Thursday at 8:30 p.m. (lasting about 15 minutes) coinciding with a happy event in the Church, on a feast-day of a martyred Saint of the Eucharist ... (this martyr is not Jesus or Mary) ... it will happen in the month of March, April, or May... between the 7th and the 17th of the month but not the 7th or the 17th... it will be seen by looking up over the area of the Pines and will be visible from all the surrounding mountainside which will serve as a 'natural' amphitheater. The sick will be cured...the unbelievers will be converted...

(Visionary) Conchita knows the nature of the great miracle as well as the exact date and she will announce the date eight days before it happens. The means of communicating the date to the world will be a miracle in itself. [The miracle] will be able to be filmed, photographed and televised.

Afterwards, a Permanent Sign will remain at Garabandal in memory of the miracle as visible proof of our Blessed Mother's love for all humanity. It will be a 'thing' never before seen upon the earth, as something not of this world, but of God. It can be photographed but not touched.[181]

Our Lady seems to be promising that **a miraculous permanent Sign will be granted in several places** where she has been reportedly appearing in our times. Besides at **Garabandal**, at **Medjugorje**, the third of the ten secrets foretold there involves a similar prophecy concerning a Sign to appear in Medjugorje as well, on the original hill of apparitions, which will also remain until the end of the world. Our Lady has also reportedly appeared recently in Cuenca, Ecuador, to visionary Patricia "Pachi" Talbot, as *"Our Lady Guardian of the Faith"*, which has received initial diocesan recognition of support.[182] Our Lady reportedly prophesied that she will also leave a Sign at the apparition and shrine site of **El Cajas, near Cuenca**, to occur in the near future when all her apparitions in the world cease.

Our Lady is asking for prayer and penance to avert the coming chastisements while there is still time. Through the effects of the Sign, conversions will be vast and great. But, many will also harden their hearts. God will have to intervene again to bring His justice to humanity. Interestingly, Our Lady had also told Conchita that there would not be another world war.[183] So too said Our Lady at Medjugorje.[184]

Joey Lomangino, who has spent his life spreading the message of Garabandal, is totally and incurably blind. At the age of 16, he was blinded and his sense of smell was destroyed when a tire he was inflating blew up in his face. He went to visit St. Pio and asked him if Garabandal was true and whether he should go there. Padre Pio said, *"Yes"* to both questions. St. Pio touched Joey's face and his sense of smell was restored. Visionary Conchita of Garabandal told Joey that when the Miracle happens there, Joey will regain his sight. He is in his 80s today. **So, the time of fulfillment is close indeed!**

Our Lady of Guadalupe

Mary appeared to St. Juan Diego in 1531 near Mexico City, where the Aztecs had been engaging in large numbers of human sacrifices to their serpent god. Mary asked him to ask the Bishop to build a basilica in her honor to combat the demonic activity and to convert the peoples. She asked him to gather some Castilian roses, which did not usually grow in that place or in that time of year, and which she then arranged in his tilma made of cactus fibers. Mary asked him to bring the roses to the Bishop as a proof of her heavenly appearance and request. When Juan did so, Our Lady's image miraculously appeared on his tilma.

The tilma of Guadalupe has maintained its structural integrity for 500 years. Photographers and ophthalmologists have located images reflected in the eyes of the Virgin. Images of Juan, the Bishop, and others, who were present during the unveiling of the Image before the Bishop in 1531, have been found in the Virgin's eyes, in the corneas of both eyes. Further, using an ophthalmoscope, doctors have observed that the Virgin's eyes have the distortion of actual normal human eyes. Noting the unique appearance of the eyes, ophthalmologist, Dr. Rafael Torrija Lavoignet, stated: *"They look strangely alive when examined."*[185] Miraculously, Our Lady sees! Our Heavenly Mother is with us. She sees us through the Holy Image of the tilma of Guadalupe!

The purpose of the Great Miracle that is prophesied to occur in our generation and soon is **to show us the love God has for us and to convert the whole world**. And this is not the first time God has given such a great miracle through the Blessed Mother to bring conversion. God sent Our Lady to the New World in the sixteenth century to give His mercy to the Aztecs. Just as God gave the Aztecs of the New World the Great Miracle image of **Our Lady of Guadalupe,** which converted them almost overnight (10 million to Catholicism in the first 10 years); so too, through Our Lady, God is about to give the whole world in our day a new Great Miracle to bring all humanity to conversion.

Just as the Aztecs were engaged in human sacrifice and Satanism, so too, today the whole world is engaging in the human sacrifice of the unborn through abortion and has handed itself over to the reign of Satan (remember Leo XIII's vision of the **100 Year's Reign of Satan**) through the onslaught of unrepented personal and social sins of our times, while today worshipping self, money, and pleasure (see 2 Timothy 3:1-5). And, just as it did the Aztecs, the new Great Miracle God is about to grant us *will* soon change the whole world forever. What a great day it will be! But, alas, some will still not listen; and so God's mercy and great miracle will be followed afterwards by His justice and divine chastisement. But, first will come the Great Renewal.

Our Lady of Guadalupe spoke to St. Juan Diego with such tender love and motherly affection, **as she speaks to each of us today, right now**, saying:

Know and understand well...

> *I am the ever Virgin Holy Mary, Mother of the True God for whom we live, of the Creator of all things, Lord of heaven and the earth...*

> *[I wish to] give **all my love, compassion, help, and protection**, because I am your merciful Mother, **to you**... and all the rest who love me, invoke and confide in me; [I promise to listen] to their lamentations, and **remedy all their miseries, afflictions and sorrows**...*

Hear me and understand well...

> *Let nothing frighten or grieve you. **Let not your heart be disturbed. Do not fear any other sickness or anguish.***

> ***Am I not here, who is your Mother? Are you not under my protection? Am I not your health? Are you not happily within my fold? What else do you wish?***

Do not grieve nor be disturbed by anything.

What a wonderful heavenly Mother we have! What consolation! We have nothing to fear or worry about when we call upon our spiritual Mother in prayer. And when we do, everything will work out for the good! Let us reflect upon these words of Our Mother often, words she is addressing to each of us today. Amen!

PHASE 5: The Great Renewal

☙

*The new era of enlightenment due to commence
in the world has now begun.*
MDM

The Special Outpouring of the Holy Spirit

Heaven revealed that special graces are now being given to the world. This gift was revealed by three prophetic sources.

First, Our Lady said through the American Locutionist:

*I will raise up **a new Church**, a Church that worships **in Spirit and in truth**. While my enemies are destroying the institutional structures, I will **raise up those individuals** whom they cannot destroy. Suddenly, it will happen. A new Church, built upon the Spirit, so that those who attack the structures will be helpless... **The lights of the structured Church will go out**. This seems hard to believe because these lights are all over the world, but much is possible for Satan, especially with the new means of communication.*[186]

And second, Jesus said through Maria Divine Mercy:

*I am gathering My army quickly now and this will swell **into a group of over 20 million souls** soon. The larger the army the more powerful will be the Holy Spirit in bringing My children together as one to fight The Deceiver. My Divine guidance is now instilled in your souls whether you realize this or not. It is like as if you have an internal switch. When My love calls, you will respond naturally to convert others. This is **the power of the Holy Spirit** and it is now being felt in every corner of the earth.*

***All religions, all creeds, all races and all nations** will respond to the light of the truth now. They are all so precious to My Eternal Father. He is now reaching out to every man, woman and child so they will hear His call. Satan will be unable to withstand the prayers which are recited by My followers. His grip will loosen and soon.* [187]

Finally, third, Our Lady confirms this trial the Church will endure, and how the Church is even now being renewed, through Fr. Gobbi as follows:

The Church is now living through her great trial, and what is awaiting her is something she has never known before. I am watching over her and arranging everything for her good... in my Immaculate Heart I am preparing for her as well the moment of her new birth in time. She will be more beautiful and radiant, holier and more godlike, after the great trial of purification...

*Thus, while my Adversary was casting darkness over the Church and reaping victims from among many of her very pastors, I was preparing secretly, in my Heart, **the new Church**, all of light.*

It is the same Church, but a renewed Church... Thus the Church will shine gloriously with a great light such as has never been known since the time of the Cenacle to this very day...

She will still be the very same Church, but renewed and enlightened, made humbler and stronger, poorer and more evangelical through her purification, so that in her the glorious reign of my Son Jesus may shine forth for all. She will be the new Church of light. [188]

A New Marian Age of the Holy Spirit

Through the American Locutionist, Our Lady reveals new lights for people of faith:

*I say all this to prepare you for these events. **Prepare**, you must. Whoever is not prepared will perish from hopelessness and despair, devoid of all light and understanding. Satan will put out all the lights of the world, all that men hoped would save them.*
*However, I will shine **my light, new lights, extraordinary lights**, seen only by people of faith, words heard only by those whom I have trained to listen. Let me explain.*
*The heavenly Father wants to communicate with his children by the powers of the Holy Spirit. This **Age of the Spirit** has already begun but too few are aware, even in the Church. I have appeared to some and have made certain places sources of divine messages. These are a sign to all, but my plan goes much further. The Father will pour out the Spirit on all mankind and I am his messenger.[189]*

Our Lady discusses a new light, of the Spirit, extraordinary yet essential to help us through these times:

Two things must happen. All must be open to this new inner light and all must be aware of false lights. There will be extraordinary true lights and extraordinary false lights.
***I will raise up leaders** in my Church who will know the true light by their own deep personal experiences and by their solid theology. They will point out the true light and will reject the false light. Follow them. Plunge into this true light for it will be the only light that you have in the darkness. Get used to the light and learn how it guides you.*

*All of this is extraordinary but the darkness will be extraordinary. **The deep personal light of the Holy Spirit guiding individuals and families** will become essential... **begin now**... My words are signs and I tell you clearly that this is **the Age of the Holy Spirit**. If you invoke him, he will give you personal signs, especially a unity with others...*

(gather in) little groups. They will be called **Marian Gatherings of the Holy Spirit.** *Even if just three or four gather, this will be enough. I will teach them and they will learn together. This advice is very easy but this is how you will prepare for the darkness. Gather with others in a Marian Gathering of the Holy Spirit. Do not put this off... What will you do when you gather? You will* **read my words.** *They will teach you. More important, you will* **give me your hearts as slaves of the Immaculate Heart as taught by St. Louis de Montfort.** *This is only the beginning. Let each one use their gift of the Spirit...* **Serve one another with the spiritual gifts.** *Do not wander into other concerns. The Spirit must do his work in you and you must learn his ways. Enough for now. I have given you a clear plan.* **Begin** *to act...*[190]

Our Lady Offers Us Some Advice

Four Pieces of Advice
First, *you must believe that I will keep you and your family safe, but* **only in my Immaculate Heart.** *That is why the heavenly Father wants to establish devotion to my Immaculate Heart. Do not follow any other path. This is the sure, the easy and the short road. You will never arrive by any other means.*

Second, *you must* **give me your heart** *so I can purify it of all its sinful desires.*

Third, *you must* **bring to me all the members of your family** *so I can purify their hearts. There is no salvation without purification.*

Fourth, *you must* **gather together in my heart.** *This is not optional. I can only bless those who gather. I can seek the scattered sheep but only so that I can gather them with the others. A scattered sheep is a lost sheep until it learns to stay with the flock.*

More Advice
Now I must go deeper. My words are true treasures that come from my heart.

First, *read God's word. Take it to heart. Love that word. Let it be a light for your path. Let the word live in your family.* **Live by the word.** *Study it. Memorize it. Too many Catholics are ignorant of the word. I* *pondered the word that I was taught at the synagogue. You, too, must ponder it.*

Second, *purify your home. Remove whatever I would not want to be there. Make it a Marian home. Clean out the secret recesses.* **Let nothing unclean enter your home**. *I will bless a purified home. I cannot bless a home which tolerates sin.*

Now, let us go still deeper. I want **love** *among the family members and* **peace** *in their relationships. I want* **truth** *to reign, together with* **honesty** *and* **purity**. *I want* **family meals** *and* **time for the children**. *I will make all of this possible if only you have faith in me and allow me to act. I ask only* **good will** *and a* **willingness** *to begin again when you have failed.*

Any home which does this, I will bless and I will make it a light for others. When the darkness comes, these lights that you and I have set in place will not go out.[191]

The Age of the Holy Spirit and the Immaculate Heart of Mary

Our Lady asks:

Why *does the heavenly Father want to* **establish devotion to my Immaculate Heart**? *Only in this way can there be an* **Age of the Spirit**. *The easiest way to understand the Holy Spirit is through my Immaculate Heart.* **My Heart is the way of entering the Age of the Spirit**. *This will not be a final Age but will prepare for the Second Coming.*[192]

Suddenly, **before all these events happen**, *there will be a gift from heaven, given without man's earning it and even without his asking, decreed by the heavenly Father. The stream of heaven will overflow into the stream of mankind.* **Divine power, divine cleansing and divine light** *will suddenly invade the mind and heart of man. Yes, I say "invade", because man makes no efforts to save himself, no efforts to cry out to God. Yet, the heavenly Father sees what is ahead. He sees the events stirred up by the Evil One. He sees the destructive powers* *that his minions have acquired... People will receive heavenly gifts without asking. What is important is that man accept these gifts and see them for what they are – the Father's final helps, the last chance to survive what is to come... First, there will be **a spirit of repentance**, wide scale repentance coming from heavenly light arising within each person. People will see what they have done... It will be like the miraculous catch of fish. The boat of the Church will be overflowing and the pastors will need to call for other boats to hold the crowds... No great event happened to bring them to their knees. This is **a gentle, hidden light** placed in the hearts of those who still retain the basic elements of belief. This is where I will begin. When the Churches notice a spirit of repentance among their fallen away members and a return to active practice, they will know that **greater graces are about to be unleashed**.*[193]

Our Lady explains that the New Gift is a covenant in the Spirit:

*Everything begins within by a fresh stirring of the Holy Spirit. Natural wisdom is not enough. Even spiritual wisdom does not hold the answers (although it offers sound guidance). My children must be aware of the method I will use. I will outline this so all can understand. First, everyone must pay attention to the **fresh stirrings of the Holy Spirit**. Yes, I say **fresh stirrings** because these **will come suddenly**. All must pay attention because the Spirit will be enlightening everyone. If they do not pay attention, they will either not notice the light, or they will not give the light much importance.*

Many in the same area, in the same group, in the same parish will receive this light. These lights must come together. One light will not survive and one light does not contain everything.

*The parish that receives this light must cherish it, live by it, and allow the light to call people together into a covenant of love. This will be a mystical joining of hearts. In this joining, the people will discover a new life. They will call it "Our life in the covenant." They will know that the covenant is a special gift which they must cherish. In the covenant will be contained all that they need. The Holy Spirit will be in their midst **as never before**.*[194]

PART 2: REVELATION 12

ୡ

Chapter Seventeen

The New Ark

ୡ

I will put enmity between you (Satan)
*and **the woman** (Mary),*
and between your seed and her seed;
he shall bruise your head, and you shall bruise his heel.
Genesis 3:15

God's temple in heaven was opened,
*and **the ark** of his covenant could be seen in the temple.*
*A great sign appeared in the sky, **a woman** (Mary)*

clothed with the sun,
with the moon under her feet,
and on her head a crown of twelve stars…
Then another sign appeared in the sky;
it was a huge red dragon, with seven heads and ten horns.
Revelation 11:19-12:6

Jesus said to His disciples:
Elijah will indeed come and restore all things;
*but I tell you that **Elijah has already come**,*
*and **they did not recognize him**.*
Matthew 17:11-12 (applied now to Mary the New Elijah)

***The time has come when the small remnant** (the Pope, bishops,*
priests, and laity), who will remain faithful and with whom Jesus will
bring about the realization of His reign,
***must enter**, in its entirety, **into my Immaculate Heart**.*
Whoever does not enter into this refuge will be carried away by the
great tempest which has already begun to rage.
Our Lady to Fr. Gobbi

In the time of the Flood, all who entered the ark were saved by God. Today, God has provided a new ark, and all who enter it will be saved. The new ark is Our Lady's Immaculate Heart. Let us pray to recognize this Gift and then to enter willingly, and quickly.

The last great spiritual battle has begun, and the lines have been drawn between the dragon and the Woman. She is calling her children to fight. God is sending the most important human person in Heaven to give us **the most important message in the history of the Church**, since the time of Christ, concerning **the fulfillment of the final biblical prophecies**. Mary is coming from Heaven to explain the signs of the times. She says:

I will bring you to the full understanding of Sacred Scripture. Above all, I will read to you the pages of its last book, which you are living. . . .

I am opening for you the sealed book.

Know how to read the signs of the times through which you are living and which are announcing to you Jesus' immanent return... **These are the times of the great battle** *between me and the powerful cohort which is under the orders of the Red Dragon and the Black Beast... mustered to lead all humanity to the denial of God and to rebellion against Him.* (Our Lady to Fr. Gobbi)

Relating the messages and Miracle of the Sun that occurred at Fatima (1917) with the messages and great Miracle that will occur at Medjugorje (and also at Garabandal), Our Lady told locutionist Fr. Gobbi:

You will see very soon the extraordinary signs which I will give, in order that you may **prepare yourselves for the very great miracle** *which is at this time about to be accomplished. The miracle of the sun, which took place during my last apparition (at Fatima), was only a prophetic sign to indicate to you that you should all* **look at the Book which is still sealed** *(Revelation).* **Today I am being sent by God to open this Book**, *in order that the secrets may be revealed to you.* [195]

God is sending Mary **to open the Book of the Apocalypse,** and to reveal its mysteries **in our times, because we are the generation of its fulfillment.**

The final battle has begun. Like never before in history, man is on the verge of inflicting a genocide on humanity to such a scale that the world's population will be depleted in huge proportions. We must ask God to intervene, and He will. What is needed now is a divine intervention. All the prophecies in the Book of Revelation will now unfold in the world. What is coming includes:

- War in the Middle East targeting Israel that will involve many other countries
- Economic disaster and collapse
- Natural disasters, which will shock many
- The takeover of the Vatican and the schism in the Church
- The fall of democracy in America due to the rejection of God and the sin of abortion; and possibly war on U.S. soil

Our Lady is being sent as the New Elijah to preach the final heavenly message of hope:

*I open the doors to the future for all to see. Some do not want to see because they must change their lives. Others will not believe my words, thinking that they cannot be coming from the Mother of God. Yet, the words are true. They come because I love mankind and because the Father has asked me to be **his Final Preacher**. Should not the Final Preacher use the clearest words, so easy to understand? Should that preacher not talk about the problems of the world and how the Father wants to help the human race?*[196]

*God is revealing my role, **so people will invoke me**. The world must invoke me. The Church must invoke me. Families and individuals must invoke me. It is not too late… Invoke me and I will turn events around. I will confront the deadly powers of the world that limit life and I will confront the demonic powers that will destroy human life entirely. I cannot speak any more clearly.*[197]

*This is why the Father has sent me, the final preacher, the **final word of warning to mankind**. He has sent me because although evil seeds are about to bring forth an evil harvest, the Father can and will intervene, even at this last moment, **if only mankind repents** of what he has done.*
*All of this seems impossible. There have been so many sins for such a long time (so many abortions for so many decades). How can, at this last minute, the harvest of death be avoided? Yes, that is what man has sown, **a harvest of death**, and that is what man is about to reap, **a***

harvest of death. *Not at the hands of the heavenly Father but* **at the hands of man himself.**
I am God's final preacher.[198]

What are my words? They are clear. They are the same as my Son's. **My message is the gospel message. Repent.** *Believe that the kingdom of God is at hand. Do penance and you shall find eternal life. This is* **a message of hope.**[199]

Mary's Heavenly Prophecy and the Signs of the Times

Mary knows that many people will not respond as they should until the 'signs' are obvious; and then they will seek her words of consolation and help. But, for those who do hear her heavenly words immediately, she says, "Prepare NOW":

At first, my words will not be accompanied by signs but the time will come when my words are challenged. Then, I will give signs, not for those who challenge, but for the little ones, that they would continue to believe...
People will come back to this word, especially as they see the events unfold... *O mankind, you are hurtling toward the cliff of total annihilation, unconscious of the forces that soon will be released in your midst. What can be done? That is why I speak and teach and try* **to show the way.**[200]

The time is short. Many disasters will befall mankind. Some are already evident, the problems which are seen and felt by all. Other problems will be new and unexpected. Together, they will squeeze the heart of mankind, which will feel sorely oppressed, unable to respond and be filled with hopelessness... **By these words**, *I am preparing my children (and all can be my children. They need only to accept me as their mother). This is not a preparation of one day nor can it be done at the last minute. The time is short.* **Prepare now.**[201]

What is Mary asking us to do? It is so simple. She herself tells us in her own words:

Repent. Turn to God. Invoke my help, praying, "Mary be with me." That is all you need to say. I will come.[202]

Mary Gives Us the Full Picture of What Is Coming

Mary is being sent to us from Heaven as the Prophetess of the Latter Times to pre-announce the full scope concerning the apocalyptic events that are coming, to call us to respond to help avert them, and to prepare us. The purpose of this book is to take the little pieces that Heaven is communicating through various heavenly messages of our times and organize them into a single summary of the full picture of the heavenly message of our times and the plan of how Heaven wants us to respond. Our Lady explains her plan:

*I give you **little pieces that fit together into a clear picture of all that will take place**. I also tell you underlying causes and what man needs to do. Although my word goes forth, **few heed it**.*[203]

***Read my words every day.** Light will come to you… Only by reading all the messages, each and every day, will I be able to form your mentality and draw you away from the illusions of the modern world. **Be faithful to reading the messages**.*[204]

What is Mary saying? Why is she speaking to us today – with such frequency and urgency? Mary comes to warn us about what is coming, and she indicates that we can avert some of it:

A Totally Different Existence
*The world… envisions the future as being like the present. No one envisions a totally different existence with **tremendous disturbances** of modern life. Yet, [what is coming] **will severely alter human existence**, especially in those parts of the world where they take place. These events are **very soon**. They are at the door. Even though*

*they are still hidden and not able to be recognized, the time is short. Some of these events **can still be avoided**, although this window of opportunity grows smaller and smaller as the true remedies are delayed and the evil is not checked.*[205]

The Two Opposing Forces of This Final Battle

Know thy enemy. Our Lady tells us through Fr. Gobbi that this is the moment of the great battle prophesied in the Book of Revelation. She says: *"These are the times of the great battle between me and the powerful cohort which is under the orders of the Red Dragon and the Black Beast... mustered to lead all humanity to the denial of God and to rebellion against Him."*

Our Lady explains that there are two opposing sides at war in this final battle. The first side is that of Satan and his cohort:

At its head is Lucifer himself, who is repeating today his act of defiance in placing himself against God to make himself adored as God. With him are fighting all the demons who are, in these times, being poured out from hell upon earth, in order to lead the greatest possible number of souls to perdition.
United with them are all the souls of the damned and those who, in this life, are walking in rejection of God, whom they offend and blaspheme, as they walk along the road of egoism and hatred, of evil and impurity. They make their one and only aim the quest for pleasures; they satisfy all their passions; they fight for the triumph of hatred, of evil, and of impiety.

Our Lady also tells us of the other cohort, the army of the Lord that she is leading on His behalf:

The cohort which I myself am leading is made up of all the angels and saints of paradise, guided by St. Michael the Archangel, who is the head of all the heavenly militia.

This is a great battle which is being waged above all at the level of spirits.

On this earth, my cohort is made up of all those who live by loving and glorifying God, according to the grace received in holy Baptism, and who are walking along the sure road of perfect observance of the commandments of the Lord. They are humble, docile, little and charitable; they flee from the snares of the demon and from the easy seductions of pleasure; they journey along the way of love, of purity, and of holiness. This cohort of mine is made up of all the little children who, in every part of the world, are answering me today with a 'yes' and are following me along the road which [in these heavenly messages] I have traced out for you.

It is with my cohort that I am bringing on my victory in these times. It is with my cohort that I am building up, each day, the triumph of my Immaculate Heart. It is with my cohort that I am preparing the way along which the glorious reign of Jesus will come to you, and it will be a reign of love and of grace, of holiness, of justice, and of peace.[206]

She continues, telling us about the kinds of weapons that are being used:

The battle is becoming more fierce and terrible, and you too, with the angels of the Lord, are being called to battle.

*The weapons used by the demons are those of **evil, of sin, of hatred, of impurity, of pride and of rebellion against God**. The weapons used by the heavenly spirits, who are at your side to do battle, are those of **goodness, of divine grace, of love, of purity, of humility and of docile submission to the Will of God**.*

The heavenly spirits have also the task of strengthening you, of healing you from your wounds, of defending you from the snares of my Adversary, of protecting you from evil and of leading you along the luminous way of my will.[207]

The Simple Solution to All Our Problems

The destructive events are coming soon, but Our Lady gives us hope and a solution to our woes:

The events will begin, pouring out one after another. In the beginning, men will just see this as another difficulty to be grappled with. Then as a second and a third event happen, they will wonder how they can respond. Then as the events pour out more and more, all will realize that the state of the world is changing…
What can I do? **I can protect all those who come to me. That is why the Father has sent me.** *This is* **the constant theme of the messages. The destructive events will pour forth but I can save those who trust in me.** *I do not say that I will save your lives. I will save your souls. Also, I will save you from much of the suffering (but not all). I will save your loved ones. You will see them return to the faith. Tell them not to despair. Tell them that all of* **this has been told to you ahead of time, so that all can believe that in these events, the Woman of Light stands in your midst calling all into the Noah's Ark of her Immaculate Heart.**[208]

Not the End of the World – Be Hopeful

After these events of the Apocalypse, the world will not end. Rather, after them, a new era of peace, joy, and happiness will evolve. Our Lady speaks about this as she describes the battle and the two opposing sides.

Mary says that it will be too late to seek the necessary virtue needed to endure the hard times ahead. Instead of waiting until it is too late, she asks to foster the necessary virtues now, while we are still able to do so:

This is what I preach. **These are the words that must go forth now,** *while the darkness grows and midnight approaches.* **I preach light. I**

preach hope. If no one else's words stir the human heart, my words will. So, listen carefully.
The greatest light that has ever shone upon mankind *(called 'the Warning') will come to it as a gift of the heavenly Father. This moment must be prepared for by hope. Yes, you must hope when there seems to be no reason to hope for the future.* **Hope,** *that is what I preach. I will explain later. For now, let all my children* **begin to hope.** *Your mother sees what you cannot see.*[209]

A New Age of Faith

Mary announces that a new age of faith is coming, but that how it comes is up to us:

I am talking about a **new Age of Faith,** *when the air is purified and the water is cleansed, when faith is the air that everyone breathes and peace is the water that everyone drinks. Who can even imagine these moments. Yet, this is* **my goal,** *brought about by a special action of the heavenly Father and which I will announce ahead of time.*
When this divine action begins, I do not want the little ones to despair. The Father does not want the destruction of the earth or the end of the human race. He wants a purified earth and a new mankind to come forth.[210]

Three Things to Do Now

Mary asks us to pray for faith, hope, and love:

First, never fear *because fear destroys hope which is needed as the darkness continues and people see no end in sight… In the darkness, keeping alive hope is the key to survival.* **Second, love one another.** *Stay close to one another. Help one another. Sacrifice yourselves. In this way, something will happen within you. You will find yourself unbelievably strong. Great heroism will be released within…* **Finally, believe these words,** *"I am coming". Yes, time and again I will come to you. Whatever you need, I will provide.*[211]

Promise of New and Lasting Hope

*Ahead of you are gigantic problems. You will face **in your lifetime more trials** than any previous generation. These trials will bring about overwhelming fears and **fear** will become your biggest problem. It will paralyze you at the very moment when you will need to take action, daily actions over a long period of time. **Survival will demand extraordinary hope**. However, fear kills hope. That will be the battle, between fear and hope. One kills the other. So, when I say **"Do not be afraid"**, I am giving **hope** a chance to save you.*

Seek Mary's Help Now

*O young reader, I see you and your generation. I see all the events that are ahead. **You will not survive without me**. Now is the time to come to know me and to experience my help in your daily trials. If you do this, when the greater trials come, hope will triumph over your fears. I say again, **"Do not be afraid"**.*[212]

*I want the whole world to come into my heart. Only there, will all be safe. Facing the world are **years ahead of destruction and disruption** of normal life. All the world will be affected. Some parts will directly experience the destruction. Other parts will experience disruption. Normal life, so to speak, will not exist... **The only place of refuge will be my motherly Immaculate Heart.** There is a place there for everyone, of any faith and of any denomination. The urgency is so great, that my heart will remain open until the last minute but no one should wait.*[213]

The Divinely Given Task of Mary Today

*In **these last times** of yours, the task of your heavenly Mother, beautiful as the moon, brilliant as the sun, terrible as an army set in battle array, is to announce that the great day of the Lord is in the very act of coming upon you... to bring my motherly announcement to every part of the world, and to call all my children to enter, through their act of consecration, into the bright and safe refuge of **my Immaculate Heart**, because **the trial** which is about to come upon you is very great,* *and you are all being called to suffer with me… [to prepare] the new times,* **when Jesus will come in the splendor of his glory and will restore his reign in the world.** Gobbi

Mary – The New Ark of Protection and Safety

God is sending Mary to be the new ark of protection:

- *And the temple of God was opened in heaven, and there was seen in his temple* **the ark** *of his testament: and there were lightnings, and voices, and thunderings, and an earthquake, and great hail.* Revelation 11:19

- *I offer to all the only safe haven in the middle of this war – my Immaculate Heart.* Locutions.org

Enter NOW into the Cenacle of Mary's Heart

I ask that all the Church be gathered together in the spiritual **cenacle of my Immaculate Heart.** *Then the Holy Spirit will bring you to the understanding of the whole and entire truth.*

He will bring you into **the secret** *of the word of God and will give you the light of wisdom to understand all the Gospel and whatever is described in it concerning the times through which you are living. The Holy Spirit will make you understand* **the signs of your time.** *They are the times foretold by Holy Scripture as those of* **the great apostasy and of the coming of the Antichrist.** *They are times of* **great tribulation** *and of innumerable sufferings for all, which will bring you to live through these final events in preparation for the* **second coming** *of Jesus in glory…*

The Holy Spirit prepares hearts and souls for the **second coming** *of Jesus… because* **you have now entered into the last times, which will lead you to the new era.**

*The task of the Spirit is to prepare humanity for its **complete change, to renew the face of creation, to form the new heavens and the new earth**.*[214]

Best Advice & Invitation

Do not be troubled. *The powerful times of the purification, of the great tribulation and of the apostasy have arrived. For this reason, I invite you all today to **enter into the temple of my Immaculate Heart**, so that I may offer you to the perfect glorification of the Most Holy Trinity... To attain these new heavens and this new earth, it is necessary to pass through the painful and bloody trial of the purification, of the great tribulation and of the chastisement.*[215]

PART 3: REVELATION 13-19

CȜ

Chapter Eighteen

The False Prophet

CȜ

Let us discuss the False Prophet by first examining what the Holy Bible and solid prophecy tells us about him:

- The False Prophet is the Beast from the land who becomes the Religious Head of the false church.

- He causes the earth to worship the first Beast (the Antichrist) (Rev. 13:12).

- He assists in reviving the Beast of Communistic Russia (who was mortally wounded).

- Three things are said in connection with the False Prophet that closely oppose the work of the Holy Spirit:

    - First, "he makes fire come down from heaven" (Rev. 13:13, Acts 2:1-4) – anti-Pentecost.

    - Second, "he had power to give life unto the image of the Beast" (Rev. 13:15, John 3:6) - opposite of being born of the Spirit.

    - Third, "he causes all to receive a mark in their right hand, or in their foreheads" (Rev. 13:16, Eph. 4:30) – against the work of the Holy Spirit of God Who seals the faithful unto the day of redemption.

- He will be the wolf in sheep's clothing that Jesus warned about (Matthew 7:15). He pretends to be something he is not, morally and spiritually.

- He performs fake miracles (Revelation 13:13). His incredible signs will fool an unrepentant world to be tricked by this "powerful delusion so that they will believe the lie" (2 Thessalonians 2:11).

- His main role will be to cause the world to worship the antichrist. He will be like a false Elijah or a false John the Baptist. He will validate the antichrist by his own work of false divine powers.

- Sure, he will claim to come in God's name. But, he will speak lies by introducing false teaching, lead others into idolatry, and do things in violation of God's will.

- He is the antichrist's Minister of Propaganda. He establishes the ideological foundation of the anti-God empire on earth. He creates new instruments and rituals of worship in his name. He uses his religious authority to help establish the authority of the antichrist.

The False Prophet – The Beast Like a Lamb

Through Fr. Gobbi, Our Lady continues to explain the other beast that will assist the dragon, from within the Church herself:

*There comes out of the earth, by way of aid to the black beast which arises out of the sea, **a beast which has two horns like those of a lamb**... The beast has on its head two horns like those of a lamb. To the symbol of the sacrifice there is intimately connected that of the priesthood: the two horns. The high priest of the Old Testament wore a headpiece with two horns. The bishops of the Church wear the mitre - with two horns - to indicate the fullness of their priesthood.*

*The **beast with the two horns like a lamb indicates Freemasonry infiltrated into the interior of the Church**, that is to say, **ecclesiastical Masonry**, which has spread especially among the members of the hierarchy. This Masonic infiltration, in the interior of the Church, was already foretold to you by me at Fatima, when I announced to you that Satan would enter in even to the summit of the Church.*

*The task of ecclesiastical Masonry is that of destroying Christ and His Church, **building a new idol, namely a false christ and a false church**.*

The False Prophet Will Rule From Rome

Mary says through Fr. Gobbi:

The Church will know the hour of its great apostasy. The man of iniquity will penetrate into its interior and will sit in the very Temple of God, while the remnant which will remain faithful will be subjected to the greatest trials and persecutions.[216]

She also says:

The hour is in preparation when the man of iniquity, who wants to

*put himself in the place of God to have himself adored as God, is
about to manifest himself in all his power. Under the bloody scourge
of this terrible trial... my Immaculate Heart will become your
strongest defense, the shield of protection which will safeguard you
from every attack of my Adversary.*[217]

*I need your help. I need your prayers. Your prayers will weaken the
work of the anti-christ as well as the **false prophet who will take up
position in the Holy See of Rome...***
*My children be aware, however, that the false prophet **will have you
believe he is also preparing you for [the new earthly] place of
Paradise**.*

*His lies will enthrall **a naïve group of Catholic followers**. He will
present a wonderful and loving external charisma and all of My
children in the Catholic Church will be confused.*
*One sign to look out for will be his pride and arrogance hidden behind
an exterior false humility. So fooled will My children be that they will
think he is an exceptional and pure soul.*
**He will be treated like a living saint. Not one word out of his mouth
will be questioned.**
*He will also appear to have supernatural gifts and people will
instantly believe he can perform miracles.*
*Anyone who opposes him **will be criticized and considered a heretic.***
*All such souls **accused of being heretics will be cast aside and fed to
the dogs.***

*All truth regarding My teachings will be twisted. Everything will be a
lie. Persecution will evolve slowly and be subtle at first.*
*My true Sacred Servants **will have to say Mass privately and in many
cases not in a Catholic Church.***
They will have to offer Masses in refuges. *Children when this
happens you must not lose hope. This will be over within a short
period of time.*

Just pray for those souls who will, in their pledge to the False Prophet, forget about the **Blessed Trinity which is the very foundation upon which the Catholic Church is built upon.**[218]

The Abolition and Abolishment of the Mass

Our Lady summarizes the culminating events of this time through Fr. Gobbi as follows:

In this period of history, Freemasonry, assisted by its ecclesiastical form, will succeed in its great design: that of setting up an idol to put in the place of Christ and of his Church. **A false christ and a false church.** *Consequently,* **the statue built in honor of the first beast,** *to be adored by all the inhabitants of the earth and which* **will seal with its mark** *all those who want to buy or sell, is that of the Antichrist. You have thus arrived at the peak of the purification, of the great tribulation and of the apostasy. The apostasy will be, as of then, generalized because* **almost all will follow the false christ and the false church.** *Then the door will be open for the appearance of the man or of the very* **person of the Antichrist!**[219]

Chapter Nineteen

Who Is the False Prophet?

The One Who Leads the False Church from Rome

ॐ

Very soon Rome will be sucked into the New World Religion, a front for satanic worship. The Church will suffer the Great Schism of division. Worship of self will be the fundamental aim of this abomination, together with the introduction of new laws, which amount to two things:

1) The abolition of the sacraments and 2) the abolition of sin.

1. The Abolition of the Sacraments

During this time they will continue to say their own version of the Holy Mass. Their offering of the Holy Eucharist, when they will desecrate the Host, will be held in Catholic churches.

- *The Sacraments will only truly be available from those priests and other Christian Clergy who remain loyal to Me.* (MDM)

- *They will offer these Sacraments in special refuge churches.* (LaSalette)

2. The Abolition of Sin

The abolition of sin will be introduced through the introduction of laws which will be seen to endorse tolerance.

- *They include abortion, euthanasia, and same sex marriages. Churches will be forced to allow same sex marriages and priests will be forced to bless them in My Eyes.* (MDM)

The False Prophet Will Take Over from Within the Church

*Gather My Church together and pray for strength for **the False Prophet is preparing and is already present in the Vatican**. But he hides his true façade very carefully.* (MDM)

During this time many false prophets will make themselves known...

These events will be widespread and they will pave the way for the false prophet as foretold who will come soon to claim his throne.

The abomination, which will be inflicted on the Catholic Church, will then be compounded by the work of the antichrist...

*The false prophet, who will profess to be a man of God, **has already planned how he will take over the ministries within the Catholic Church.***

He and the antichrist work already in unison, in order to bring about desolation upon the world, which will result after the abomination in the Catholic Church has been fulfilled. (MDM)

*The **false prophet will take up position in the Holy See of Rome…***

His lies will enthrall a naïve group of Catholic followers. He will present a wonderful and loving external charisma and all of My children in the Catholic Church will be confused.

One sign to look out for will be his pride and arrogance hidden behind an exterior false humility. So fooled will My children be that they will think he is an exceptional and pure soul.

He will be treated like a living saint. Not one word out of his mouth will be questioned.

*He will also appear to have supernatural gifts and people will instantly believe he can perform miracles. Anyone who opposes him **will be criticized and considered a heretic.***

*All such souls **accused of being heretics will be cast aside and fed to the dogs.***

All truth regarding My teachings will be twisted. Everything will be a lie.

Persecution will evolve slowly and be subtle at first. (MDM)

Chapter Twenty

The Antichrist

&

The son of perdition,
who opposes and exults himself
against every so-called god or object of worship,
(will take) his seat in the temple of God,
proclaiming himself to be God...
and the Lord Jesus will slay him with the breath of his mouth and
destroy him by his appearing and his coming.
The coming of the lawless one by the activity of Satan will be with all
power and with pretended signs and wonders,
and with all wicked deception for those who are to perish,
*because **they refused to love the truth** and so be saved.*
2 Thessalonians 2:3-10

Every spirit that does not acknowledge Jesus, that spirit is not from
*God. This is **the spirit of the antichrist**, which you have heard is*
coming and even now is already in the world.
1 John

Let us discuss the Antichrist by first examining what the Holy
Bible and solid prophecy tells us about him:

- By stealth and fraud he will seize leadership and world power – Daniel 11:21.

- He will align with the False Prophet, the visible head of the one world church – Daniel 11:22-23.

- He is the "man of sin" of 2 Thess. 2.

- He receives his power, seat, and great authority from the Dragon (the devil) – Rev. 13:2, 2 Thess. 2:9.

- "All the world" wonders after him – Rev. 13:2, 2 Thess. 2:11,12 – "And for this cause God shall send them strong delusion, that they should believe the Lie; that they all might be damned."

- He exults himself and is "worshipped" – Rev. 13:4, 2 Thess. 2:4 – "He as god sits in the temple of God."

- He has a mouth "speaking great things" – Rev. 13:5, 2 Thess. 2:4 – "Who...exalts himself above all that is called God." He "has a mouth speaking great things and blasphemies." Is not this one of the chief characteristic marks of the Antichrist?

- He makes war on the saints (Rev. 13:7, 2 Thess. 2:4 – "Who opposes...all that is called God," that is, he will seek to exterminate and obliterate everything on earth which bears God's Name.

- *Antichrist will exceed in malice, perversity, lust, wickedness, impiety, and heartless cruelty and barbarity all men that have ever disgraced human nature... He shall through his great power, deceit and malice, succeed in decoying or forcing to his worship **two-thirds of mankind**; the remaining third part of men will most steadfastly continue true to the faith and worship of Jesus Christ.* (St. Cyril of Jerusalem)

- **The wars in the Middle East will actually give rise to the Antichrist**, who will emerge as a military hero.

- The Antichrist will become head of the New World Religion and he, and the False Prophet, who will head up the shell of the Catholic Church on earth, will work closely to deceive all of God's children.

- This will occur when the world will soon be presented with the most deceitful lie.

- *The Antichrist will engage in "a **religious deception** offering men an apparent solution to their problems at the price of apostasy from the truth."* Many will be misled. (CCC 675)

- **Rome will lose the faith and become the seat of the antichrist... all the universe will be struck with terror, and many will let themselves be misled.** (LaSalette)

The Antichrist Is Alive Today

Jesus explains through Maria Divine Mercy:

*This is the most important time in the history of the world. All the signs have been given to My visionaries throughout the last century yet they are ignored and shoved aside as they bury their heads in the sand. It is precisely at this time that My sacred servants must preach about **the importance of My return to earth**. They must prepare souls by reminding them of the consequences of failing to redeem themselves while they are still on this earth. For they cannot ask for forgiveness after death. I call on My Sacred Servants now. Why won't you emphasize this to your flock? Why do you not actively discuss the repercussions for My Children during the great chastisement? Don't you know that many of My children will lose their souls to **the Anti-Christ who is already here on this earth ready to spring** as he waits in the wings.*[220]

Many people will not be aware of the antichrist and as such will cooperate with him:

*Now you must be told that My Mercy (the Warning) will soon wash over humanity like a flame of fire and it will engulf the soul of every man. When this happens the world will be steered into a calmer place. So many will convert and that is good. But **like a storm in the night, the antichrist will arrive and dismantle this sense of peace.***

*He will interrupt people's lives, **although they will not notice** at first. He will become a very powerful world leader and you must never look him in the eye. Cast your eyes downwards. Place your trust in Me and pray that those he infests can be redeemed...*

This man has been given many powers by the beast, so you must protect yourselves from him or he will be responsible for causing you to stain your soul.

*The problem with this war is that **those who side with the antichrist and the false prophet will be seen to be doing great good in the world**.*

Those who follow the Laws of God will be demonized and sought out.[221]

We need to flee to the refuge of the Two Hearts of Jesus and Mary, and then we will be safe.

Chapter Twenty-One

Who Is the Antichrist?

The One Who Brokers the Middle East Peace Plan

CB

We know some details about the Antichrist, as reported by Our Lord through Maria Divine Mercy, as follows:

> *The Antichrist and the False Prophet, between them, are already finishing planning their wicked reign and the first thing they will bring about will be the **escalation of the war in the Middle East**.*

The Antichrist will be the main man pulling the strings in the background. **Then he will come forth and be seen to broker a peace plan.**

So sophisticated will their plan be, that many will be fooled by the loving humane exterior which they will present to the world of their wicked plan.

It will be then when **the world will fall under his spell.**

My children will lose their souls to **the Anti-Christ who is already here on this earth ready to spring.**

When armies surround Jerusalem, and afterwards a 7-year peace treaty will be signed between Israel and a rising world ruler called "the man of lawlessness," also known as the "Antichrist", then these events have arrived.

The Antichrist, directed by Satan, will be seen to become a friend of Israel. Then he will appear to defend it with the support of Babylon, which is the European Union.

All wars, instigated deliberately in the Middle East, will spread into Europe.

The antichrist will spread atheism, behind the guise of the New World Religion, which will be headed up by the false prophet.

St. Hildegard, Newest Doctor of the Church, adds:

The son of perdition is this very wicked beast who will put to death those who refuse to believe in him; who will associate with kings, priests, the great and the rich; who will mistake the humility and will esteem pride; who will finally subjugate the entire universe by his diabolic means.

Chapter Twenty-Two

The Chastisements Are Necessary

೮ყ

The coming chastisements are necessary, and God brings good out of them for those who love Him. Jesus explains why the chastisements are necessary through mystic Luisa Piccarreta:

*The chastisements are necessary; they will serve to prepare the ground so that the Kingdom of the Supreme Fiat may form in the midst of the human family. So, many lives, which will be an obstacle to the triumph of my Kingdom, will disappear from the face of the earth, and therefore **many chastisements of destruction** will take place; other [chastisements] will be formed by creatures themselves to destroy one another. Destruction of entire regions, turmoil of nature, earthquakes, wars, places in desolation, cities deserted, entire streets with houses* *closed, with no people present, and dead people... human bodies mutilated, floods of blood, towns destroyed, churches profaned...*

Entire cities destroyed, rebellions, the withdrawal of grace from the evil, and also from the very religious who are evil, so that those poisons, those wounds which they had inside, might come out... Ah! I can take no more, the sacrileges are enormous; yet, this is still nothing compared to the chastisements that will come!

The chastisements will serve to purify the face of the earth *so that the Divine Will may reign on it... So, let Me do it, do not oppose My chastising the people.*

The great chastisements that Divine Justice has prepared *– how all the elements will put themselves against man;* ***the water, the fire, the wind, the rocks, the mountains, will change into deadly weapons, and strong earthquakes will make many cities and people disappear*** *– and in all nations... And then, the revolutions which will engulf them. Now, the Supreme Fiat wants to get out... the chastisements, cities collapsed, destructions – this is nothing other than the strong writhing of its agony... It wants freedom, dominion...* ***What disorder in society, My daughter, because My Will does not reign!***

All Countries Deserve Chastisements, particularly Italy & France

Almost all nations have united in offending God, and have conspired against Him. Jesus told me:

'My daughter, you cry over the present times, and I cry over the future. Oh! In what a maze will the nations find themselves, to the point that one will become the terror and the massacre of the other, such that they will be unable to get out by themselves. They will do things as though crazy, as though blind, to the point of acting against themselves. And the maze which poor ***Italy*** *is in... How many shocks she will receive! Remember how many years ago I told you that she deserved the chastisement of* ***being invaded by foreign nations*** *- this is the plot that they are hatching against her. How humiliated and annihilated she will remain! She has been too ungrateful with Me. The nations for which I had a predilection,* ***Italy and France, are the ones which have denied Me the most;*** *they held hands in offending Me.*

Just chastisement: they will hold hands in being humiliated. They will also be the ones which will wage war more against the Church.

Man has lost religion. *Religion is ignored by some of the very ones who call themselves religious...* **this is why man lives like a beast – he has lost religion.** *But even sadder times will come for man, because of the blindness in which he has immersed himself... But the blood which I will cause to be shed by every kind of people – secular and religious – will revive this holy religion, and will water the rest of the people... Here is the necessity for blood to be shed and for churches themselves to be almost destroyed.*

Therefore, see how necessary the chastisements are in these times, and how necessary it is for death to almost destroy this sort of people, *so that the few who will be left may learn... to be humble and obedient. So, let Me do (it); do not... oppose my chastising the people.'*

Our Lady also gives an explanation about the necessity of the chastisements, saying through Luisa Piccarreta:

The Church is so full of interior bitterness, and in addition to the interior bitterness, She is about to receive exterior bitternesses.
I saw people starting **a revolution,** *entering churches, stripping altars and burning them, making attempts on the lives of priests, breaking statues... and a thousand other insults and evils. While they were doing this, the Lord was sending more scourges from Heaven, and many were killed; there seemed to be a general uproar* **against the Church, against the government, and against one another.**

Luisa speaks of a vision she received about the Church:

I saw many priests running away from the Church and turning against the Church to wage war against her. *(They have become this way because they focused on human and worldly things which in turn hardened their hearts to divine things.)*

In the religious, in the clergy, in those who call themselves Catholics, My Will not only agonizes, but is kept in a state of lethargy, as if It had no life.

About the religious: **How many pretend to be my children, while they are my fiercest enemies! These false sons are usurpers, self-interested and incredulous; their hearts are bilges of vice. These very sons will be the first to wage war against the Church – they will try to kill their own Mother! Oh! How many of them are already about to come out into the field. Now there is war among governments and countries; soon they will make war against the Church, and Her greatest enemies will be Her own children.** *My Heart is lacerated with sorrow. But in spite of all this, I will let this storm pass by, and the face of the earth and the churches be washed by the blood of the same ones who have smeared them and contaminated them. You too, unite yourself to my sorrow - pray and be patient in watching this storm pass by.*

Hope

Mary continues, saying:

May all happen for the Triumph of the Divine Will.

Luisa also speaks about why these things must happen:

But how can It ever come to Reign on earth if evils and sins abound so much as to be horrifying? Only a Divine Power, with one of Its Greatest Prodigies, could do it; otherwise the Kingdom of the Divine Will will be in Heaven, but not on earth.

And Jesus shows us His Plan:

How can the Kingdom of the Divine Fiat come if the earth abounds with evil, and (thus) Divine Justice is arming all the elements to destroy man and what serves man?... *Everything you [see] will serve to purify and prepare the human family. The turmoils will serve to* *reorder, and the destructions to build more beautiful things... **I will stir everything for the fulfillment of my Divine Will.***

Reason for Chastisements

*My daughter, I am not concerned about the cities, the great things of the earth - **I am concerned about souls.** The cities, the churches and other things, after they have been destroyed, can be rebuilt. Didn't I destroy everything in the Deluge? And wasn't everything redone again? But if souls are lost, it is forever - there is no one who can give them back to Me. **Ah! I cry for souls.** They have denied Heaven for the earth, and **I will destroy the earth; (then) I will make the sanctity of living in my Will reappear, (and the sanctity of future generations) will be so high that, like suns, they will eclipse the most beautiful stars of the saints of the past generations. This is why I want to purge the earth:** it is unworthy of these portents of Sanctity (that will come afterwards).*

PHASE 6: The Great Persecution

ॐ

*Then the dragon was angry with the woman, and went off to make war on the rest of her offspring, on those who **keep the commandments** of God **and bear testimony** to Jesus.*
Revelation 12:17

*As The Warning will now take place so too will the **ecological disasters** befall mankind. **Prayer** is your only weapon now My children to save yourselves and mankind from the fires of Hell. Once The Warning is over, **peace and joy** will prevail. And then **the [great] persecution** by the New World Alliance will commence.* MDM

What does the Great Persecution entail?

1. Persecution – *The bloody persecution of those who remain faithful to Jesus and his Gospel and who stand fast in the true faith. (See Matthew 24:9-10, 14)*

2. The Horrible Sacrilege – *The horrible sacrilege, perpetrated by him who sets himself against Christ, that is, the Antichrist. He will enter into the holy temple of God and will sit on his throne, and have himself adored as God. In this abolition of the daily sacrifice consists the horrible sacrilege accomplished by the Antichrist. (See 2 Thessalonians 2:4, 9; Matthew 24:15)* (Gobbi)

Satan Hates YOU

Satan has sung his victory *because he has brought sin into souls and division into families, into society, into nations themselves and between nations.*
Our Lady to Fr. Gobbi

The battle is between heaven and hell *and because you do not seek heavenly help, **hell is destroying the world**.*
Locutions.org

We must realize that this battle is predominantly a spiritual one. We must know our enemy, and we must be aware of his allurements and entrappings. And you must know how to respond, how to 'fight' back:

- *Lest you forget, he, Satan, hates all of you. Yet, because of his powerful and subtle seductive ways **you follow his pursuit of power like slaves**.* (MDM)

- *Choose power on this earth, which may exalt you and bring your recognition over the ways of the Lord, and you will be cast away.* (MDM)

- ***Prayer** will help dilute the impact of **the [great] persecution** by the New World global alliance which will follow [the Warning]. If enough of you remain loyal to me, My teachings and continue to **pray** as well as **receive the sacraments** you can change the course of events which would follow... **Your prayers will help prevent much of the [great] persecution*** *which will happen as foretold. So out of deference to Me, your ever Loving Savior, follow me now.* (MDM)

The real and final spiritual war has begun! Choose a side, or the enemy might choose it for you.

Chapter Twenty-Three

The Two Witnesses

ೞ

I, John, heard a voice from heaven speak to me:
Here are my two witnesses:
These are the two olive trees and the two lampstands
that stand before the Lord of the earth.
When they have finished their testimony,
the beast that comes up from the abyss
will wage war against them and conquer them and kill them.
Revelation 11:4

Let's summarize what the Bible and prophecy says about the Two Witnesses:

- The Two Witnesses mentioned in Revelation (11:3-4) are also called the two olive trees and the two lamps stands.

- The two olive trees represent: the Law & the Prophets.

- The two lamp stands represent: Israel (the Jews) & the Church (particularly the Catholics).

- The Church and Israel will gather as one in Jerusalem and will be a light to the nations during the Great Tribulation.

- They will witness the truth to the world, but will be persecuted.

- *As the falsities and depravities of the world **escalate**, so too will the faith of those who lead My army. **The 2 witnesses will be persecuted; namely, the Catholic Church and the House of Israel.*** (MDM)

- This event has to do with the temporary fall of both religions, though Revelation says *"the temple and altar"* will remain standing. The temple and the altar are the core foundations of both religions, which will never fall.

- But, **the Antichrist will overthrow the pope and usurp his see.**

- **The remnant Church, the** loyal members of the Christian churches **will be cast aside into the desert for 1,260 days, where they will take refuge.**

- The faithful remnant will read the Holy Bible and understand it.

- They will inform the world of the full meaning of the seals contained in the Book of Revelation.

- **Catholics will have to honor Jesus in secret because the Mass will change beyond recognition under the rule of the False Prophet.**

- **The False Prophet will persecute the Jews as well.**

- **Together, we will be the two witnesses against the false christ and the false church.**

- **God will give us strength and protection** to survive the terrible evil monarchy, which will arise under the dual leadership of the False Prophet and the Anti-Christ, both of whom will be cast into the lake of fire that is Hell.

- *The churches will be persecuted; namely, the Catholic Church and the House of Israel.* (MDM)

Two Recent Prophecies About the 'Two Witnesses'

I. From the American Locutionist

Our Lord spoke through the American Locutionist, saying:

*Churches will see what they have never seen and do what they thought they would never do. Seeing **the union of Israel and the Catholic Church**, they will say, "We must be one". All the barriers to unity, put up over the many centuries, will be swept away in one breath of the Spirit.*

*There will be the ingathering prophesied by Isaiah. All the riches of the nations will come to Israel. This will be true wealth, the spiritual wealth of **all the Churches gathering as one in Jerusalem with Israel and the Catholic Church**. My prayer will be fulfilled, that all would be one as the Father and I are one.*

*Also, the world will see something quite different, what they have never seen. They will see the **Churches united and all the Churches united with Israel**. The world will experience a powerful call to come out of darkness. **The Church and Israel will be a light to all nations**. The light will not be lessened or covered over by divisions of the Churches or divisions between the Churches and Israel. The world will not be able to escape the invitation. The unity will stand before them inviting them to accept Me as Lord. (Jesus)[222]*

Mary explains to the American Locutionist how this will happen:

A moment will come when I will take my beloved son, the Pope. I will walk with him to Jerusalem. For the second time I will go to Jerusalem to witness the death of a son.

When this happens the eyes of the Jewish people will see for the first time. They will see in the Pope's death what the Catholic Church has done for them. There will be no mistake about which Church has blessed them, because it will have been done by the head of the Church and by the greatest of sacrifices. **Israel will embrace the Catholic Church**.

All Catholics will welcome Israel *because all will have seen the decision of the Holy Father (the bishop dressed in white) to offer his life for Israel.* **The union between the Catholic Church and Israel will be a union of hearts** *brought about by the events that the whole world will have seen and can never forget.*[223]

Jesus says through the American Locutionist:

The Pope will enter Jerusalem like I entered it. The city will already have suffered much and Israel will begin to despair, wondering what can be done. Then this figure clothed in white will come, sent by the Father just as He sent me. He will come to save Israel, just as I came. He, too will die in Jerusalem but his death will have a profound effect upon the whole world. For the whole world will weep at his death and his death will bless Israel. Why do I reveal these things now? Why do I bring you to the center of the mystery so quickly? Because the time is short. The events are near. They are not far away.[224]

How long will it be? **Keep your eye on Israel**. *This is the center. By keeping your eye on Israel you will get to know the time. Not exactly, but you will see it coming closer. The more danger there is to Israel, the closer the time will be.*

I love Israel and I love Jerusalem. In Jerusalem, I shed my blood, redeemed the world and rose from the dead. It is a sealed city, sealed in my blood and in my Holy Spirit. Even more than geography, I love the Jewish people. They are my people. But Jewish lips do not call out, "Jesus is our Messiah". I like to hear these words from anyone's lips. But I have my greatest joy when I hear those words from the lips of a Jew and from the lips of Israel. This is the deepest hope of my heart.
(Jesus)

Our Lady prophesizes that Israel will unite with the Catholic Church:

I am a daughter of Israel and I dreamed of Israel gathered around the Messiah, for whom they had waited so long.
*But then, what did I experience? I saw Israel reject my Son, call him a false Messiah, reject his claims and nail him to the cross. But that was only my first sorrow as a daughter of Israel. After He rose from the dead and the apostles began to preach, I held new hopes. Certainly now, Israel would accept my Son as Messiah. Instead, I experienced a second rejection. My own people did not accept Him as their Messiah. Twice, I have been broken in heart. Twice, they have rejected Jesus as Messiah. But **it will not happen a third time**. I look forward to the day when all of **Israel will proclaim my Son as Messiah**.*
*__The moment of the greatest darkness is the moment before the greatest light__. The very moment when it seems that Israel will be destroyed is the moment when **I will save Israel** and all will proclaim that Jesus is the Messiah. I have revealed the deepest sorrow of my heart. (Mary)*[225]

II. From Maria Divine Mercy

In March 2012, Jesus told locutionist Maria Divine Mercy, who has received many heavenly messages about "the Warning", that she will open the seventh seal. Jesus explains that the Two Witnesses, the Jews and the Christians, will be blessed with new miracles to help the world believe. He says that they will include *"**ecological wonders which will be given by My Father out of His love for His two witnesses the Christians and the Jews. Power will be given to these two faiths when they are being persecuted.** Their enemies will suffer as they inflict terrible punishment on them."*[226]

He also confirmed to her the meaning of the prophecy of the two witnesses, as follows:

My dearly beloved daughter, the time for the opening of the seals, **which will result in you opening the seventh seal,** *is almost upon you. Because of your prayers much upheaval is being averted.*

You, My followers are accepting My cross and you will unite **with the Immaculate Heart** *of My Mother as you march towards My Glorious Kingdom.*

As the falsities and depravities of the world **escalate,** *so too will the faith of those who lead My army.*

The churches will be persecuted; namely, the Catholic Church and the House of Israel.

Many will be pleased. These two religions will be tormented and every effort, **both externally and within,** *will be made to eradicate any trace of either.*

There will be great rejoicing around the world when they have fallen.

Many will consider them to be destroyed. People will then **ignore their corpses.**

But this would be foolish. **For they will rise again to form the New Heaven and the New Earth as the gates of My Paradise are opened** *(as described in Revelation 21).*

No one can nor will destroy My chosen people on earth.

They may inflict pain, torture, death and demolish the very buildings and temples set up by them to honor My Father.

But then they will rise and reclaim their rightful thrones when they will reign with Me in Paradise.

Never reject God.
Never reject his Churches.

For, if you do, you will be following the path of deceit to eternal damnation. (Jesus)[227]

Chapter Twenty-Four

The Anti-Trinity of Evil

൭

The Trinity of Evil is:

1. The Devil (the Dragon)

2. The Antichrist (the Beast) – Leader of the One World Government

3. The False Prophet (Beast like a Lamb) – Leader of the False Church

The three entities of the anti-trinity are discussed in the Book of Revelation, as follows:

*And I saw three unclean spirits like frogs come out of the mouth of **the Dragon**, and out of the mouth of **the Beast**, and out of the mouth of **the False Prophet**. For they are the spirits of demons, working miracles.* (Rev. 16:13-14)

*And **the Beast** was taken, and with him **the False Prophet**... these both were cast alive into the lake of fire burning with brimstone.* (Rev. 19:19-20)

*And **the Devil** that deceived them was cast into the lake of fire and brimstone, where **the Beast** and **the False Prophet** are, and shall be tormented day and night forever and ever.* (Rev. 20:10)

The Anti-Trinity Opposes the Trinity

1. Satan – opposes God the Father

2. The Antichrist – opposes God the Son

3. The False Prophet – opposes God the Holy Spirit

These two persons, the antichrist and the false prophet, are under the influence of Satan, and will bring all humanity to the brink of destruction. While God the Father sent Jesus to redeem all humanity, and Jesus sent the Holy Spirit to bless us and make us holy... Today, Satan is sending the Antichrist to seek to destroy all humanity, and he will use the False Prophet to misguide us and trick us into following his evil plan of destruction and persecution.

Chapter Twenty-Five

The Image of the Beast

ଓଃ

Let's summarize what the Bible and prophecy says about the image (idol) of the Beast (Antichrist):

- The false prophet sends out a universal order to "set up an image (idol) in honor of the beast" (Rev. 13:14).

- Then, a strange thing happens. We are told the false prophet, "was given power to give breath to the image of the [antichrist], so that it could speak and cause all who refused to worship the image to be killed" (Rev. 13:15).

- This will eventually lead him to set *up the abomination of desolation* (Daniel 9:27, Matthew 24:15, and 2 Thessalonians 2:3-4). This is an idolatrous image set up in the holy place of a rebuilt temple.

- It is an *abomination* in the sense of being supreme idolatry.

- The false prophet causes all, both small and great, rich and poor, free and slave, to receive a mark on their right hand or on their foreheads, and that no one may buy or sell except one who has the mark or the name of the beast (antichrist), or the number of his name (666).

- *The Antichrist will enter into the holy temple of God and will sit on his throne, and have himself adored as God.*

  The horrible sacrilege will be set up, perpetrated by him who sets himself against Christ, that is, the Antichrist. The horrible sacrilege accomplished by the Antichrist is the abolition of the daily sacrifice of the Mass. (Fr. Gobbi)

About the mark of the Antichrist, St. Hildegard comments:

The mark (of Antichrist) will be a hellish symbol of Baptism, because thereby a person will be stamped as an adherent of Antichrist and also of the Devil in that he thereby gives himself over to the influence of Satan. Whoever will not have this mark of Antichrist can neither buy nor sell anything and will be beheaded.
He will win over to himself the rulers, the mighty and the wealthy, will bring about the destruction of those who do not accept his faith and, finally, will subjugate the entire earth.

Eternal Father will prevent New World Order from final persecution of His Children

Jesus offers some reflection through Maria Divine Mercy as follows:

*Many reading this message will smile and question this fact but they should also know that unless they stand up and defend their rights they will be forced to accept **the Mark of the Beast** to access their money.*

New World Currency will be presented to an incredulous world
*The **New One World currency**, which will be presented to an incredulous community, is designed to control you. Then once that*

*happens they will try to **deprive you of food**. Unless My children accept this reality now, they will be defenseless when they are under the control of a **New World Order led by Masonic forces**. Prepare now, My children, because, although The Warning will convert millions, including those loyal to the One World Order, it will not be enough to stop these evil slaves of Satan and **the Anti-Christ**. With control of your money you will find it hard to defend your right to **property, food and health,** the three things which they will be in charge of if you do not start shouting your opposition now. Stop your leaders in their tracks. Don't let them bully you. If enough of you are alert to this evil monstrous plan then you can warn others.*

Plan your food supplies now

Plan your food supplies now. Grow and buy seeds that will keep you alive. Buy silver coins or gold so that you can buy what is necessary. Most importantly find locations where, as a group, you can meet to offer the Holy Sacrifice of the Mass. For in time your churches will be burned to the ground.

Satan's minions are like ants they multiply in their thousands

*Never accept **the Mark, the chip of the Beast**. Pray, Pray that your home will be given the special blessings to safeguard you from the army which will try to put you out of your home. Satan's minions are like ants. They multiply in their thousands by the hour. You, My children, must pray now and **fight this series of atrocities being planned by the New World Order** who salivate at the prospect of controlling the world. Plan to have blessed candles in your home. Stock up now for they will keep you in the light of protection. Unless you wish to become a slave to this hideous doctrine then you must plan now.*

*Buy gas stoves, blankets, dried and tinned food, water purification tablets, candles along with religious images to sustain you and your families **during the great chastisement, which will follow the Warning**.*

Prayers are already diluting the impact of the Great Chastisement but you, My children, must be alert at all times. By being careful in your *preparations you will be able to survive the great bombardment being orchestrated which will be worse than **what happened to the Jews under the reign of Satan's disciple Hitler.***

*Heed this warning calmly. For by preparing in advance **you will spare yourselves from the indignation being planned by the New World Order**. For those of you are involved with the New World Order hear Me now. Repent. Heed The Warning for what it offers you – **a chance to turn your back on Satan and the flames of Hell.***

Advice for Servants of the Church

*For My Sacred Servants this is what I must inform you. Fix your eyes on Me now and pray to The Holy Spirit to keep you on your toes so that you will recognize the False Prophet as soon as he shows himself within your midst. Then you need to gather in groups to ensure that My **children will be able to receive the Most Holy Eucharist during the persecution**.*

*My Father's hand is ready to fall now with great force on those wicked arrogant leaders of banks, Western and Eastern powers who plan in secret how they aim to control all of you. My **Eternal Father will destroy everything in their wake to prevent them from the final persecution** they are planning against His children...*

*It is because of the love of His children He does this. For those who say God, the Father, cannot be angry for he loves all know this. **Yes, he is angry and his anger is justified** because of the **evil injustice which is being perpetrated on his precious family**. Once again He will unite all His children to live in peace finally for all of eternity.*

*Remember children to see the signs all around you, the multitude of **wars, lack of money, lack of food, lack of healthcare** and accept that this is the work of the Evil One. It is not the work of God the Eternal Father. He will no longer accept this behavior. Be thankful He is taking action for if He did not His creation would be destroyed. And He will not allow that to happen.*[228]

*As The Warning will now take place so too will the **ecological disasters** befall mankind. **Prayer** is your only weapon now My children* to save yourselves and mankind from the fires of Hell. Once The Warning is over **peace and joy** will prevail. And then **the persecution by the New World Alliance will commence.** Their power will be weakened if enough of you spread conversion and pray hard.

Don't be afraid My beloved followers you will work closely together to pray for the salvation of mankind. And **you will save millions** of souls in the process.[229]

Prophecy at Garabandal will now become a reality

The prophecies given at Garabandal (the Global Warning, Great Miracle, and Chastisement) will now become a reality. Prepare now for this event for you have **only a few months left to prepare your souls.**

Please do not fear My daughter for I know that these events have made you sad because you are thinking of your children's future. **The Warning will change everything.** But it will present a fork in the road. Mankind, when having been woken up to the truth of the existence of God will then, through his own free will, choose one of two paths. The path of salvation. Or the path of damnation.

Chastisement will wipe out much of the world

Pray hard that man chooses the first. For if he doesn't **the world will suffer the most severe chastisement with much of it wiped out...** The world will now seem to become quieter and somewhat strange in the coming months leading up to The Warning. For when it happens , spectacular though it will be visually in the sky, so quiet will this mystical experience be, that you will be more prepared for this silent encounter with your own conscience.

Remember the more people that are forewarned of this event the more souls will be saved. Pray, pray My Divine Mercy (Chaplet) for those souls who will die during The Warning. They need your prayers.[230]

The Remnant Faithful of Christ Will Not Be Fooled (But So Many Others Will Be)

Let's summarize what the Bible and prophecy says about the remnant faithful:

- To the elect people of God, it will be clear that the false prophet is bringing a spiritually corrupting message.

- His attempt to establish idolatry will be revealed in the fact that **he orders mankind to worship a human leader and system** rather than God (Rev. 13:14-15).

- There will occur the bloody persecution of those who remain faithful to Jesus and his Gospel and who stand fast in the true faith.

PART 4: REVELATION 20-22

ᏮᏃ

PHASE 7: The Great Chastisement

ᏮᏃ

If men do not repent and better themselves,
*the Father will inflict **a terrible punishment** on all humanity.*
*It will be a punishment **greater than the deluge**,*
such as one will never have seen before.
Fire will fall from the sky
***and will wipe out a great part of humanity**,*
the good as well as the bad, sparing neither priests nor faithful.
The survivors will find themselves so desolate
that they will envy the dead.
Our Lady of Akita

What does all this mean for us today?

- The European Union worships the Beast

- Communistic Russia will arise again and take over Europe

- The Beast like a Bear (Russia) will join with the Red Dragon (China) and pose a threat to the **'Beast with the Ten Horns'** (European Union), and will overcome them to introduce communism.

- Led by the Antichrist, this force will mislead the people for 7 years through some sort of agreement.

- When the people see Russian Communism, which died now come back, they realize it is unstoppable and they cannot defeat it. He is powerful and has everything at his disposal to keep everyone else in subjection to it.

- At this point, they will also be afraid of Russia. They know no one can come up against it and win, especially because of his dying and coming back showing the world he is "immortal." And it gets better, because he does not just come back, but now acts in the place of God Himself.

- The European leaders worship the dragon (Satan). Revelation 13:4 reveals they are Satan worshipers. They are all part of the brotherhood, occult, secret societies, illuminati, freemasonry.

- Half way through the 7-year period, as the Antichrist has risen to power, he will begin the Great Persecution of the remnant faithful Catholics and Protestants and Jews. He will abolish the Mass publicly.

- He will utter evil — blasphemy — though the world does not recognize it for what it is. He *"will exalt and magnify himself above every god and will say unheard-of things against the God of gods"* (Daniel 11:36). He will even seek to put himself in the place of God, establishing the abomination.

- As part of His Providence, God allows the beast to appear supreme in the affairs of mankind during this time.

The Coming Divine Chastisement

At the reported apparitions of **Garabandal** Our Lady prophesied about a great Chastisement, a divine punishment, that would soon befall humanity. The visionary, Conchita, has written:

I cannot reveal what kind of punishment it is except that it will be a result of the direct intervention of God, which makes it more terrible and fearful than anything we can imagine. It will be less painful for innocent babies to die a natural death than for those babies to die because of the punishment. All Catholics should go to confession before the punishment and the others should repent of their sins. When I saw IT (the punishment), I felt a great fear even though at the same time I was seeing Our Blessed Mother. The punishment, if it comes, will come after the miracle.

The final message of Garabandal is understood as follows:

The final prophecy depends on whether or not mankind has heeded the message of Our Lady... *The vision of this 'conditional punishment' brought terror and tears to the children...* **If it happens, it will be** *more terrible than anything we can possibly imagine because it will be the result of* **the direct intervention of God. It will have nothing to do with wars, revolutions or the hardness of men's hearts.** *If the punishment comes, and I believe it will come, it will come after the promised miracle.*[231] But, visionary Conchita also said: *"The Chastisement cannot be (altogether) avoided, because we have lost even the meaning of sin."*[232]

In a similar apparition, on October 13, 1973, which is the anniversary of the 1917 miracle of Fatima, Our Lady appeared to visionary and stigmatist, Sr. Agnes Sasagawa of **Akita**, in what has since been recognized as a Church-approved apparition,[233] stating as follows:

*As I told you, **if** men do not repent and better themselves, the Father will inflict **a terrible punishment** on all humanity. It will be a punishment **greater than the deluge**, such as one will never have seen before. **Fire will fall from the sky and will wipe out a great part of humanity**, the good as well as the bad, sparing neither priests nor faithful. The survivors will find themselves so desolate that they will envy the dead.*

***The only arms which will remain for you will be the Rosary and the Sign** left by my Son. Each day, recite the prayers of the Rosary. **With the Rosary, pray for the Pope, the bishops and the priests.** The work of **the devil will infiltrate even into the Church** in such a way that one will see cardinals opposing cardinals, and bishops against other bishops. The priests who venerate me will be scorned and opposed by their Confreres. The churches and altars will be sacked. The Church will be full of those who accept compromises and the demon will press many priests and consecrated souls to leave the service of the Lord. The demon will rage especially against souls consecrated to God. The thought of the loss of so many souls is the cause of my sadness. If sins increase in number and gravity, there will no longer be pardon for them.*

While in Akita, Fr. Gobbi received this confirmation of the warning and chastisement that will soon purify the world, as had been foretold to Sr. Agnes:

*I now announce to you that the time of **the great trial** has come, because during these years all that I foretold to you will come to pass. **The apostasy** and **the great schism in the Church** is on the point of taking place **and the great chastisement**, about which I foretold you in this place (Akita), is now at the very doors. **Fire will come down from heaven and a great part of humanity will be destroyed.** Those who survive will envy the dead, because everywhere there will be desolation, death, and ruin... in order to be protected and saved, [you] must all enter right away into the safe refuge of my Immaculate Heart.[234]*

The Marian messages to Fr. Gobbi include details of the chastisement, as follows:

*Because this humanity has not accepted my repeated call to conversion, to repentance, and to a return to God, there is about to fall upon it **the greatest chastisement which the history of mankind has ever known**. It is a chastisement much greater than that of the flood...*
***In appearance everything remains calm and it seems that all is going well. In reality, [the Church] is being pervaded with an overwhelming lack of faith which is spreading the greatest apostasy everywhere.** Many bishops, priests, religious and faithful no longer believe and have already lost the true faith in Jesus and in his Gospel. For this reason **the Church must be purified with persecution and with blood**...*
*These are the times foretold by me, when cardinals will be set against cardinals, bishops against bishops, and priests against priests and the flock of Christ will be torn to pieces by rapacious wolves who have found their way in under the clothing of defenseless and meek lambs. Among them there are even some who occupy posts of great responsibility and, by means of them, **Satan has succeeded in entering and in operating at the very summit of the Church... The activity of my Adversary to extend his reign over all humanity, will become stronger.** Thus evil and sin, violence and hatred, perversion and unbelief will increase everywhere. **Wars will spread**...*
*Even **in the Church, the darkness** will descend more densely yet, and will succeed in enveloping everything. Errors will spread much more and many will wander away from the true faith...*
*The contestation directed against the Pope will become stronger; theologians, bishops, priests and laity will openly oppose his Magisterium... You have entered the conclusive period of **the great tribulation**, and the hour of the great trial... has now arrived for you. It is **a trial so great and painful, that you cannot even imagine it, but it is necessary** for the Church and for all humanity, in order*

that the new era, the new world, and the reconciliation of humanity with the Lord, may come upon you.[235]

Through mystic Luisa Piccarreta, Jesus says:

The more it seems *that the world is apparently at peace and they sing the praises of peace, the more they hide wars, revolutions and tragic scenes for poor humanity, under that ephemeral and* **disguised peace.** *And* **the more it seems** *that they favor my Church, singing hymns of victories and triumphs, and practices of union between the State and the Church, the nearer is* **the brawl that they are preparing against Her.** *The same was for Me. Up to the moment when they acclaimed Me as King and received Me in triumph, I was able to live in the midst of peoples; but after my triumphant entrance into Jerusalem, they no longer let Me live; and after a few days they shouted at Me:* **"Crucify Him!",** *and all taking arms against Me, they made Me die.*[236]

Chapter Twenty-Six

The People of God Will Be Crucified & RISE AGAIN

ᚸ

Jesus said to the crowd:
They will seize and persecute you…
because of my name.
It will lead to your giving testimony…
You will even be handed over by parents,
brothers, relatives, and friends,
and they will put some of you to death.
You will be hated by all because of my name,
but not a hair on your head will be destroyed.
By your perseverance you will secure your lives.
Luke 21:12-19

Our Lady states through one locutionist the connection between Christ's Passion and that of the Church today:

*Just when it seems that darkness has conquered the world and Satan's victory seems inevitable, **the power of the resurrection will burst forth**. O you who believe, never despair. Your faith in my Son's resurrection is not in vain. The resurrection is God's final word and that power will not be destroyed. Wait for Jesus! He is coming!*[237]

Let's summarize what the Bible and prophecy have to say about the Church in these latter times:

- The Church is the Body of Christ in the world.

- By God's Providence, the Church lives out the life of Christ in history.

- The Antichrist will lead the Great Persecution to crucify the Church.

- It will seem as though the Church is dead.

- Then, after 3 days of darkness, the Church will resurrect.

- And God will grant peace to humanity in the great victory!

Our Lady reveals the divine plan for the Church to experience her crucifixion so as to prepare for Christ's Second Coming in glory:

*In **these last times, when she must live through the bloody hour of her purification and of the great tribulation**.*

*For her also, the plan of the Heavenly Father must be carried out, and thus she is being called to climb the Calvary of her immolation. This most beloved Daughter of mine will be stricken and wounded, betrayed and despoiled, abandoned and led to the gibbet, where **she will be crucified**. **The man of iniquity will*** *enter into her interior, and he will bring to its culmination the abomination of desolation, foretold in the Holy Scriptures.*

*Spread my prophetic announcement in every part of the earth: prepare yourselves, one and all, to receive **my Son Jesus, who is even now about to return among you, on the clouds of heaven, in the splendor of His divine glory.***[238]

Chapter Twenty-Seven

The Antichrist Will NOT Fully Succeed

☾

I, John, saw in heaven another sign, great and awe-inspiring:
seven angels with the seven last plagues,
for through them God's fury is accomplished.
Then I saw something like a sea of glass mingled with fire.
On the sea of glass were standing those
who had won the victory over the beast
and its image and the number that signified its name.
Revelation 15:1

He shall speak against the Most High and oppress the holy ones of the
Most High, thinking to change the feast days and the law. They shall
be handed over to him for a year, two years, and a half-year.
But when the court is convened,

and his power is taken away by final and absolute destruction,
then the kingship and dominion and majesty of all the kingdoms under
the heavens
shall be given to the holy people of the Most High.
Daniel 7:25-27

Then I saw the beast and the kings of the earth and their armies
gathered to fight... The beast was caught and with it the false prophet
who had performed in its sight the signs by which he led astray those
who had worshipped its image. The two were thrown alive into the
fiery pool burning with sulfur.
Revelation 19:19-20

Let's summarize what the Bible and prophecy say about how the antichrist will seemingly succeed, but how he will ultimately fail:

- The inhabitants of the world won't just fear the new Communistic empire.

- They will also love and worship it.

- In Revelation, the world is shown to willingly accept the beast's authority, and to give no regard to God.

- *"All inhabitants of the earth will worship the beast"*(Revelation 13:8).

- The antichrist captures the hearts and souls of men and women everywhere.

- But he will not capture the spirit of the remnant faithful Catholics and Christians (and people of good will).

Our Lady reveals what kind of chain decisively and ultimately will bring Satan, the Antichrist, and the False Prophet down:

Satan's pride will again be conquered by the humility of little ones, and the Red Dragon will find himself decisively humiliated and defeated when I bind him not by a great chain but by a very frail cord: **the holy rosary.** (Fr. Gobbi)

More on this 'secret weapon' to come…

PHASE 8: The Great Victory

 C3

*Then I saw an angel coming down from heaven, holding in his hand
the key of the bottomless pit and **a great chain**. And he seized the
dragon, that ancient serpent, who is the Devil and Satan, and bound
him for **a thousand years,** and threw him into the pit, and shut it and
sealed it over him, that he should deceive the nations no more.*
Revelation 20:1f

How shall the Great Victory come about?

***Extraordinary Phenomena**, which occur in the skies – The miracle
of the sun, which took place at Fatima during my last apparition, is
intended to point out to you that you are now entering into the times
when those events will take place, events which prepare for **the
return of Jesus in glory**. (See Matthew 24:29-33)* (Gobbi)

Chapter Twenty-Eight

The 3 Days of Darkness

☙

*Immediately after the distress of those days the **sun will be darkened**,*
the moon will not give its light, the stars will fall from the sky and the
powers of the heavens will be shaken.
*And then **the sign of the Son of man will appear** in heaven;*
then, too, all the peoples of the earth will beat their breasts;
and they will see the Son of man coming on the clouds of heaven with
power and great glory.
Matthew 24:30

Jesus said to his disciples:
For just as lightning flashes
and lights up the sky from one side to the other,
so will the Son of Man be in his day…

As it was in the days of Noah,
so it will be in the days of the Son of Man;
they were eating and drinking,
marrying and giving in marriage up to the day
that Noah entered the ark,
and the flood came and destroyed them all.

Similarly, as it was in the days of Lot:
they were eating, drinking, buying,
selling, planting, building;
on the day when Lot left Sodom,
fire and brimstone rained from the sky to destroy them all.
So it will be on the day the Son of Man is revealed...

Whoever seeks to preserve his life will lose it,
but whoever loses it will save it.
Luke 17:24-33

Those from every people, tribe, tongue, and nation
will gaze on their corpses for three and a half days,
and they will not allow their corpses to be buried...
*But **after the three and a half days**,*
a breath of life from God entered them.
Revelation 11:9-11

The sun will be turned into darkness,
*and the moon into blood before **the great Day of the Lord**.*
*But **whosoever calls upon the name of the Lord shall be saved**.*
Joel 3:4; Matthew 24:29-31; Acts 2:20-21; Revelation 16:10

The Bible relates a unique event in the times of the Israelite captivity in Egypt, at the time of the redemption of Israel by Moses and the ten divine plagues. The ninth plague of Egypt was a plague of three days of darkness. The Book of Revelation and various mystics have prophesied that a similar event will occur again in our times. Jesus seems to be referring to the three days of darkness in the Gospel, when He says in Matthew: *"Immediately after the tribulation of those days the sun will be darkened, and the moon will not give its light, and the stars will fall from heaven, and the powers of the heavens will be shaken."*[239] Several Saints have prophesied about the three days of darkness.

Visionary **Bl. Anna Maria Taigi**, whose body is incorrupt, prophesied about the earthly scourge and the heavenly scourge of three days of darkness, saying:

*God will send **two punishments**: one will be in the form of **wars, revolutions and other evils**; it shall originate on earth. The other will be sent from Heaven. There shall come over the whole earth **an intense darkness lasting three days and three nights**. Nothing can be seen, and the air will be laden with pestilence which will claim mainly, but not only, the enemies of religion. It will be impossible to use any man-made lighting during this darkness, except blessed candles. He, who out of curiosity, opens his window to look out, or leaves his home, will fall dead on the spot.*

During these three days, people should remain in their homes, pray the Rosary and beg God for mercy. All the enemies of the Church, whether known or unknown, will perish over the whole earth during that universal darkness, with the exception of a few whom God will soon convert. The air shall be infected by demons who will appear under all sorts of hideous forms.[240]

Our Lady has prophesied about the three days of darkness[241] **at La Salette**, saying:

*[The Antichrist] **will be smothered by the breath of the holy Archangel Michael**. He will fall, and the earth which for **three days** will be in continual evolutions will open its bosom full of fire; he will be plunged for ever with all his own into the eternal chasms of hell. Then **water and fire will purify the earth** and will consume all the works of the pride of men, and **all will be renewed**: God will be served and glorified.*[242]

Christ has also revealed details about the three days of darkness and the great consummation, as described **to stigmatist and priest, St. Pio**, whose body is incorrupt, as follows:

The hour of My coming is near! But I will show mercy. A most dreadful punishment will bear witness to the times. My angels, who are to be the executioners of this work, are ready with their pointed swords! They will take special care to annihilate all those who mocked Me and would not believe in My revelations...

Hurricanes of fire *will pour forth from the clouds and spread over the entire earth! Storms, bad weather, thunderbolts and earthquakes will cover the earth for two days. An uninterrupted rain of fire will take place! It will begin during a very cold night. All this is to prove that God is the Master of Creation.* ***Those who hope in Me, and believe in My words, have nothing to fear*** *because I will not forsake them, nor those who spread My message. No harm will come to those who are in the state of grace and who seek My Mother's protection...*

The weight of the Divine balance has reached the earth! The wrath of My Father shall be poured out over the entire world!

The sins of men have multiplied beyond measure: irreverence in Church, sinful pride committed in sham religious activities, lack of true brotherly love, indecency in dress, especially at summer seasons...The world is filled with iniquity... The godless shall be annihilated, so that afterwards the just shall be able to stand afresh (one fourth of humanity will remain)...

The ***darkness shall last a day and a night, followed by another day and a night, and another day*** *– BUT on the night following, the stars will shine again, and on the next morning the sun shall rise again, and it will be* ***SPRINGTIME!!***

Be courageous soldiers of Christ! At the return of light, let everyone give thanks to the Holy Trinity for Their protection! The devastation shall be very great! But I, Your God, will have purified the earth. I am with you. Have confidence!

Our Lady confirms the coming chastisement through Fr. Gobbi, as she says:

*You are close to **the greatest chastisement**, and so I say to you: entrust yourselves to me, and remember that the weapon to use in these terrible moments is that of the **holy rosary**. Then you will form my cohort which I am leading, in these times, to its **greatest victory**.*[243]

Chapter Twenty-Nine

The Second Coming of Christ –

NOT the Final Coming at the End of Time

CB

And then they will see the Son of Man
coming in a cloud with power and great glory.
Luke 21:27

I saw one like a Son of man coming,
on the clouds of heaven...
His dominion is an everlasting dominion
that shall not be taken away,
his kingship shall not be destroyed.
Daniel 7:13-14
Behold, he is coming amid the clouds,
and every eye will see him,

even those who pierced him.
All the peoples of the earth will lament him.
Yes. Amen.
Revelation 1:7

Jesus said to his disciples:
In those days after that tribulation
the sun will be darkened,
and the moon will not give its light,
and the stars will be falling from the sky,
and the powers in the heavens will be shaken.

And then they will see 'the Son of Man coming in the clouds'
with great power and glory,
and then he will send out the angels
and gather his elect from the four winds,
from the end of the earth to the end of the sky...

But of that day or hour, no one knows,
neither the angels in heaven, nor the Son, but only the Father.
Mark 13:24-32

For this we declare to you by the word of the Lord, that we who are
alive, who are left until the coming of the Lord, shall not precede those
who have fallen asleep.

For the Lord himself will descend from heaven with a cry of command,
with the archangel's call, and with the sound of the trumpet of God.
And the dead in Christ will rise first;

then we who are alive, who are left, shall be caught up together with
them in the clouds to meet the Lord in the air; and so we shall always
be with the Lord.
1 Thessalonians 4:15-17

Our Lady reveals details of the Second Coming:

*And then the sign of **the Son of Man will appear** in heaven. All the tribes of the earth will mourn, and men will see the Son of Man coming upon the clouds of heaven, with great power and splendor. (See Matthew 24:30) Gobbi*

Our Lady distinguishes between the Second Coming, which is now upon us, and the Final Coming, which will occur at the end of time, through Fr. Gobbi:

*His **second coming**, beloved children, will be like the first. As was His birth... so also will be the return of Jesus in glory, before His **final coming** for the last judgment... The world will be completely covered in the darkness of the denial of God, of its obstinate rejection of Him and of rebellion against His Law of love... 'When the Son of Man comes, will He still find faith on the earth?'... He will come to establish His kingdom in the world, after having defeated and annihilated His enemies.*

Even in this second coming, the Son will come to you through His Mother...

*I am the Mother of Hope and Trust... As I was the virginal Mother of the **first coming** of Jesus, so also today I am the glorious Mother of His **second coming**... Live in my Immaculate Heart, blessed in the expectation of the blessed hope and the glorious coming of my Son Jesus...*

*Thus too it must be for His **second coming**, when He will return in the splendor of His divinity and will come upon the clouds of heaven to establish His reign in glory... know how to read **the signs of the times** through which you are living and which announce to you His immanent return...*

*[Prepare for] His **second coming**, when He will return in the **splendor of His divinity** and will come upon the clouds of heaven to **establish His reign in glory**...*

*Jesus Christ, our Redeemer, our Savior and our King, is about to come to you **in the splendor of his glorified body**.[244] "*

Jesus reportedly says through Maria Divine Mercy:

My dearly beloved daughter, many people wonder what The Second Coming really means, so let Me explain…
Much confusion exists in the world regarding this event. Many people believe that My Second Coming indicates that the end of the world has come. That is not the case for, instead, it will mean the End Times when Satan and his followers who create untold misery in the world will be banished from earth for 1,000 years.[245]

We Are NOW in the 'Second Advent' Before the Second Coming

Our Lady discusses how she will again be the precursor of the coming of her Son:

Today, many are the false prophets who are spreading lying messages in order to cast many of my children into anguish and fear.

*I am the Mother of Hope and of Trust. Live with me through these times of your **second Advent**. As I was the virginal Mother of the first coming of Jesus, so also today I am the glorious Mother of his **second coming**.*

Live in this expectation, and you will be blessed (in 3 circumstances).

***(1) Blessed in the midst of trials and sufferings** of every kind, because you have the certitude that the time of the present tribulation is preparing the time of the glorious return of my Son Jesus.*

***(2) Blessed in the midst of misunderstandings and persecutions**, because your names are written in my Immaculate Heart and because you are being guarded in my secure and motherly refuge.*

(3) Blessed also if you are living in a Church which is darkened, *wounded, and divided because this, her hour of agony, is preparing for* *her the radiant dawn of a second Pentecost.* Gobbi

Mother of the Second Advent

*I was chosen by the Most Holy Trinity to become **the Mother of the*** ***Second Advent**, and thus my motherly task is that of preparing the* *Church and all humanity to receive Jesus, who is returning to you in* *glory. His **second coming** will take place in the light of his divinity,* *because Jesus will return to you on the clouds of heaven, in the* *splendor of his royalty and will make subject to Himself the peoples* *and the nations of the earth, and all his enemies will be crushed under* *the throne of his **universal dominion**.* (Gobbi)

Chapter Thirty

The Era of Peace

CB

*For behold, I create **new heavens and a new earth**; and the former
things shall not be remembered or come into mind. But be glad and
rejoice forever in that which I create; behold, I create Jerusalem a
rejoicing, and her people a joy. I will rejoice in Jerusalem, and be
glad in my people; no more shall be heard in it the sound of weeping
and the cry of distress.*
Isaiah 65:17-19

*We do confess that **a kingdom is promised to us upon the earth,
although before heaven, only in another state of existence;
inasmuch as it will be after the resurrection for a thousand years in
the divinely-built city of Jerusalem**…*
*We say that this city has been provided by God for receiving the saints
on their resurrection, and refreshing them with the abundance of all
really spiritual blessings, as a recompense for those which we have
either despised or lost.*
Tertullian, *Adversus Marcion*

*I and every other orthodox Christian feel certain that there will be a
resurrection of the flesh followed by a thousand years in a rebuilt,
embellished, and enlarged city of Jerusalem, as was announced by the
Prophets Ezekiel, Isaias and others…*

*A man among us named John, one of Christ's Apostles, received and foretold that **the followers of Christ would dwell in Jerusalem for a thousand years**, and that afterwards the universal and, in short, everlasting resurrection and judgment would take place.*
St. Justin Martyr, *Dialogue with Trypho*

*In the tender compassion of our God
the dawn from on high shall break upon us,
to shine on those who dwell in darkness and the shadow of death,
and to guide our feet into **the way of peace**.*
Luke 1:79

Twenty Aspects of the New Era of Peace

There are certain aspects of the Era of Peace that we know about from Scripture and from prophecy. Some of them include:

1. A new Pentecost:

*Behold **a new Pentecost is coming**. A new heaven and a new earth is dawning but first the old will be destroyed. Fire will fall down from Heaven. Lightning will flash from one end of the sky to the other and the earth will plunge into a darkness it has never seen. The world has chosen these punishments.* (Our Lady through Nancy Fowler)

2. The first resurrection of the flesh:

*There will be **a resurrection of the flesh**, followed by a thousand years in the rebuilt, embellished, and enlarged city of Jerusalem.* (St. Justin Martyr)

*The time for the beast to be cast into the abyss is near, and then **the twelve nations will enjoy peace and unity**. During this time the saints in Heaven, and all those who died in My Favor, will be raised with the righteous who will survive the Tribulation. All will be resurrected and be given the Gift of perfect bodies, which will overcome the death* *known to humanity since the sin of Adam. They will enjoy peace and prosperity under My Spiritual Reign until My Kingdom is handed over to My Father. This will be **the first resurrection and will be followed by a one thousand year reign of perfect harmony according to the Divine Will** of My Father.[246]* (MDM)

3. We will want for nothing:

*[If you remain faithful], you will be rewarded with the New Paradise on Earth where **you will want for nothing**.* (MDM)

4. Our bodies will become immortal:

*In my New Paradise they **will become perfect immortal bodies. Those on the earth will become immortal at the Second Coming** in the blink of an eye.* (MDM)

5. No more death:

*As the trumpet of My messenger rings out, the dead will be raised, as well as, those whose names are in the Book of the Living, to enjoy Eternal Life in the 1,000 years of My New Kingdom, promised to Me by My Father. It is called the New Paradise and everything that is mortal up to the end will no longer be. You will be united with Me, your Jesus. **Death will no longer matter, for it will not exist.*** (MDM)

6. No disease, no worries, only love in its purest form:

I can steer you properly towards the new paradise on earth where you, your family and your loved ones will enjoy the Glorious Life that awaits you for one thousand years. No disease. No shortage of food. No worries. Just love in its purest form. (MDM)

7. Restored terrestrial paradise:

***The glorious reign of Christ [will] bring all humanity... back to the state of his terrestrial paradise...** and all creation will become again that marvelous garden, created for man to reflect in a perfect manner the greatest glory of God... That which is being prepared is* *so great that its equal has never existed since the creation of the world.*[247]

*Then all creation, set free from the slavery of sin and of death, will know the splendor of a **second terrestrial paradise**, in which **God will dwell with you, will wipe away every tear, and there will no longer be day or night, because the former things have passed away and your light will be that of the Lamb and of the new Jerusalem come down from heaven upon the earth, ready as a bride for her Spouse.***[248]

*All humanity will return to **a new marriage of love** with its Lord, who will take it in his arms and lead it into **the terrestrial paradise** of **a full and perfect communion** of life with Him.* [249] (Gobbi)

8. A New Pope and Renewal:

Then there will be a new Pope after Peter the Roman and the Great Persecution. John of the Cleft Rock prophesied in the fourteenth century what would come in the new era, saying: "***But [then] God will raise a holy Pope**, and the Angels will rejoice. Enlightened by God, this man will rebuild almost the whole world through his holiness. He will lead everyone to the true Faith... He will lead all erring sheep back to the fold.* "[250]

The prophecy of Bl. Anna Maria Taigi indicates what will happen after Rome falls, and after the Antichrist is dethroned and the three days of darkness has occurred:

After the three days of darkness**, St. Peter and St. Paul, having come down from Heaven, will preach in the whole world and designate **a new Pope**. A great light will flash from their bodies and will settle upon the cardinal who is to become Pope. Christianity, then, will spread throughout the world. He is the Holy Pontiff, chosen by God to withstand the storm. At the end, he will have the gift of miracles, and his name shall be praised over the whole earth. Whole nations will come back to the Church and **the face of the

earth will be renewed. Russia, England, and China will come into the Church.

9. Heaven and earth will merge:

*This New Paradise I have promised will come about when **Heaven and Earth merge** to become one. This new life I bring to all My devoted followers is one of love and glory. You, My followers, will have to endure much suffering, however, while this **transition** takes place (MDM)*

10. There will be no suffering:

*It **will bring to an end all suffering in the world**. It will ignite a fount of love and glory for all My children to share. (MDM)*

11. It will be beyond our comprehension:

*This New Paradise will be **beyond your comprehension** but hear this. This new life will offer you all of My devout followers a **life free from worry**. You will **want for nothing**. All will be provided by Me. Each and every one of you who chose this Glorious Kingdom will be astonished at the Precious Jewel that awaits you. Pray now that your brothers and sisters open their eyes to the truth of the promises I have made so they, too, can enter this new life on Earth.[251] (MDM)*

12. Not the end of the world:

This does not mean the end of the world. Because it does not.
It is simply the end of Satan's reign on earth which is to be welcomed children.
The time is drawing closer for My Son to take up His rightful throne when he will come, for the Second time, to reign over the New Perfect Paradise on earth. (MDM)

13. A new heavens and a new earth:

*This, his glorious return, will **bring to fulfillment the fullness of time, when He will initiate the new time of the new heavens and the new earth**.*[252]

*[He will] return in the power of his divine glory and will bring **time and history to its fullness. Time and history will reach their completion;** with his divine and glorious presence, He will **make all things new**.*[253] (Gobbi)

*My heart bursts with joy when I tell you children of the new earth which I have prepared for you. My **children will live for 1,000 years** in the Paradise I created for Adam and Eve.* (MDM)

14. Peace, love and harmony, even with the animals:

*There will be **peace, love, harmony** and you will want for nothing.*
People will marry, have children and the flowers, rivers, seas, mountains and lakes will take your breath away.
Animals will live with My children in harmony and you will be governed with love under the reign of My Son, Jesus Christ.
*And then will come the new Heaven and Earth where you will all live **peaceful, long and blissful lives** in union with Me.*[254] (MDM)

*The Lord will soon restore on earth his glorious reign **of love, of holiness and of peace**...*[255] *the **new era of holiness and of grace, of light and of purity, of love and of peace**.* (Gobbi)

It will be a ***"Celestial and Divine Era of Love."*** (Luisa Piccarreta)

15. All will live in the Divine Will:

*Christ Risen is now bringing **the Will of the Father to perfect fulfillment**, through his **second coming** in glory, to restore his reign, in which **the divine Will** may be accomplished by all on earth...*[256] *[In the new era, the Holy Spirit will] **free every creature from the slavery*** *of evil and of sin. The Holy Spirit pours out in fullness his holy gifts, leads to the understanding of the whole truth, and renews the face of the earth.*

*The new era, which I announce to you, coincides with **the complete fulfillment of the divine Will**, so that at last there is coming about that which Jesus taught you to ask for, from the Heavenly Father: 'Your Will be done, on earth as it is in heaven.' (Mt 6:10)*

*The glorious reign of Christ will coincide, then, with **the perfect accomplishment of the Will of God on the part of every one of his creatures, in such a way that, as it is in heaven, so it will also be on this earth**.*

But this is not possible unless there first takes place the defeat of Satan, the tempter, the lying spirit, who has ever intervened in the history of mankind in order to lead men to rebellion against the Lord and disobedience to his Law. (Gobbi)

Only then will My Holy Will be done on earth as it is in Heaven. (God the Father)[257] (MDM)

16. There will be no sin:

My New Paradise on earth will be an era of peace and happiness without sin.
This is the divine will of My Father and has been His promise to mankind right from the start.
I love you children.[258] (MDM)

17. Man will still be free:

*Man will **still be free**, still able to choose good and evil, **but man will be so filled with light that good will be easily chosen and evil will be easily rejected**. All of this can only take place after the world is purged.*[259] (American Locutionist)

18. Humanity will live in deep communion with God and with the Saints:

*From the perfect fulfillment of the **divine Will**, the whole world [will become] renewed, because God finds there, as it were, his new garden of Eden, where **He [will] dwell in loving companionship with his creatures.***

*The new era, which is just now beginning, brings you to a full communion of life with those who have preceded you and who, here in paradise, enjoy perfect happiness. You see the splendor of the heavenly hierarchy; you **communicate with the saints of paradise;** you **relieve the purifying sufferings of the souls who are still in purgatory**. You experience, in a strong and visible way, the consoling truth of the communion of saints.* (Gobbi)

19. As it begins, Christ will judge the living and the dead and reign over the New Heavens and Earth:

*I will come again, as foretold, and this time is almost upon you. **I will judge** the Living and the Dead and only those who are worthy can enter My Kingdom.*[260]

*I will Reign over the New Heavens and the New Earth. This will be **a Spiritual Reign** and My Church, the New Jerusalem, will be at peace and My Word will be heard amongst all nations. Satan will be bound during My Reign and will no longer deceive God's children. This Reign, will not be a symbolic one, but where the Tree of Life will breathe Love and Peace so that all those who are blessed to enjoy My New Paradise will **not suffer death** even when Satan will be released, albeit for a short time, at the end of this period.*[261]

He will come on a great cloud and His Majesty will overcome every single soul who will fall at His Feet in ecstasy.[262]   (MDM)

20. It will come in this generation, and soon:

*Because you, of this generation, have been selected to enjoy this Paradise you must not stop in your work to **help Me take all of My children with Me into My Glorious Kingdom...***
This is the chosen generation for My New Paradise on Earth...
Be joyful and happy for you have much to look forward to children.
The trials ahead will pale into insignificance when you will witness the glorious Kingdom which is waiting for you...
***Accept that My Second Coming will be witnessed by you, of this generation...** All of God's children, favored to enter this new Glorious Existence, will become as one. **Love will be everywhere.** Peace, joy, laughter, companionship, wonders and the Adoration of God, will be part of every moment.*
***Death will not exist. Hatred will be dead. Evil will be banished. The whole of mankind will no longer suffer or experience pain or imperfection of any kind. This is My New Paradise. The time for tears will be no more.** Trust in Me, My followers, for the pain and suffering you are experiencing is almost over. I know how you suffer because of the unjust regimes under which you must live. This is the final period, for the Hand of My Father will now intervene. **The world will change.** The old will be cast away and a New Dawn will emerge in all God's Glory when **His Power will Reign**, as it was meant to be, since the Creation of the world.* (MDM)

Chapter Thirty-One

Triumph of the Immaculate Heart of Mary

&

New Global Reign of Eucharistic Heart of Christ

CB

I heard a loud voice from the throne saying, 'Behold, God's dwelling is with the human race. He will dwell with them and they will be his people and God himself will always be with them [as their God]. **He will wipe every tear from their eyes, and there shall be no more death or mourning, wailing or pain, [for] the old order has passed away.***'*

*The one who sat on the throne said, 'Behold, **I make all things new.** '*
Revelation 21:3-4

Nothing accursed will be found anymore.
The throne of God and of the Lamb will be in it,
and his servants will worship Him.
They will look upon His face,
and His name will be on their foreheads.
Revelation 22:3-4

New Reign of Eucharistic Heart of Christ

The Great New Era of Peace will usher in the Great New Reign of Christ through His Second Coming in glory. Christ's new reign will not be a physical one, but a Eucharistic one. And it will usher in the new Kingdom of the Divine Will:

*This **New Era will coincide with the greatest Triumph of the Eucharistic Jesus**... The New Era, which I announce to you, coincides with **the complete fulfillment of the Divine Will**.*

The glorious reign of Christ will coincide with the triumph of the Eucharistic reign of Jesus, because in a purified and sanctified world, completely renewed by love, Jesus will be made manifest, above all, in the mystery of his Eucharistic presence. (Gobbi)

Triumph of the Immaculate Heart

The world is about to enter a new age, the age of the Spirit and of peace, but only through a divine chastisement and the great tribulation. This will be the Age of the Two Hearts, of the Triumph of the Immaculate Heart and the Reign of the Sacred Heart together. This echoes the promise of Our Lady at Fatima, when she said:

"In the end, My Immaculate Heart will triumph."

Our Lord also told Lucia of Fatima:

Put the devotion of the Immaculate Heart besides the devotion of My Sacred Heart.

Mankind will love God and God's people will dwell in unity, under the reign of the Two Hearts.

Two Hearts in the New Era

Our Lady discusses the Two Hearts in the New Era through Fr. Gobbi:

*The new era, which I am preparing for you, coincides with the defeat of Satan and of his universal reign. All his power is destroyed. He is bound, with all the wicked spirits, and shut up in hell. Herein, **Christra reigns** in the splendor of His glorified body, and the Immaculate Heart of your **heavenly Mother triumphs** in the light of her body, assumed into the glory of paradise...*

*-- The glorious reign of Christ **will be established after the complete defeat of Satan and all the spirits of evil, and the destruction of Satan's diabolical power**. Thus he will be bound and cast into hell, and the gates of the abyss will be shut so that he can no longer get out to harm the world. And Christ will reign in the world.*

*-- The glorious reign of Christ **will coincide with the triumph of the Eucharistic reign of Jesus**, because in **a purified and sanctified world, completely renewed by love**, Jesus will be made manifest, above all, in the mystery of **his Eucharistic presence**.*

*The Eucharist will be the source from which will **burst forth all his divine power**, and it will become **the new sun**, which will shed its bright rays in hearts and souls and then in the life of individuals, families, and nations, making of all one single flock, docile and meek, whose sole shepherd will be Jesus.*

*Your heavenly Mother is leading you on toward these **new heavens and this new earth**, the Mother who is gathering you today from every part of the world to prepare you to receive the Lord who is coming.*[263]

Mystic Ven. Mary of Agreda (17th Century) spoke about Mary's role **concerning the great renewal to come**, saying:

*It was revealed to me that through the intercession of the Mother of God, **all heresies will disappear**. This victory over heresies has been reserved by Christ for His Blessed Mother... Before the Second Coming of Christ, Mary must, more than ever, shine in mercy, might, and grace in order to bring unbelievers into the Catholic Faith. The powers of Mary in the last times over the demons will be very conspicuous. **Mary will extend the Reign of Christ over the heathens and Mohammedans (Muslims), and it will be a time of great joy when Mary, as Mistress and Queen of Hearts, is enthroned.**[264]*

Our Lady adds through Fr. Gobbi concerning these times saying that *"**the reunion of all Christians in the Catholic Church** will coincide with the Triumph of my Immaculate Heart in the world."*[265] Through Mary the Church will enter the new Age of Obedience and Love. **Jesus will reign in hearts, in souls, in individuals, in families, and in all society! It will be a universal reign of grace, of beauty, of harmony, of communion, of holiness, of justice, and of peace! It will be the time of the renewed and more beautiful earthly paradise!**[266]

The Thousand Years of Peace

The Kingdom of God will soon be manifest in a great way. And thus will begin the celebration of the building of the *New Jerusalem*. And *you* are helping to bring about this great Plan of God. Our Lady said to Fr. Gobbi: *"Thus **you are already contributing to the forming of the new Jerusalem**, the holy city, which must come down from heaven, as a bride adorned for her husband."*[267]

During this new era of peace, Jesus will come in glory in His Spirit. Jesus will not be present in the flesh, but will reign in our hearts and, in a most powerful way, by means of the Eucharist. This will be a mighty triumph of Christ here on earth before the final consummation of all things. This is not related to the heresy of Millenarianism, which is the condemned position that Jesus Christ would come down to earth in the flesh (in His glorified human form) and reign as an earthly king with His Saints for a literal one thousand years before the end of time. Instead, the new era of peace will be a *"spiritual," "temporal," "second"* (but not final), *"intermediate"* or *"middle"* coming of Christ to take place before the end of the world. This renewed coming of Christ in the Spirit upon the earth for a significant period or *"age"* has been taught in different degrees and expressions by the Church Fathers, among them Papias, St. Justin Martyr, St. Irenaeus, Tertullian, St. Hippolytus, Lactantius, St. Bernard of Clairvaux, St. Augustine and others, and is based on Revelation 20.[268]

This period of *"a thousand years"* is symbolic, biblical language for a long period of time, but not necessarily a literal thousand year period of time. Christ's intermediate coming is a *"returning"* insofar as He will manifest Himself to this world in a glorious way and will bring His Kingdom to this world. Christ will not descend bodily in His resurrected glory until the end of time, but He will come by way of his glorified Spirit who will purge, illuminate and unify all creation in the intermediate coming. He will reign within His Church and within His people. Evidently, we will still have our weakened human nature, but without the great influence of Satan and with the special presence of the Spirit of Christ. Our Lady spoke about this to Fr. Gobbi:

*And then the Holy Spirit will work **the new miracle of universal transformation** in the heart and the life of all: sinners will be converted; the weak will find support; the sick will receive healing; those far away will return to the house of the Father; those separated and divided will attain full unity. In this way, the miracle of the Second Pentecost will take place. It will come with **the triumph of my***

Immaculate Heart in the world,[269] together with a new Eucharistic Reign of Christ.

The universe will be renewed in a form of universal restoration. God will bring forth a renewed creation where *both* the material world and humanity will be transformed. Eventually, He will restore the world to its original state.[270] And at some point, God will begin to establish the new heavens and the new earth,[271] and make all things new. St. Bernadette spoke a prophecy of our time, saying:

The Virgin has told me that when the Twentieth Century passes away... ***A new Age of Faith will dawn around the world...*** *There will follow a century of peace and joy as all the nations of the earth lay down their swords and shields. Great prosperity will follow... Millions will return to Christ ...The Twenty-First Century will come to be known as* ***the Second Golden Age of Mankind.***

Our Lady tells Fr. Gobbi:

And ***then Jesus Christ will bring his glorious reign in the world****... the triumph of my Immaculate Heart in the glorious coming of my Son Jesus.*[272]

Our Lady also revealed that ***"the glorious reign of Christ will be established after the complete defeat of Satan and all the spirits of evil, and the destruction of Satan's diabolical power.*** *Thus he will be bound and cast into hell, and the gate of the abyss will be shut so that he can no longer get out to harm the world. And Christ will reign in the world."*[273]

After the fire of Justice and the defeat of Satan, which is soon to occur, the Church shall revive, the earth shall be set aflame with love, and all creation shall be restored in Christ.

The Great Gift and Heavenly Invitation – Consecration to the Two Hearts

The great gift of our times is the consecration to the Two Hearts, as Our Lady advocates:

*Therefore, little children, I am inviting you today to **the prayer of consecration to Jesus**, my dear Son, so that each of your hearts may be His. And then, I am inviting you to consecration **to my Immaculate Heart**. I want you to consecrate yourselves as persons, as families, and as parishes so that all belongs to God through my hands.* (Medjugorje)

While the consecration is a most powerful devotion in itself, it must be lived with a spirit of self-reform and renunciation to bear fruit that will last. Our Lady of America says:

*My children… think they have done enough in consecrating themselves to my Immaculate Heart. It is not enough. That which I ask for and is most important many have not given me. **What I ask, have asked, and will continue to ask is reformation of life.** There must be sanctification from within. **I will work my miracles of grace only in those who ask for them and empty their souls of the love and attachment to sin and all that is displeasing to my Son.** Souls who cling to sin cannot have their hands free to receive the treasures of grace that I hold out to them.*[274]

Chapter Thirty-Two

The Two Hearts – Side by Side

CB

The greatest secret that Heaven is revealing to us in these times is the secret of the Two Hearts. Heaven is telling us that the promise of safety and protection comes through devotion to the Two Hearts, especially when placed side by side.

The Triumph and Reign of the Two Hearts – Together

Thus, reader, let us look forward with HOPE to and dedicate our lives to bringing about **the coming Triumph and Reign of the Two Hearts, the great Era of Peace, and the establishing of the universal Kingdom of the Divine Will on earth**; and let us spread this 'good news' with urgency and love!

St. John Eudes, who St. Pius X calls the father, doctor, and apostle of the Hearts of Jesus and Mary Devotion, enunciates this doctrine saying: *"I shall only tell you that you must never separate what God has so perfectly united. So closely are Jesus and Mary bound up with each other that whoever beholds Jesus sees Mary; whoever loves Jesus, loves Mary; whoever has devotion to Jesus, has devotion to Mary."*[275] He continues elsewhere, saying:

Although the Heart of Jesus is distinct from that of Mary... and infinitely surpasses it in excellence and holiness nevertheless, God has so closely united these two Hearts that we may say with truth that They are but one, because They have always been animated with the same spirit and filled with the same sentiments and affections... Jesus is enshrined in the Heart of Mary so completely that in honoring and glorifying her Heart, we honor and glorify Jesus Christ Himself.[276]

In 1830, the Blessed Mother appeared in a vision to St. Catherine Labouré, whose body is now incorrupt in Paris. Mary asked her to have a medal made of the vision, which showed Mary with rays of light coming forth from her hands encircled by the words: *"O Mary, conceived without sin, pray for us who have recourse to Thee."* On the back of the medal, there was to be an *"M"* and a cross, with the Two Hearts of Jesus and Mary, all encircled by twelve stars. Mary promised: *"All who wear it will receive great graces."* This medal quickly became known as the Miraculous Medal.

Our Lady instructs us to enter into the safety of her Immaculate Heart. Shortly before her death, Blessed Jacinta of Fatima told her cousin Lucia:

*In a short time now I am going to heaven. You are to stay here and say that God wishes to establish in the world **the devotion to the Immaculate Heart of Mary**. . . . Tell everybody that God grants graces through the Immaculate Heart of Mary, and that they must ask them from her. Tell them that **the Heart of Jesus wishes that by His side should be venerated the Immaculate Heart of Mary**. Tell them to ask peace through the Immaculate Heart of Mary; God has placed it in her hands. Oh that I could put into the heart of everybody the flame* *that I feel burning within my breast and which makes me love so much the Heart of Jesus and the Heart of Mary.*

Bl. John Paul also stated: *"In the History of Salvation therefore the Two Hearts are inseparably united, and this definitive alliance is integral to the Church's doctrine... to her piety and the liturgical celebration... and to her pastoral pedagogy."*[277] Bl. Mother Teresa of Calcutta explains the relation between the Two Hearts, saying: *"The Heart of Mary is the door which leads us directly to Jesus. She is the gate through which we enter His Sacred Heart. Each 'Hail Mary' we pray opens our heart to His love and leads us into a deeper union with the Eucharistic Heart of Jesus."*[278]

The Heavenly Secret of Our Times – Now Revealed:

Devotion to the Two Hearts

I. Enter the Ark of the Immaculate Heart

Make the Marian Consecration to Jesus through Mary (to the Two Hearts)
Pray the (family) Rosary daily
Fulfill the 5 First Saturdays Devotion
Wear the Brown Scapular (and Miraculous Medal)

II. Foster Devotion to the Sacred Heart

Attend Daily Mass (with Bible reading)
Receive the Eucharist Worthily (with regular Confession)
Make Weekly Holy Hours of Adoration
Pray the Chaplet of Divine Mercy Daily
Fulfill the 9 First Fridays Devotion

How To Practice the Devotion to the Two Hearts

The way to practice the Two Hearts Devotion is three-fold:

1. Attain an image of the Two Hearts and enthrone them in your home (and office, parish, community center). You can order sets at www.TwoHeartsPress.com
2. Consecrate yourself and family to the Two Hearts by reciting a consecration prayer.
3. Practice the devotion by personal prayer directed to the Two hearts and by fulfilling the various devotional aspects listed above.

The Source of All Man's Problems

A free will that does not share in the Father's plan.[279]

Let's look in more detail at **the TWO-FOLD heavenly plan** that is the solution to all man's problems:

I. The Immaculate Heart: Our Only Safe Haven in These Times

American Locutionist offers some reflections, as follows:

I offer to all the only safe haven in the middle of this war – my Immaculate Heart.[280] American Locutionist

The Antidote to the Problems of Today

*The antidote is to **turn to my Immaculate Heart.***

1. The **turning** must be with the whole heart.
2. It begins with **believing** my words.
3. It continues with **calling** on my name.
4. It is nourished by [**praying**] the Rosary, but
5. It is only completed by a **complete change** of life, a total turning away from all darkness and toward a life that is **free from every sin**.

Is the world capable of this? Is America ready for this? The antidote that I am offering is strong medicine but **nothing else will have any effect**. The time is so short![281]

...I cannot save anyone who does not come into my Immaculate Heart. Yes, the world will be aflame with destruction, but my heart will be aflame with salvation. I give you this prayer, **"Mary, draw me into the saving fire of your Immaculate Heart"**. Say this and I will save you.[282] Let us not wait. Let us begin now. Open your heart. Say this prayer with me,

Jesus, I am a sinner and I believe that You can forgive my sins.

I believe You are the Savior of the world and that You want to save me. I open my heart to You and I invite You to enter it. Amen.

Keep asking Jesus to come. I will be at your side.[283]

This is the secret to persevere to the end – carry little baggage and walk with others in deep love.[284]

True Devotion of St. Louis De Montfort

You are a child and you need to be nursed. As you grow, I will help you to walk. And as you come to adulthood, I will guide your every step. This is called "The Secret of Mary" and has been revealed, especially to St. Louis de Montfort. **I call all to learn this "True Devotion"**, so that the spring of living water is yours. Learn it now. Do not delay. So many helps and favors are not distributed because

people do not know about the True Devotion of St. Louis de Montfort.
Read his books *and they will open your eyes to hidden treasures.*[285]

The Five First Saturdays

On the evening of Thursday, December 10, 1925, after supper, Sister Lucia received a visit by the Child Jesus and the Virgin Mary in her convent cell.

The Divine Child was the first to speak to Lucia: *"Have pity on the Heart of your most Holy Mother. It is covered with thorns with which ungrateful men pierce it at every moment, and there is no one to remove them with an act of reparation."*

Showing the young nun a heart surrounded by thorns, then Our Lady made known her request for **Communions of reparation:**

*My daughter, look at my Heart encircled with the thorns with which ungrateful men pierce it at every moment by their blasphemies and ingratitude. Do you at least try to console me and announce in my name that I promise to assist at the hour of death with the graces necessary for salvation all those who, on the **first Saturday of five consecutive months,** go to Confession and receive Holy Communion, recite the Rosary and keep me company for 15 minutes while meditating on the mysteries of the Rosary with the intention of making reparation to me.*

*The great work is still to be done, left to the last minute, so to speak, the work I spoke about at Fatima and which I later commanded to be done – **the consecration of Russia to my Immaculate Heart and devotion to the five First Saturdays**. These two are joined together, the mutual work of the Pope and the faithful. Do not ask why the Pope delays. That is in my hands. My desire is that the faithful do not delay. No one holds them back. They must begin to practice the Five First Saturdays immediately. The power will build and sweep the Holy Father along, then both head and members will be ready with full heart to consecrate Russia to my Immaculate Heart.*[286]

To fulfill Mary's request, you must do four things on the First Saturday of five consecutive months:

1. Receive Jesus in Holy Communion (If this is not possible on Saturday, then the Sunday following)
2. Receive the sacrament of Reconciliation (or a week before or a week after)
3. Say a Rosary (5 decades)
4. Keep Our Lady company for fifteen minutes while meditating on the mysteries of the Rosary

Your motive for doing these must be to make reparation for sins and offenses against Mary's Immaculate Heart.

The Most Holy Rosary

Praying my Most Holy Rosary each day is important for it will protect you from the Evil One.[287] Especially pray the Holy Rosary for that is the prayer that will crush Satan.[288]

*So many do not know of the power of this devotion to **the rosary** which can save the world.*

*When I came to the children at **Fatima**, I carried the rosary. I taught them to say it fervently and I told Francisco, in particular, that he had to say it properly. He responded with great fervor and said the rosary daily with great devotion.*

My servant, St. Louis de Montfort, wrote "The Secret of the Rosary", which all should read. It is a small book but will inculcate devotion. He writes that he does not know why, but the rosary is the most powerful of prayers.[289]

Jesus speaks through Maria Divine Mercy:

Patience, silent prayer daily, the formation of prayer groups, daily recital of the Divine Mercy chaplet, fasting and the Holy Rosary to My

*Beloved Mother combined act as **the perfect formula** for saving souls.*[290]

Prayer, especially the recital of the Divine Mercy (Chaplet), will spread conversion and by saying the Holy Rosary this will dilute the work of these evil persons.[291] *Praying The Divine Mercy (Chaplet) can save millions, even if it is only a small group of devout loving followers*[292] who are praying it.

Importance of the Holy Rosary and the Divine Mercy Chaplet

*While **ecological disasters** will occur please remember that prayer including the recital of the Holy Rosary and the Divine Mercy (Chaplet) will help avert much of it. Remember My cherished children that you who believe in Me and My Eternal Father and who follow My instructions have **nothing to fear**. Also let me remind you that because of the **two great acts of Mercy** being given to you – the gift of the Holy Spirit which burst upon the entire world a few days ago (May 2011) and the Great Warning millions will be converted to the truth. This will be a great miracle and one which will bring **joy** to the multitudes.*[293]

*So, if you feel the need to pray for those closest to you, then I urge you to consider your brothers and sisters in every corner of the world. All of you are My children. By praying the Divine Mercy (Chaplet) for all My children everywhere you, My followers, **can save mankind** from the darkness of Hell. The power of this prayer will guarantee that My Mercy will cover everyone around the world... Pray, **Pray My Divine Mercy (Chaplet) at 3pm every single day and you can save the world**.*[294]

Pray, pray all of you My Divine Mercy (Chaplet) and the Most Holy Rosary every day as often as you can to alleviate the impact of this devious and demonic plan. Pray too for those souls who will be lost in the imminent global ecological disasters brought about by the Hand of God, the Father. They need your prayers.[295]

Our Lady through Maria Divine Mercy:

*Tell people to pray my Most Holy Rosary, even non-Catholics, for this is the greatest weapon against the influence of **The Deceiver who groans in pain** when it is said. His power is weakened when my children say this prayer. The more my children pray the Holy Rosary the more souls can be saved.*

*You, my child, have a very difficult mission, much harder than any of the prophets in history. This is because of the **darkness of spirit in the world**. Never before has such a darkness descended when My children turn their back on my Son. He who died a terrible death to save them. Yet they have not only forgotten this but choose to deny His very existence.*

*Prayer to me, your Blessed Mother, **hurts the Evil One who cringes** and loses his power when My Rosary is recited. This is the weapon that has been given to me so I can help save lost souls **before I crush the serpent's head** finally. **Never underestimate the power of the Rosary** for even just one group of people dedicated to the regular devotion of my Holy Rosary can save their nation. Tell my children to be careful when turning their back on prayer for when they do this they are leaving themselves wide open for The Deceiver to ensnare them by his charming but dangerous path to darkness. Bring my children into the light by spreading devotion to My Most Holy Rosary.*[296]

*The prayer to St Michael and the recital of the Most Holy Rosary are your **most powerful weapons** against Satan.*[297]

The Family Rosary

Our Lady of Fatima says:

Say the Rosary every day to obtain peace for the world.

Lucia of Fatima said:

*God is giving **two last remedies to the world**. These are **the Holy Rosary and the Devotion to the Immaculate Heart of Mary**... the Most Holy Virgin in these last times in which we live has given **a new efficacy to the recitation of the Rosary** to such an extent that there is no problem, no matter how difficult it is, whether temporal or above all spiritual, in the personal life of each one of us, of our families, of the families of the world, or of the religious communities, or even of the life of peoples and nations that cannot be solved by the Rosary. **There is no problem I tell you, no matter how difficult it is, that we cannot resolve by the prayer of the Holy Rosary**. With the Holy Rosary, we will save ourselves. We will sanctify ourselves. We will console Our Lord and obtain the salvation of many souls.*

The Hail Mary

St. Teresa of Avila appeared to one of her religious sisters from Heaven to tell her of the great worth of the Hail Mary, saying:

I would be willing to return to a life of suffering until the end of time to merit the degree of glory which God rewards one devoutly recited Hail Mary prayer.

Our heavenly Mother is asking each of us to four acts of reparation:

Prayer
Acts of Penance
Mortification of the Senses
Fasting

Our Lady's Admonition: Restore Purity

Our Lady at Fatima spoke about fashions which *"will be"* introduced which *"will offend"* the Lord greatly. Ten year old Jacinta lay dying in a hospital bed in Lisbon, Portugal in 1920 when Our Lady said to her: *"**Certain fashions will be introduced which will offend Our Divine Lord very much.** Those who serve God ought not to follow these fashions."* Then Our Lady revealed to Jacinta that *"**the sins that lead most souls to hell are the sins of the flesh.**"* Our Lady of America has asked us to especially restore the purity of our lives as well.

Fr. David Knight says:

I think we would have to be deliberately naive in this age to ignore the fact that certain visual stimuli are objectively and normally provocative to the sex drive of the ordinary male. We might close our eyes to this, but the merchants don't. In the measure that a particular style of dress is consciously and deliberately provocative - whether the deliberate intent is on the part of the designer, or the wearer, or of both - this way of dressing must be recognized as [sinful], by which a person arouses unsolicited sexual desire in another person.[298]

The Catholic Catechism teaches says:

*Modesty means **refusing to unveil what should remain hidden.** Modesty is decency. **It inspires one's choice of clothing.***[299]

A women's bodily beauty is a gift for her husband alone.

Modesty Must Be the Goal of Every Christian

Just because a Catholic shouldn't dress "sexy" for others doesn't mean that we should look ugly and boring!

What Are Immodest Styles?

We must buy (and wear) clothes with modesty in mind. So what types of dress are the worst offenders? The most common is short skirts, formfitting tops, and bikinis…

"That's kind of radical, isn't it?"

"Very. Almost as radical as the Gospel itself."[300]

In summary, Our Lady is telling us that **women have nothing to lose by dressing modestly**. But, they have much to gain, including good treatment, decent male friends, and eternal life.

II. The Sacred Heart – Eucharistic Adoration Makes Us Stronger and Calmer

From Maria Divine Mercy, Our Lord speaks to us about the Eucharist:

The graces received by My children at the Eucharistic Adoration are powerful. They not only give you the graces to cope with life's suffering they make you stronger in your love for Me, your devoted and loyal Savior.

The love that is poured out over souls during the Adoration is given in abundance. *The souls feel this flood of My graces in so many different ways. The first gift is one of **peace** in your soul. You will feel this instantly after you have completed your time in close union with Me.*

*So many, many of My children are denying themselves the **many gifts** I have to offer at Adoration, where you spend one hour of your time before My presence on the altar. While Catholics are aware of the power of the Eucharist, many do not acknowledge the importance of this most important time with Me in contemplation. They simply ignore this gift. It bores them to have to spend this extra time with Me.*

*Oh, if only you knew how strong this would make them. Their fears and worries would be dissipated were they to just keep Me company in quiet intimate reflection. **If My children could see the light that*** *envelops their souls during this special Holy Hour they would be astonished.*

*Children it is during this hour that **you become very, very close to Me.** This is where your voice, your pleas, your pledges of love for Me will be heard. Many wonderful graces are given to you children at this time, so please do not ignore My pleas to spend this time in My company.*

The rewards will make you free of worry

*The rewards will **make you free of worry, light of heart mind and soul and calmer** in yourself. When you receive me during the Eucharist, I will fill your soul. But when you come to Me in adoration, I will envelop you to such an extent that **the floodgates of My merciful love will saturate your mind, body and soul.** You will feel a strength which will yield a quiet confidence that you will find difficult to ignore.*

Come to Me children now. I need your company. I need you to speak with Me when My Divine presence is at its strongest. I love you and want to pour all My graces on you so you can infuse your souls to My Sacred Heart.[301]

The Promises of Eucharistic Adoration

Jesus said to modern-day mystic and stigmatist Catalina Rivas (whose heavenly messages received the imprimatur):

I promise to the soul that visits Me frequently in this Sacrament of Love, that I will receive it affectionately together with all the Blessed and the Angels in Heaven, and that each of its visits will be written down in the Book of its Life and I will grant to it:

1. *Every petition that is presented before the Altar of God in favor of the Church, the Pope and consecrated souls.*
2. *The annulment of Satan's power over its person and its loved ones.*

3. *Special protection in case of earthquakes, hurricanes and other natural disasters which otherwise would affect it.*
4. *It will be lovingly withdrawn from the world and its attractions, which are the cause of perdition.*
5. *The elevation of its soul, desiring to attain sanctification, in virtuous eternal contemplation of My Face.*
6. *Relief of its loved ones from the pains of Purgatory.*
7. *My blessing on every material and spiritual project it undertakes, if they are for the good of its own soul.*
8. *The receiving of My visit in company with My Mother at the moment of its death.*
9. *To listen to and to look after the needs of the persons for whom it prays.*
10. *The intercession of the Saints and Angels at the hour of its death, in order to diminish temporal punishment.*
11. *That My Love will cause holy vocations consecrated to God among its loved ones and friends.*
12. *That the soul which preserves a genuine devotion to My Presence in the Eucharist will not be condemned or die without the Sacraments of the Church.*

To the priests and nuns that propagate the devotion of Adoration, I will grant many special graces, the complete recognition of their sins and the grace to amend them. I will help them to form communities of devout and holy faithful, and they will attain many privileges.

I promise these things to all persons, under only two conditions which are the fruit of genuine love towards My Real Presence in the Eucharist, and which are absolutely indispensable for My promises to become a reality in their lives:

a) *That they strive to preserve the dignity of My Altars.*
b) *That they be merciful towards their neighbor.*

At weekly **Adoration of the Blessed Sacrament,** *special graces are being granted.* **Pray until prayer becomes a great joy** for us, and as St. Paul says, pray unceasingly. The saints tell us the great secret of all secrets about the great gift of all gifts:

Bl. John Paul: *YOU have great need for Eucharistic Adoration!*

Pope Paul VI: *In the course of the day, the faithful should not omit visiting the Blessed Sacrament.*

St. Alphonsus Liguori: *Of all devotions, that of adoring Jesus in the Blessed Sacrament is the greatest after the sacraments, the one dearest to God and the most helpful to us.*

Bl. Mother Teresa: *The time we spend with Jesus in Eucharistic Adoration is the best time we can spend on earth.*

Our Lord revealed to St. Gertrude: *Each time (we go to Eucharistic Adoration) raises our place in Heaven forever.*

St. John Vianney: *In Heaven we will consider these moments with the Lord as the happiest of our earthly lives.*

Bl. John Paul: *The worship of the Eucharist is of inestimable value.*

Bl. John Paul: *I hope that ... perpetual adoration, with permanent exposition of the Blessed Sacrament, will continue into the future. Specifically, I hope that the fruit of this Congress results in **the establishment of perpetual Eucharistic Adoration in all parishes and Christian communities throughout the world**.*

Our Lady through Fr. Gobbi summarizes the call to restore Eucharistic devotion:

And so, my beloved ones and children consecrated to my Heart, it is **you who must be today 'a clarion call'** *for the full return of the whole Church Militant to Jesus present in the Eucharist. Because there alone is to be found the spring of living water which will purify its aridity and renew the desert to which it has been reduced; there alone is to be found the secret of life which will open up for it a second Pentecost of grace and of light; there alone is to be found the fount of its renewed holiness:* **'Jesus in the Eucharist!** *'[302]*

The Two Hearts Together with St. Joseph

St. Joseph too will come with the Holy Child
to bring peace to the world.
Our Lady of Fatima

God wishes me to be honored in union with Jesus and Mary
to obtain peace among men and nations...
The Divine Trinity has placed into our keeping
the peace of the world.
Our Lady of America apparitions

In the Church-recognized apparitions of Our Lady of America, St. Joseph spoke to visionary Sr. Mildred, giving great insights to bring countless souls to a new way of life, saying:

My spiritual fatherhood extends to all God's children. I am the protector of the Church and the home, *as I was the protector of Christ and His Mother while I lived upon earth. Jesus and Mary desire that my pure heart, so long hidden and unknown, be now honored in a special way.* **I desire souls to come to my heart** *that they may learn true union with the Divine Will.* **The Holy Trinity desires thus to honor me** *that in my unique fatherhood all fatherhood might be blessed. So* **the head of the family must be loved, obeyed, and respected, and in return be a true father and protector to those under his care.** *Receive my blessing. May Jesus and Mary through my hands bestow upon you eternal peace.*

So what are we to do? Through American Locutionist, Our Lady calls us to 1) read the messages in this book, and to 2) spread them to others as her messengers:

Someone to Carry the Message

*How can I speak from the housetops, when I have no one to carry the message of light and hope? That is what these people will be. That is why I call them together. What is the light on the mountain? It is **the messages themselves**. These messages will attract people. They will see them as true light. They will ask, "Why did Mary gather us together in this light?" They will realize, "We are called together **to spread this light**. We are **to take the messages to everyone, by every means**. Our Lady wants to speak from the housetops. We will be **her messengers**." So, I speak to you who are reading these messages. How did you find out about them? Who told you? With whom have you shared the messages?" How many of you are deeply interested to find your call in these messages. This is what you are to do. **You are to gather together with one purpose**, that you will **spread these messages in every possible way**. Right now, I call you to this and I give you my full permission.*

Mary's Housetop

*You do not need to be learned or clever. **I place this gift in your hands. Just give it to others.** Let your numbers increase. Many will find light in these words. Some, besides finding light, will want to spread the light. Let them join with you so that you grow in numbers. I will provide the teachings. You will be my housetop from which the words go forth.*[303]

Here is your mission; here is the reason you have found this book and are reading it. Now, go quickly and act. But, pray first:

PRAYER OF CONSECRATION TO THE TWO HEARTS

Hail, most loving Hearts of Jesus and Mary! We venerate You. We love and honor you. We give and consecrate ourselves to You forever. Receive us and possess us entirely. Purify, enlighten, and sanctify us so that we may love You, Jesus with the heart of Mary, and love you, Mary, with the Heart of Jesus.

O Heart of Jesus, living in Mary and by Mary! O heart of Mary, living in Jesus and for Jesus! O Heart of Jesus pierced for our sins and giving us Your Mother on Calvary! O heart of Mary pierced by sorrow and sharing in the sufferings of your Divine Son for our redemption! O sacred union of these Two Hearts.

Praise be God, the Father, the Son, and the Holy Spirit. Praise be the Holy Spirit of God Who united these Two Hearts together! May He unite our hearts and every heart so that all hearts may live in unity, in imitation of that sacred unity which exists in these Two Hearts.

Triumph, O Sorrowful and Immaculate Heart of Mary! Reign, O (Eucharistic and) Most Sacred Heart of Jesus! In our hearts, in our homes and families, in Your Church, in the lives of the faithful, and in the hearts of those who as yet know You not, and in all the nations of the world. Establish in the hearts of all mankind the sovereign triumph and reign of Your Two Hearts so that the earth may resound from pole to pole with one cry:

"Blessed forever be the (Eucharistic and) Most Sacred Heart of Jesus and the Sorrowful and Immaculate Heart of Mary!"

O dearest St. Joseph, I entrust myself to your honor and give myself to you that you may always be my father, my protector and my guide on the way to salvation. Obtain for me a greater purity of heart and a fervent love of the interior life. After your example, may I do all my actions for the greater glory of the Triune God in union with the (Sacred) Heart of Jesus and the Immaculate Heart of Mary. O Blessed St. Joseph, pray for me that I may share in the peace and joy of your holy death. Amen.

Two Hearts Media

Chapter Thirty-Three

The Universal Kingdom of the Divine Will

ℭℨ

When you see these things happening,
know that the kingdom of God is near*.*
Luke 21:31

*There will be **a resurrection of the flesh**, followed by **a thousand
years** in the rebuilt, embellished, and enlarged city of Jerusalem.*
St. Justin Martyr

*[If you remain faithful], you will be rewarded with the New Paradise
on Earth where you will want for nothing.*
***There will be My Second Coming, the greatest miracle since My
resurrection.*** *This will be the day I come to judge the living and the
dead.* ***This is the day I come to gather My family so that we become
one.*** *This will be the beginning of My reign as Heaven and earth
merge to become one for 1,000 years.* ***At this time all will live by the
Divine Will of My Father.***
MDM

The Church will be renewed and the face of the earth transformed
through a universal abandonment to the Divine Will... *The world is*
exactly at the same stage when I was about to come upon earth.
All were awaiting a great event, a New Era; as it indeed occurred. The
same now; since the great Event is coming – the New Era in which **the**
Will of God will be done on earth as it is in Heaven.
Our Lord to Luisa Piccarreta

As the new Era of Peace begins, humanity will be renewed and brought into the new Kingdom of the Divine Will. The petitions of the Our Father will come to pass. The petition of "Thy Kingdom come, Thy Will be done on earth as it is in Heaven" will come to pass. So will the petition, "Deliver us from evil." In the new Era, we will all be given the extraordinary grace to live in the divine Will and be preserved from all evil.

Living *in* the Divine Will, *the Sanctity of Sanctities*!

One of the greatest ways to grow in holiness and prepare for the new Era is to live according to God's will, to embrace His will in everything. But, there is more. Through mystic Luisa Piccarreta, the Little Daughter of the Divine Will, God is asking us not only to seek and obey His divine Will, but to live *in* the Divine Will, which is *"the most beautiful and the brightest among all other sanctities."* Jesus promises: *"If you put yourself at the mercy of my Will, you will no longer have concerns for anything."*[304] Living constantly in this way, we will have nothing on our own, but everything will be in common with Jesus. In this, Our Lady's *FIAT* (*"Let it be done to me according to Your Word"*) becomes our constant motto. Our passion is the Divine Will, to *live in* God's Will. This is the fruit of living united to the Two Hearts. As we commit to living our consecrated lives in Jesus and Mary, let us pray to do so by living in the Divine Will. Our Lord tells Luisa that this will become common in the era to come; we can begin now:

It will be a time in which God gives a great **grace to the creature as to make him return almost to the state of origin; and only then, when I see man just as he came out from Me, will my Work be complete, and I will take my perpetual rest in the last FIAT.** Only the life in my Volition will give back to man his state of origin. Therefore, be attentive, and together with Me, help Me to complete the sanctification of the creature.

The [New Era of the] FIAT - my 'Fiat Voluntas Tua (Let it be done according to Your Will), on earth as it is in Heaven' - will be like the rainbow which appeared in the sky after the deluge, which, as a rainbow of peace, assured man that the deluge had ceased. So will the third FIAT be. As It comes to be known, loving and disinterested souls will come to live in my FIAT. They will be like rainbows – rainbows of peace – which will reconcile Heaven and earth, and dispel the deluge of so many sins which inundate the earth. These rainbows of peace will have the third FIAT as their own life; therefore my 'Fiat Voluntas Tua' will have Its completion in them. And just as the second FIAT called Me upon earth to live among men, the third FIAT will call my Will into souls, and It will reign in them 'on earth, as in Heaven.'

In this Kingdom, a new era, a new continuous creation, **will begin for My Will**. It will put out everything that It had established to give to creatures, had they always done Its Will, and that It had to keep within Itself for many centuries, as though in deposit, to then release them for the good of the children of Its Kingdom.

Too perfidious and ungrateful will be those who will not recognize in these manifestations of Mine the echo of Heaven, the long chain of love of the Supreme Will, the communion of goods of our Celestial Father, that He wants to give to creatures; and as though **wanting to put aside everything that has passed in the history of the world, He wants to begin a new era, a new creation**, as if the new history of Creation were just now beginning. Therefore, let Me do, because whatever I do is of highest importance.

When the knowledges about My Divine Will have done their course, in view of the great good that they contain—goods that no creature has thought about until now, that the Kingdom of My Will will be the outpouring of Heaven, the echo of the celestial happiness, the fullness of terrestrial goods—so, in view of this great good, unanimously, [then the people] will yearn, they will ask that My Kingdom come soon... Therefore, one will be the echo from one end of the earth to another, one the sigh, [and they will pray]: 'May the Kingdom of the Supreme Fiat come.' Then, triumphantly, It will come into the midst of creatures.

The Will of God that the Writings of My Divine Will come to light is absolute, and as many incidents as may occur, It will triumph of everything. And even if it should take years and years, It will know how to dispose everything so that Its absolute Will be fulfilled. The time in which [the Will of God] will come to light is relative and conditional upon when creatures dispose themselves to receive a good so great, and upon those who must occupy themselves with being its criers, and make the sacrifice so as to bring the new era of peace, the new Sun that will dispel all the clouds of evils.

However, when my love will make arise the Era of my Will... those who want to resist the current will run the risk of losing their lives.

Afterwards, He added: *The whole world is upside down; everyone is waiting for changes, for peace, for new things. They even gather to discuss about it, and they are surprised at not being able to conclude anything and come up with serious decisions. So, true peace does not arise, and everything comes up to words, but no facts. And they hope that more conferences may serve to take serious decisions, but they wait in vain. In the meantime, in this waiting, they are all fearful, and some get ready for new wars, some hope for new conquests. But with this, peoples are impoverished and are stripped alive; and while they are waiting, tired of the sad era, which, dark and bloody, enwraps them, they wait and hope for a New Era of peace and of light...*

*The world is exactly at the same stage when I was about to come upon earth. All were awaiting a great event, a New Era; as it indeed occurred. The same now; since the great Event is coming – **the New Era in which the Will of God will be done on earth as it is in Heaven – everyone is waiting for this new Era**, being tired of the present one, but not knowing what this novelty, this change is, just as they did not know it when I came upon earth. This wait is a sure sign that the Hour is near. But **the most certain sign [that this renewal is near] is that I am manifesting what I want to do [through Luisa]**; and turning to a soul, just as I turned to my Mama in descending from Heaven to earth, I communicate to her my Will and the goods and effects It contains, in order to give It as gift to all humanity.*

Luisa continues: I continue in my painful state. My sweet Jesus came for just a little, and drawing me strongly to Himself, told me: *My daughter, I repeat it to you - **do not look at the earth. Let them do what they want. They want to make war - so be it**; when they get tired, I too will make my war. Their tiredness in evil, their disenchantments, the disillusions, the losses suffered, will dispose them to receive my war. **My war will be war of love.** My Will will descend from Heaven into their midst. All of your acts and those of others done in my Volition will wage war on the creatures - **but not a war of blood; they will wage war with weapons of love, giving them gifts, graces and peace.** They will give such surprising things as to astonish the ungrateful man. This Will of Mine, militia of Heaven, will confuse man with Divine weapons; it will overwhelm him, and will give him the light in order to see - not evil, but the gifts and the riches with which I want to enrich him. **The acts done in my Will**, carrying the Creative Power within themselves, will be the new salvation of man; and descending from Heaven, they will bring all goods upon earth. They **will bring the New Era**, and the triumph over human iniquity. **Therefore, multiply your acts in my Will to form the weapons, the gifts, the graces, so as to be able to descend into the midst of creatures and wage the war of love on them.***

*... **And when he (the Father) sees them almost lost, he [will go] into their midst** to make them richer; he [will offer] remedies for their wounds, and [bring] peace and happiness to all. Now, conquered by so much love, [His] children will bind themselves to their father with a lasting peace, and will love him.*

*Everyone is waiting for this new Era... Peoples -- wait and hope for [this] New Era of peace and of light... **the great Event is coming – the New Era in which the Will of God will be done on earth as it is in Heaven.***

Our Lady confirms this through Fr. Gobbi:

*In the hour of the great trial, paradise will be joined to earth, until the moment when the luminous door will be opened, to cause to descend upon the world the glorious presence of Christ, who will restore his reign in which the **divine Will** shall be accomplished in a perfect manner, as in heaven, so also on earth.[305]*

How to Approach the End of Our Times with Peace

Chapter Thirty-Four

What Is God Asking Us to Do RIGHT NOW?

ЄӠ

During the times to come, Jesus promises that He will take care of those who put their trust in Him:

*There is nothing to fear in this world if you will trust in Me completely. I have wonderful plans for all of you who will come closer to My sacred heart. The most extraordinary gifts await you. Have no fear of worldly unrest. For I will protect all those who believe in Me and **will provide for your needs of the flesh**.*[306]

*There is nothing to fear in this world if you will trust in Me completely. I have wonderful plans for all of you who come closer to My Sacred Heart. The most precious gifts await you. Have no fear of worldly unrest. For **I will protect all those who believe in Me and provide for your needs of the flesh.**[307] (MDM)*

No Blaming God

No one understands. No one grasps the destructive forces that will soon be unleashed. They will be unleashed by men themselves. No one should blame God. Yet, when these forces are released, many will ask, "Why did God let this happen?" So, I must explain the deeper truths, the greater realities...

Now, all is clear. What is happening in the world? The world rejects God and he withdraws. When he withdraws, there is no force/power present to restrain the destructive forces that men carry in their own hearts. There are destructive forces everywhere and the divine presence has withdrawn.

What are you to do? Invite God back. Ask him to return. He will come. He listens to his children. Invite him into every part of your lives, your homes and your communities. Restore the statues that remind people of God. Let hearts join in public prayer. Especially, invite him into your own heart. You will see the forces of evil withdraw, because a greater power confronts them.

When these destructive forces break out, make the right conclusion. Do not ask "Why did God allow this?" Say rather, "This happened because we have rejected God's presence and protection".[308] (American Locutionist)

Never judge other religions, creeds or sexual preferences

***Never tell those of different creeds or sexual preferences they are doomed.** To push My teachings in a manner where you tell those who are not followers that they will perish or come to harm by brandishing* *their ways as 'evil' will simply render them weaker than before. Many will simply turn their backs on you. Then you will have failed. Instead of lecturing, show compassion. Teach through example. Never tell or attempt to say to these people that they are doomed in My eyes. Because they are not.*

I love every single soul of all religions. Of all persuasions. Of all creeds. Of all sexual preferences. Each one is a precious child. No one better than the next. While sin will always be there – you are all sinners remember that – it will be up to each one of you to follow My teachings and spread My word.

Embrace each other. Show compassion to each other. Don't exclude anyone irrespective as to whether they are Catholics, Other Christian Denominations, Islam, Hindu, Jews, Buddhist – even those new cults which have emerged who do not believe in God, The Eternal Father. Pray for them. Teach them the importance of opening their hearts to the truth. Teach through example. Spread conversion. But never ever inflict judgment on others or attempt to differentiate yourself from those who do not understand the truth.

Never believe because you have been given the graces from Heaven because of your allegiance to Me that you are better than your brothers or sisters. Yes you bring joy to My Sacred Heart but you must deal with others in a loving but not dictatorial manner.

None of you is worthy to judge others. *Remember this lesson – not one of you is worthy to judge or access others. No one has the power or divine knowledge to make any moral assessment of others. Keep an open mind always and remember the day you believe you are more important in My eyes than those you deem to be sinners is the day you become lost to Me.*

I will not exclude any creed from these messages.*[309]* (MDM)

The Two Options

*Now, he has mankind on the edge of a greater precipice. The heavenly Father will not allow Satan to fulfill his plan but he has only two options. Mankind can **return to God** and walk in his ways. Or, the heavenly Father can allow the **divine chastisements** to stop mankind in its tracks. The second is just the lesser of two evils. There will be the chastisements of heaven so there is not the destruction planned by Satan.*[310]

Approaching a Disastrous Moment

*The world is approaching that moment when the power of Satan will have **two aspects**. First, he will have linked his evil into what is truly **a worldwide system**. Second, this system will contain the **power to destroy most of the world**.*

*I say this. The heavenly Father will not allow this but he has **only two alternatives**. Either he purifies creation by **divine chastisements** that totally disrupt what Satan is putting in place so that all of creation is not destroyed. **Or, the world comes into my Immaculate Heart** and I reveal a much easier salvation, by which hearts are touched and the evil attached to progress and inventions is purified. In this way, the power is used for good and not evil.*

*The choice is a solemn one, filled with a thousand ramifications which touch the hearts of people and the fibers of society. I say this again and again – **the secrets of God lie in my Immaculate Heart**. That is where the Father has placed them.*[311] (American Locutionist)

A Chastisement of Mercy

*A **time of great trial** will come upon the world, a **great distress** of the nations. **Many will die**. Others will not know what to do. However, those who know me and know my words will have enough light to get through this period of darkness.*

*The world will be **purged by this extraordinary divine intervention**. This is the purpose of the trial because the Father would not do this if he had any other choice. He cannot allow the world to go on as it is. If he did not intervene, as drastic as this is, life on earth would be even worse. Man would inflict on man unheard of sufferings as the weapons of mass destruction are released by those who are under the control of the evil one. So, **what looks like divine chastisements are really acts of his mercy**. God will purge the world before man destroys it.*

God's Care for the Living and the Dead

*Those who live in light and believe my words will know this is true. Even in the worst moments, they will see God's purposes and know what to do. **Some will die but they will accept their deaths in a spirit of faith**, knowing that they have used their lives to love and serve God. They will have no regrets and the Spirit will console their inner being.*

***Others will be preserved from death by the Spirit so they can form the new Church** that will arise, the light of the new mankind that will be fashioned by the Father. This will include people from all over the world. They will be people of faith, even if they did not believe before. They will have come to faith in the middle of the trials because of the signs in the heavens and the wonders upon earth. They will know that God has saved them and they will tell the story to their children and their children's children.*[312] (American Locutionist)

The Goal of Divine Justice

When mankind fails in the basic duties of justice, the heavenly Father must inflict Divine Justice to remove darkness and restore truth to the land. During this time, my children must remain in hope and light. When Divine Justice removes the architects of darkness, I will place the children of light on the lampstand. Until then, they must live in faith until the powers of darkness are toppled.

Need For Words

To prepare for this cleansing of Divine Justice, I give my words to the little ones... If they do not hear my words, they will not be prepared for my helps. I will provide many helps, but my words are needed to reveal these. If they do not listen, they will not have my helps and very few will survive the times of Divine Justice.

Revealing the Problems

To my children, I will reveal the enemy strongholds which Divine Justice must destroy. If my children stay away from these strongholds, they will not be harmed by Divine Justice, which is like a surgeon's scalpel, cutting only what is infected...

Protecting the Little Ones

How can I protect the little ones? Listen to my words. In the present, they must gather together in love for one another and in their desire to safeguard the family. **I will open to them the doors of economic security to provide all that they need.** *Trying to act only at the moment of economic collapse will be too late. Let them make decisions now. They must love one another. Be of one mind and one heart.* **Let the father be the head of the family,** *listening to the words of all the members...*

I must unmask these evil movements and reveal them for what they are...

Each chastisement will be perfectly suited to cleanse each evil. If the evil is violence, there will be death. If the evil is hatred and false denunciations, the evil will fall on those who spew these out. If the evil is dishonesty, they will be caught and exposed. For each evil, there will be a chastisement...

Divine Justice touches the problem like a surgeon's scalpel, cutting away only what is infected. To prepare for the time of Divine Justice, I give my words to the Little Ones. My words, my words, I am always speaking about my words. Yet this is the way I enlighten them. If they do not hear my words, they cannot prepare for the other helps I will offer.

There will be many other helps, but my words will reveal them. I speak these words from the deepest love of my heart. If they do not listen, very few will survive the time of Divine Justice.

Preparing for the Time of Divine Justice

I will reveal to my children the enemy stronghold which Divine Justice must destroy. By staying away from those areas, the little ones will not be harmed by Divine Justice. This is easy to understand. God restores justice by destroying places of injustice. He destroys greed by attacking those who control wealth. To avoid suffering seek only the necessities of life, which the heavenly Father will always provide.[313] (American Locutionist)

Three Ways to Respond

1. Do not fear. Repent. Then, act by love. That is the secret. Never despair. Join together in community. **Gather together privately** and weekly in a prayer group that is dedicated to the Two Hearts.

Know that all that I have told you and more will come to pass. Repent. Repent. Repent. If you have ears, open them. If you have eyes, open them. (Mary to Nancy Fowler)

2. Pray the Holy Rosary and the Divine Mercy Chaplet, as part of the Two Hearts Devotion, for both combined will help wipe out much of this pending evil.

*Pray, pray all of you **My Divine Mercy (Chaplet) and the Most Holy Rosary every day** as often as you can to alleviate the impact of this devious and demonic plan. Pray too for those souls who will be lost in* *the imminent global ecological disasters brought about by the Hand of God.* (MDM)

*Say the Rosary every day to obtain **peace** for the world.* (Our Lady of Fatima)

There is no problem I tell you, no matter how difficult it is, that we cannot resolve by the prayer of the Holy Rosary. (Lucia of Fatima)

One day, through the Rosary and the Scapular, I will save the world. (Mary to St. Dominic)

The Rosary is THE WEAPON. (St. Pio)

3. Fast and offer sacrifices of reparation and penance for souls.

Pray, fast, and make sacrifices *for your sins and for the sins of all sinners and unbelievers.* (Our Lady of Fatima)

*Christians have forgotten they can **prevent war** and even natural calamities by prayer and fasting. Only by prayer and fasting can war be stopped.* (Our Lady of Medjugorje)

Chapter Thirty-Five

Three Heavenly Requests for the Church Leaders

☙

I noted in my research that Heaven is requesting three things of the Church in these times, to avert the calamities and to bring humanity safely through this period into the Era of Peace. They are:

1. To Stop Communist Russia

The First Request from Heaven: Our Lady of Fatima requested the Consecration of Russia to her Immaculate Heart. She said it would be done, but not until very late.

Our Lady of Fatima said:

If people do as I shall ask many souls will be saved, and there will be peace.... **But if** *people do not cease offending God... war, famine, persecution of the Church and of the Holy Father.*

To prevent this, I shall come to ask the **consecration of Russia to my Immaculate Heart, and Communions of reparation on the first Saturdays.** *If my requests are heard, Russia will be converted and there will be peace.* **If not, she will spread her errors throughout the world, fomenting wars and persecution of the Church. The good will suffer martyrdom; the Holy Father will suffer much; different nations will be annihilated.**

The 1984 Marian Consecration of Bl. John Paul II was done and accepted (thus bearing some good fruit), but not complete as requested by Heaven:

The consecration of Russia to the Immaculate Heart and the moving of the papacy from Rome to Jerusalem – *these are the two important goals of [the Pope after Benedict XVI].* (American Locutionist)

While this consecration will not be done until the end, the good news of this prophecy is that it will be done in the end, as Our Lady foretells:

But **in the end** *my Immaculate Heart will triumph. The Holy Father will consecrate Russia to me, which will be converted, and some time of peace will be granted to humanity.*

2. To Prevent a War on U.S. Soil and Nuclear War

The Second Request from Heaven: Our Lady of America requests the US Bishops to process with her statue into the National Basilica in Washington DC and crown her. She then promises more miracles than at Lourdes and Fatima… IF we do this… Otherwise, war is coming to our land.

In the United States, Our Lady has given messages for our times and for our country. This devotion to the Blessed Virgin Mary under the title of Our Lady of America enjoys canonical approval through former Archbishop of Cincinnati, Ohio, Archbishop Leibold, who approved for public devotion this private apparition of the Blessed Virgin Mary to Sister Mary Ephrem (Mildred Neuzil), who died on January 10th, 2000.

Furthermore, many other Bishops have also shown their approval by their promotion of this devotion. Archbishop Raymond L. Burke, a canon lawyer, in 2007, confirmed that the devotion was approved.

Sr. Mary Ephram was told by Our Lady of America:

America, the United States in particular, is being given the tremendous, yet privileged opportunity to lead all nations in a spiritual renewal never before so necessary, so important, so vital."

Mary said that she was coming to America now as a last resort. Sr. Mary Ephram wrote that Mary *"promised that **greater miracles than those granted at Lourdes and Fatima** would be granted here in America, the United States in particular, if we would do as she desires."* Mary promised *"miracles of the soul."* Our Lady taught Sr. Mary Ephram to pray:

By the Holy and Immaculate Conception,
O Mary, deliver us from evil.

On the fifty-third anniversary of Our Lady of America, Our Lady told Sr. Mary Ephram:

*From the beginning of time **every prophecy, every vision,** throughout the centuries, **will have its fulfillment in Our Lady of America and her message of the Indwelling Trinity living in every soul,** which will renew the whole world and destroy Lucifer and all the evil spirits in the fight he is making against the Indwelling Trinity.*

Our Lady of America's Prophecy

Our Lady instructed that a statue of her be constructed as she appeared, and that the statue be placed after a solemn procession into the National Shrine of the Immaculate Conception, in Washington, D.C. Our Lady said that **if this is done**, the United States of America would turn back toward morality and the national shrine would become a place of *"wonders."* Let us turn to Our Lady of America and ask for her to be enshrined in the National Basilica of the United States, that this prophecy might be fulfilled.

Our Lady of America is calling the United States to lead the world, to establish peace, to restore the virtue of purity, and to protect the family. She calls for us to renew the family by inviting **the Most Holy Trinity to be the center of the Christian family**, and **to recognize the Holy Family of Joseph, Mary, and Jesus as the model of family life**. Let us honor Our Lady of America as she requests, so that she might bring faith and hope to our world and to families.

3. To Bring a Period of Peace to the World

The Third Request from Heaven: Our Lady of All Nations said that when the new and final Marian Dogma of Co-Redemptrix, Mediatrix, and Advocate is proclaimed, then she will grant a period of peace to the world.

Our Lady of All Nations prophesied about **warning signs** to come as indication of the apocalyptic time, including meteors and natural disasters, along with political conflicts and economic disasters. She also promised that if we seek her help, she would bestow **Grace, Redemption, and Peace** to stave off **degeneration, disaster, and war**.[314]

The Our Lady of Akita statue (which is of Our Lady of All Nations) wept 101 times. In the end, Our Lady of Akita said: *"Whoever entrusts themselves to me will be saved."* What more do *you* need? Respond now, Our Lady is pleading!

Our Lady of All Nations, the twentieth century, Church-approved apparitions of Our Lady and Our Lord to Ida Peerdeman of Amsterdam,[315] speaks of a victory and period of peace that will arrive after the final dogma of Mary is proclaimed by the Church – that of **Mary Co-redemptrix, Mediatrix, and Advocate**. *When exactly this new Marian dogma will be proclaimed is unknown*, but that it will be proclaimed is assured by Our Lady of All Nations. Mary also stated that the new dogma will be proclaimed only after a period of struggle and upheaval for the Church. The final and greatest Marian dogma will come, that is assured, but only through a struggle that will arouse much controversy that will be hard and bitter, and the dogma will be much disputed. Giving us hope and commissioning us, Our Lady says:

*Let the following words sink in well: the Lady of All Nations can and will bestow on all peoples of the world who have recourse to her – grace, redemption, and peace. To you all, however, falls the task of introducing the Lady of All Nations to the whole world... Do **fight and ask for this Dogma**, it is the Crowning of your Lady!*

Our Lady speaks of the urgency of proclaiming the fifth Marian dogma and what fruits it will bring to humanity, through Fr. Gobbi, saying:

I am the Woman clothed in the sun. I am in the heart of the Most Holy Trinity. **Until I am acknowledged there where the Most Holy Trinity has willed me to be, I will not be able to exercise my power fully**, *in the maternal work of co-redemption and of the universal mediation of graces.*[316] *... The task which the Most Holy Trinity has entrusted to me will be acknowledged by all; I will be able to exercise my great power fully, so that the victory of my Son Jesus may shine forth everywhere, when He will restore, through you, his glorious reign of Love.*[317]

Our Lady reminds us of the importance of **our role** in assisting her in the great victory, saying through Fr. Gobbi: *"***You are an important part of my plan*** as Mediatrix and Coredemptrix... I want you thus to be associated in my motherly work of coredemption, and I am making you more and more a participant in my great sorrows.*"[318]

Already in our time, the Popes, like Pius XI and Pius XII, have called Mary by the title of *Co-redemptrix*. **John Paul II used the title of *Co-redemptrix* for Mary at least six times during his pontificate**; and he told mariologist Mark Miravalle: *"The fifth dogma will be."*[319] The God-Man came to us by means of Mary in the Incarnation; He comes to us now in grace by means of Mary; and He will come again in our time in the Second Coming by means of her as well.

A special Prayer of Our Lady of All Nations was also given through this apparition, so *"that under this title and through this prayer,* **she may deliver the world from a great world catastrophe... Through this prayer the Lady shall save the world.***"* After giving this special prayer for the world, Our Lady said to Ida about **The Lady of All Nations Prayer**:

You do not know how great and how important this prayer is before God! You cannot estimate the great value this will have. You do not *know what the future has in store... This prayer is short and simple so that everyone in this quick and modern time can pray it. It is given in order to call down the True Spirit upon the world... **This prayer has been given for the conversion of the world**. I am the Lady of All Peoples... 'Who once was Mary.' Here is the meaning of this formula: Mary was known as Mary by a great number of men, but now, **in the new era which is opening, I wish to be known as the Lady of All Peoples**. And everyone will understand that.*

Mary is not relinquishing her name, but publicly expanding her office and heavenly role (Revelation 12) for the conversion and salvation of all souls.

The fifth dogma of Mary will bring a period of peace to the world and to humanity. Our Lady of All Nations prophesied to visionary Ida Peerdeman on May 31, 1954:

*The Lady of All Nations wishes for unity in the true Holy Spirit. **The world is covered by a false spirit, by Satan. Once the dogma, the final dogma in Marian history, has been proclaimed, the Lady of All Nations will grant peace, true peace, to the world.** The nations, however, must pray my prayer, together with the Church. They shall know that the Lady of All Nations has come as Coredemptrix, Mediatrix and Advocate.*

And twenty-five years later, to the day, Our Lord promised through visionary, Ida: *"The Holy Father will proclaim her Co-redemptrix, Mediatrix and Advocate."*[320]

Mark Miravalle summarizes, saying:

***Mary's titles are her functions.** Her roles as the Co-redemptrix, the Mediatrix of all graces, and the Advocate are titles which refer to Mary's motherly spiritual functions of grace which she performs for humanity. If these roles are solemnly proclaimed by the Holy Father, the greatest spiritual authority on earth in the name of all humanity,* *then the Immaculate Virgin will be able to fully exercise these functions for the human family in a greater and more dynamic way than ever.*[321]

Our Lady promises the nations of the world a new spring of *"grace, redemption, and peace"* that will save the world from *"degeneration, disaster, and war"*. As humanity's Queen Mother, she is, and will soon become known to all as, **the Co-Redemptrix of redemption, the Mediatrix of grace, and the Advocate of peace** for all nations and peoples. What a great hope we should place in Mary. She is our Mother of mercy; our life, our sweetness and our hope!

In one of her prophetic messages, Our Lady warned about a series of events that would cause great harm to Rome. Our Lady seemed to indicate that such events would occur 51-53 years after the apparitions, which ended on May 31, 1959… that would mean 2010-2012 or soon afterwards. Our Lady said:

Era of Decline

*Child, do not be afraid… Earlier I already showed you, '51-53'. Do you know, child, what kind of an era this is? Throughout the centuries the world has not yet experienced such an era, such **a decline of faith**; and that is why I want this to be carried out, quickly and without fear…*

Rome in Danger

Then the Lady says to me again,

*I already told you earlier: the Cross has to be brought back into the world in these years, 51-53. You do not know what is lying hidden in the future. You do not realize **the great danger facing Rome**. Rome still thinks that she is standing strong, but she is not aware of how she is being undermined. Do you realize how quickly action needs to be taken?*

Do Not be Afraid

Next the Lady says,

*... Spread this. Otherwise the world will fall into **degeneration**. Otherwise the world will **destroy itself**. Otherwise there will be **war upon war** and no end to destruction.*

False Prophets

*Rome must know her task in this time. Does Rome realize which enemy is lying in wait and creeping like a snake throughout the world? And by this I do not mean **communism** alone; other prophets will come— **false prophets**. That is why those means should be made use of.*

I stand as the Lady before the Cross, as the Mother before my Son, Who through the Father entered into me. And this is why I stand before my Son, as the Advocate and bearer of this message to this modern world.[322]

Our Lady seems to be warning about the new rise of Communism and about the False Prophet who will rise up in Rome in this period.

Our Lady then asks that in the year '53' for her to be brought to all the nations. This would seem to be in 2012 or around that time. She then promises if this is done, that in '54' (which could mean 2013), she will bring some relief. She asks the Pope to bring her new title to the nations in '54', or what seems to be 2013. Then, Our Lady indicates the apostasy and coming of false prophets in the Church that would take place soon afterwards (after 2013). Here are some excerpts as follows:

Degeneration, Disaster and War

I see the Lady standing before me. She says,

*Mary, the Lady of All Nations, has been sent today in order once again **to warn the world, the Church of Rome, and all peoples of degeneration, disaster and war**...*

The Lady Will Bring Peace

Then the Lady gazes before herself and says very slowly and clearly, *The year 53, that is the year in which the Lady of All Nations must be brought into the world.*

For a long time the Lady remains silent, and then she says, *The Lady of All Nations will be allowed to bring peace to the world. Yet she must be asked for it under this title. The Lady of All Nations will assist the Church of Rome. The Church of Rome, the community, shall invoke Mary, the Mother of the Lord Jesus Christ, under this new title, 'The Lady of All Nations'. They shall pray my prayer against degeneration, disaster and war, and bring it among all nations. I shall help the Church of Rome, the community. The nations shall invoke me under this title.*

The Redeemer and the Coredemptrix of All Nations

The Lady gazes before herself again for a long time. Then she says clearly and with emphasis,

The Lord is the Redeemer of all nations. Mary, the Mother, was chosen from the beginning as Coredemptrix. She became Coredemptrix at the departure of the Lord Jesus Christ to the Father. She became Mediatrix and Advocate of all nations.

The Lady pauses again for a moment and then says,

Because Mary was destined as Coredemptrix, Mediatrix and Advocate, she comes now in this time as the Lady of All Nations. Because Mary is given the title 'Lady of All Nations', she has come under this title to different places, to different countries.

Destined for the World

Then the Lady gazes before herself and says,

... The Lady of All Nations is not destined for one country, for one place, but is destined for the world, the peoples.

The Crowning of Mary

Now the Lady pauses for a moment and then says very clearly and slowly,
*Then the great work begins: the crowning of Mary, the proclamation of the dogma of Coredemptrix, Mediatrix and Advocate. First, however, let the Church and the nations invoke Mary under her new title and pray her prayer so that degeneration, disaster and war may be staved off from this world. **If they do so, the nations of Europe will breathe a sigh of relief after 54.***

And now the Lady looks over the globe on which she is standing and says - *Then the great worldwide task follows.*

[Our Lady then warns about the apostasy, the split within the Church, saying:]

Black and White Sheep

Then the Lady looks about her, and, pointing at the sheep, she says,
Look at my black sheep.

I then see lots of black sheep. **Separated from them** I see white sheep on the opposite side. The Lady warns very seriously, *White sheep, beware. The time is still here in which all of you can cooperate to achieve unity.*

As she says this, I see those **two groups of sheep changing into two groups of people, black people and white people, standing apart from one another**.

The Crowning of the Mother of the Lord

Then the Lady says,

*Church of Rome, the Lady of All Nations will come only a few more times. She is still warning about **the false prophets**. Read carefully the messages the Lady brought you…*

The Lady says this with great emphasis. Now the Lady raises her forefinger as if in warning and says,

Holy Father, *you have a great task to accomplish before you… See to the final dogma, the crowning of the Mother of the Lord Jesus Christ, the Coredemptrix, Mediatrix and Advocate. **In 54 you are to bring this new title among the nations.** See to those countries in which the Lord Jesus Christ is being persecuted.*

This can and will become a great world action, above which Mary will stand as the Lady of All Nations. I am helping; I shall be allowed to help the world and peoples through my Lord.[323]

We need to respond, as she has requested, and pray and spread her powerful prayer, which is as follows:

The Lady of All Nations Prayer

Lord Jesus Christ, Son of the Father,

send now Your Spirit over the earth.

Let the Holy Spirit live in the hearts of all nations,

that they may be preserved

from degeneration, disaster and war.

May the Lady of All Nations,

who once was Mary,

be our Advocate. Amen.

Chapter Thirty-Six

No Time Left to Delay!

℃ℬ

And he said to John,

These words are trustworthy and true,
and the Lord, the God of prophetic spirits,
sent his angel to show his servants what must happen soon.
'Behold, I am coming soon.
Blessed is the one who keeps the prophetic message of this book.'
Revelation 22:6-7

The time to prepare is now! So says the American Locutionist:

The **relationships of faith must be made strong**. This is **the way to survive**. People must strengthen their ties to others, the bonds of their faith.

Prayer and conversion can dilute the impact of the havoc which will come about through the reign of both the Anti-Christ and the False Prophet.

Get Ready for What is Coming

Institutions will be washed away in the floods of bankruptcy and mismanagement. People will search for other alternatives but nothing will be ready. No one has prepared adequately. Life for many will be very different. Parents will worry about their children and how they will provide for the future. Anxieties will increase and, in some places, even panic and breakdowns of social life will occur. What do I have to say about this darkness? What advice can I give?

... Survival will come only from faith that life still has a purpose, from hope that the heavenly Father will provide sufficiently as Jesus promised, and from love which binds people together, each one looking out for the other.

As institutions fall and as the other sources of help are ineffective, faith, hope and love will bind people together. There will arise a new, living set of relationships composed of people who refuse to give up and are determined to help each other, just as Jesus taught his disciples.

... To these faithful souls who will endure the darkness, I speak the words from Jeremiah which they must always remember, "I know well the plans I have in mind for you, says the Lord, plans for your welfare, not for woe! Plans to give you a future full of hope." (Jer. 29:11)

Yes, in the darkness, I have plans for a future full of hope and my children must believe that those plans exist.[324]

I will open up gatherings of faith and my children will be aware of them. They will not know why I have led them to these gatherings. They will just know that I am leading them in this way. Only when Satan's attacks begin will they see that these are saving gifts – the windows and doors that I have opened so they can escape. Yes, I say "escape" because to remain is to be lost. To foolishly cling to homes or material goods is to be swallowed up. Just as a place was prepared for me in the desert (12:6) where I was kept safe, so I will prepare *places for all those who hear and receive my words. People must learn to go out into the desert, those places of solitude where I can gather my children. Did I not go into the desert? Would I not go to prepare a place for my children? This is how I will save them in **the times of great trials that lie ahead**.*[325]

How to Survive

*When the time comes, it will be too late to prepare. Those who have called on my name will know what to do to survive. Their hearts will tell them and **I will guide them**. Those who are selfish will act selfishly. They will condemn themselves because they will see all their past efforts destroyed in one moment. They will have nothing to live for. They will make efforts to control the situation, but their efforts will be in vain and they have never learned how to live in faith.*

*This is my teaching, how to **live in faith**. People with few resources will survive because of a deep rooted faith. People with more resources will not, because they cannot find any faith in their hearts...*

In the chastisement, the earthly kingdoms fall. Terrible jolts come upon society. In the beginning, no one notices. However, as the jolts continue, all begin to see that their society, which provided all these goods, is collapsing. For a person without faith, this is all they have. They have nothing and do not know how to turn to God for their security. They are lost and each day is worse than the last one. They stumble in an insurmountable darkness. For them, everything is destroyed. They cannot go on. Indeed, many choose not to go on. They destroy themselves...

*I will teach you **a prayer**. Say it often and I will come to you and you will see a flower **of faith** growing in your heart. This is the prayer,*

O Mary, when I am alone, I realize I am empty.
I believe this feeling is my search for faith.
O Mary, plant the seed of faith in my heart and I will let it grow.[326]

Pray... Now and Every Day for God's Will

*My life was filled with sorrows, yet I never swerved. Whatever the heavenly Father wanted, I wanted. What he did not want, I did not want. My free will never swerved. Yet, it remained free because that alone gave glory to God. My will never swerved because he surrounded me with so many graces. These same graces are stored in my Immaculate Heart... I stored them up for you and I am ready to pour them out on whomever asks for them. They have only one purpose – **to unite your will to the Father's will**, just as my will was so united. This is the greatest gift. It will last forever. In heaven, the will of every angel and every saint is perfectly in tune with the divine will. By pouring out these graces, I give you **two gifts**. On earth, you will fulfill your call, the reason God created you. In heaven, you will be perfectly united to God, to me, to all the angels and saints.*
*Let me teach you a **simple prayer** that will be so effective because it seeks these graces.*

O Mary, in your Immaculate Heart, are stored up all the graces of divine union. If you place these in my heart, I will always do God's will. Amen.[327]

*My first task is to separate those who are in the forces of darkness so they do not encourage one another. I must turn them against each other... I will sow these seeds of discord in **the Taliban**, in **Al-Qaeda** and in all the **terrorist groups**. Let my people pray for this. Let them lift up their voices, asking me. This is the **simple prayer** they are to say,*

O Blessed Virgin, Mother of the Savior, scatter the forces of evil so they are not engrossed in darkness but can come to light.

Notice the prayer. I do not want these people's destruction, but their scattering. If they are scattered, then I can surround them in light and they can believe and turn to me...
What is important is that millions of my children begin to pray that I scatter the forces of darkness. Say the prayer right now.[328]

Two Ways to Act

All must begin now to prepare…
(First,) **take only what is needed**. *Otherwise, the baggage you carry will be too heavy for you and you will never complete the journey. So, you must grow detached. Many will mourn their losses saying, "I used to have this. I used to have that." They will spend valuable time in trying to salvage what is useless. Think of yourselves on a journey and prepare for a journey, taking all that is needed but only what is needed. I will give you the wisdom. Do not live as those settling in, providing yourselves with every possible luxury. See yourselves like those on a journey and you will survive.*
Second, **draw close to one another**. *Do not wander. Do not separate. To spread out and to go your own way is a luxury of settled existence. On a journey, all must stay close because nothing is settled. There are always new questions and last minute decisions that must be communicated to all. Many have chosen individual life styles, having the luxury of independent living. They go off. They isolate themselves and immerse themselves in things. On a journey, things are a burden. People are an asset. Having others to help you is what gets you to the end. Recapture the family relationships. Recapture the extended family. Come back home. Gather again. This will prepare you for the trials ahead.*[329]

Advice for the Trials

No one knows the trials which lie ahead. For now, I can only promise mankind that I will provide a road for all who call on me. Many will trust in their own wisdom and will take the wrong road. They will say, "Let us go here and we will be safe". Others will turn to me and I will show them the true path. These decisions are very important. The first steps often decide the future course.

Acting in Love
As the trials begin, they must not act from fear but from **love**. **That is the secret**. *Do not just think about yourself.* **Think about others**. *Do*

not exclude anyone of good will who is willing to cooperate. By opening your heart to others, the trial can become a great moment. Those who reach out and who help others, I will bless and show the way.

Never Despairing

*Never despair. This is so important. Many with great resources will give up. However, those who share love will be bonded together in a cocoon of my protection. These bonds of love will grow. People will be reunited. Families which dispersed amid surpluses will gather again as resources shrink. Individualism will give way to **relationships and helping one another**.*

*Do not forget. I will be acting in everyone's life and in every event. These events have already begun like **the first signs of labor pains**. The contractions will quicken and grow more noticeable. My words must be acted on now. **First**, love one another. **Second**, simplify your lifestyle. Cut your expenses. **Third**, lessen your individualism. Multiply your oneness. Develop your relationships. If you always move along this road, you will make great progress and will be ready as the trials increase.*[330]

*By your faith in my promises, you will call on me and, even more important, you will be open to **my extraordinary helps**. This help **will begin with a light** that reviews your whole life. This light will give you a choice, an opportunity to begin again. The graces will be extraordinary and will motivate you to the greatest purity of heart and mind.*

*Then, I will infuse **great courage and unbelievable charity** to help others. Other virtues will also be given. You will be surprised at how **peaceful** you are. You will experience **great inner strength**, which you had never had before.*

Helps Along the Road

*In these trials, do not turn back because greater helps await you along the road. I will send you **special friends** who will guide you and support you. You, yourself, will become that special friend to others.*

*Now, I will explain my greatest gift. You will experience **my presence and my love** as you have never experienced them before.*

*Right now, the trials have not begun, so you do not need these extraordinary help. When the trials begin, they will be released. So, **do not fear**.*[331]

A Stream of Heavenly Blessings

*The heavens will open, slowly at first. A **continuous stream of blessings** will descend. Then, as the whole world is gradually awakened and as many hearts begin to receive, the heavens will open even more, and a gigantic river of blessings will descend. This will be a continuous river, flowing into every heart that is open. The Church will never have seen such a river since the early days of Pentecost with its signs and wonders.*

Theologians will wonder what is taking place. They will examine it and be unable to discredit it. They will be forced to say that these are valid blessings, extraordinary in nature but seemingly ordinary, that is, abundant to all. In this way, they will put their seal upon these phenomena...

*What are the rivers? **Every type of blessings**, beginning with **repentance and sorrow** for sin but leading quickly to a personal relationship with my Son through my intercession.*[332]

Summary of What to Do NOW!

We must balance our perspective of these heavenly messages. While it is easy to be curious about what Heaven is warning us about concerning near and future events, we must realize and acknowledge that Heaven is more importantly revealing to us what we must do, what God and Our Lady need us to do, to avert the events that are coming. Mary expresses her concern about the curiosity we have to hear about future events, but the lack of enthusiasm we have to actually do what Heaven is asking us to do to change those events:

*All the world is filled with questions of what will take place. There is a fascination with the future, to know what will come. But, **what good is it to know the future when mankind is not willing to repent?** Yes, the future is dark and I could reveal the future events. I have already revealed these **secrets** to the visionaries of **Medjugorje**. I have also given messages to the world for over thirty years. O reader, do you know those messages? Do you know the story of Medjugorje?*

*To highlight my teachings, I will contrast the two parts of Medjugorje. I have revealed ten secrets of future events to these visionaries, the children whom I have chosen. I have also said that **many of these future events could be eliminated if people just prayed and repented.***

Curiosity for the Secrets

*My teaching is this. Everyone wants to know the secrets because they are curious. They want to know the future. **Is it not much more important to be able to influence future events?** My messages ask for periods of **prayer** every day, for frequent **Communion**, for monthly **confession**, for saying the **Rosary each day**, for **fasting** on bread and water on Wednesday and Friday. Assuming these devout practices **will change future events**.*

You can see the foolishness of the world. Everyone wants the future events to be revealed. Yet, when I reveal how these events can be changed, few are interested.[333]

Chapter Thirty-Seven

Become the Great Apostles of the Latter Times!

෬

But when these signs begin to happen,
stand erect and raise your heads
because your redemption is at hand.
Luke 21:28

*I also saw the souls of those who had been beheaded **for their witness to Jesus and for the word of God**, and who had not worshipped the beast or its image nor had accepted its mark of their foreheads or hands. They came to life and they reigned with Christ for a thousand years... This is **the first resurrection**.*
Revelation 20:4-5

***Many of YOU will become saints** in My New Paradise and, having helped build My Remnant Church on earth,* *will reign with me in the New Heaven and Earth which will emerge at My Second Coming.*

MDM

*The **small number of souls, who hidden, will preserve the treasures of the Faith and practice virtue** will suffer a cruel, unspeakable and prolonged martyrdom.*

*BUT, during all this time, **men possessing great wealth will look with indifference** while the Church is oppressed, virtue is persecuted, and evil triumphs.*

Our Lady of Good Success

Cardinal Joseph Ratzinger (Pope Benedict XVI) wrote an article, "The Church Will Become Small":

The Church will become small and will have to start afresh more or less from the beginning.

She will no longer be able to inhabit many of the edifices she built in prosperity. As the number of her adherents diminishes . . . she will lose many of her social privileges. . . As a small society, [the Church] will make much bigger demands on the initiative of her individual members....

It will be hard-going for the Church, for the process of crystallization and clarification will cost her much valuable energy. It will make her poor and cause her to become the Church of the meek . . . The process will be long and wearisome as was the road from the false progressivism on the eve of the French Revolution — when a bishop might be thought smart if he made fun of dogmas and even insinuated that the existence of God was by no means certain . . . But when the trial of this sifting is past, a great power will flow from a more spiritualized and simplified Church. Men in a totally planned world will find themselves unspeakably lonely. If they have completely lost sight of God, they will feel the whole horror of their poverty. Then they will discover the little flock of believers as something wholly new. They will discover it as a hope that is meant for them, an answer for which they have always been searching in secret.

And so it seems certain to me that the Church is facing very hard times. The real crisis has scarcely begun. We will have to count on terrific upheavals. But I am equally certain about what will remain at the end: not the Church of the political cult, which is dead already, but the Church of faith. She may well no longer be the dominant social power to the extent that she was until recently; but she will enjoy a fresh blossoming and be seen as man's home, where he will find life and hope beyond death.[334]

In the Great Tribulation and Great Persecution, God will allow Satan to persecute the Church, and then God will exercise His just wrath as a punishment for our sins and finally overthrow Satan's dominion in the world with a divine intervention. In the midst of this, the remnant faithful will hold fast to the Tradition of the Faith and the faithful souls will glorify God with their lives as witnesses of hope. Our Lady of Fatima indicates that the Pope will have much to suffer, and so will his faithful children.

Are YOU Listening?

Concern for Salvation

Being concerned about your soul *is not a matter of being rich or poor, healthy or sick. It is a personal gift, a value which the person holds dearly. It is to value the only goal that really matters. "What does it profit a man to gain the whole world and lose his soul?" said Jesus. No matter what you had on earth, no matter what you accomplished on earth, no matter how highly you were praised on earth, you have lost everything – completely and forever.*

If you had nothing on earth, if you seemed to accomplish little, if you were forgotten and set aside, yet my Son Jesus said to you "Come into my kingdom", you will enjoy life forever and ever. How can I get this across? The greatest gift of God is to be concerned about the state of your soul, to be concerned with being in God's favor, to be concerned with how God thinks of you.

God's Perspective

Understand clearly. God has his opinion of you. **Right now you are in his favor or you are in his judgment.** *You should be very concerned about what his opinion is of you. His opinion is based upon the state of your soul and the state of your soul depends totally on your decision. You must want to be a friend of God, do nothing to lose that friendship, and do everything to gain it. O reader, your greatest call is to be a child of God through my Son.*[335]

Help from Heaven

*I speak **to you who have faithfully read these messages and tried to put them into practice**. Do not fear and do not panic. You must trust your heavenly Mother. I speak to you every day so you know what to do.*

(1) First, you must have the daily practices of devotion, that is, Holy Communion and the rosary.

(2) Also, you must show mercy and kindness toward everyone.

(3) Finally, you must have a simplicity in your life. These are the basic practices that will prepare your soul for the patient endurance that is always required during a time of trial.

Able to Receive

*If you read and live my messages, you will be capable of receiving my help. Notice **the purpose of the messages** – to fashion you so you can* *receive my help. What will you receive? This is important to know so you can cooperate.*

(1) First, I will guide your inner thoughts. I will place desires and hopes within you. Do not set them aside. They are my words to you.

(2) I will also send people into your life, people who are faithful to me. These will be your friends and companions on the journey. Again, do not set them aside. They are important friends.

(3) Finally, I will give you an attraction to prayer and to a heavenly goal. Do not set these attractions aside because they are meant to give you peace.

I ask you to read my messages and to live them. *Then,* **be sensitive to all the help** *that I will pour down from heaven.*[336]

Peace the World Has Never Known

This time of preparation is soon giving way to the period of increasing upheaval, to the time of the Great Conversion, caused by the love, mercy, *and* justice of God, and to the time of the Tribulation and the Antichrist, a time which will afterwards see the ushering in of the Restoration, and the era of love and peace. Peace is God's gift to man; it is the result also of the human project in conformity with the divine plan.[337] Scripture reveals that peace is an attribute of God Himself: *"the Lord is peace."*[338] When the resurrected Jesus meets His disciples, and every time He meets us in the Mass, He says: **"Peace be with you."** He is inviting us to join Him and His Mother in *"the battle for peace!"*[339] Let us share *the good news of peace*; let us build the culture of peace and love! Our Lady of Fatima promised that in the end there would be peace. And so it will be as Mary had prophesied:

"In the end, my Immaculate Heart will triumph" **and there will be a great era of peace.**

Now is a time of peace, of mercy, of forgiveness and conversion, and of reconciliation. For soon comes justice, which will also bring us peace as well, but with greater difficulty, because peace is the fruit of justice and love. Now is the time for victim souls to offer their lives as a sacrifice of love to save humanity. It is time for the whole Church and all the faithful to acknowledge that the Devotion to the Two Hearts, which are united as one Heart, is a single true Devotion of greatest importance for our world today, and for the Renewal of our world in what will be the greatest Renewal in the history of the world since Christ and the Church's first Pentecost.

We are being called to help usher in the Age of the Two Hearts! We are united to Jesus through the Heart of Mary. Let us pray that the Two Hearts triumph and reign to bring upon humanity a new dawn and the new era of peace!

YOU – The Apostles of the Latter Times – Will Help Save the World

*I want YOU to comprehend that **God has chosen each one of you in order to use you for the great plan of salvation of mankind**. YOU cannot comprehend how great your role is in God's plan.*
Our Lady of Medjugorje

Our Lady calls us and sends forth, saying:

*I am joining you in your prayer, to obtain for you the gift of the Holy Spirit, that He may transform you into **apostles of these last times**.*

*The moment of your public witness has come. Show yourselves to all as my little sons, as the apostles formed by me for the great task of **the new evangelization** which is awaiting you.*

*As in the Cenacle of Jerusalem I opened the door so that the Apostles could go out and preach the Gospel, initiating the first evangelization, so also, in this cenacle of yours, I am calling you all to **be apostles of the second evangelization**.* (Gobbi)

Jesus confirms, saying:

Many of YOU will become saints in My New Paradise and, having helped build My Remnant Church on earth, will reign with me in the New Heaven and Earth which will emerge at My Second Coming. (MDM)

Perhaps most inspiring of all, Our Lady calls each of us to help her and her Son to save the world:

There are many plans that I cannot fulfill without YOU...

I cannot do anything without YOU...

I want to draw you closer to the Heart of Jesus.

Therefore, dear little children, pray that YOU may comprehend the greatness of this message which I give YOU.

Our Lady of Medjugorje

Chapter Thirty-Eight

Fight... Children of the Light!

CB

In those days, I Daniel,
heard this word of the Lord:
At that time there shall arise
Michael, *the great prince,*
guardian of your people;
it shall be a time unsurpassed in distress
since nations began until that time.
At that time **Your people shall escape,**
everyone who is found written in the book.
Many of those who sleep in the dust of the earth shall awake;
some shall live forever,
others shall be an everlasting horror and disgrace.
But the wise shall shine brightly
like the splendor of the firmament,
and **those who lead the many to justice**
shall be like the stars forever.

Daniel 12:1-3

Then the dragon was angry with the woman,
and went off to make war on the rest of her offspring,
*on those who **keep the commandments** of God*
and bear testimony *to Jesus.*
Revelation 12:17

Fight, dearest children, my apostles,
in these last times of yours.
This is the hour of my battle.
This is the hour of my great victory.
Our Lady to Fr. Gobbi

Enter NOW Into the New Ark

The most important heavenly message of our times is the divine secret that will save us:

There are disorders everywhere – in the family, in society, in governments and in international relationship. Nowhere is there peace. Cannot men discern that this universal unrest comes from the Evil One who stirs everywhere? Wherever there is turmoil, he is there, exploiting it to his own purposes.

*I am here on the scene to actively engage in battle. I am the woman (of Genesis 3:15 and Revelation 12:1). The evil one and I are foes, eternal foes. **The battle will be fought to the end**. Let no one doubt that I will win and that he will be vanquished. Let no one doubt that peace will be restored, that human life will again gain a tranquility of order. Yet, let no one doubt that until that special moment brought about by my Son's blood happens, **there will be endless wars**.*

*I will fight him everywhere. I will raise up **my army**, with new skills and greater powers of the Holy Spirit. I will give **new signs and wonders** to encourage them. I will hold them close to my heart so that they **will never be deceived**. I will give them **the greatest of comforts*** *for the trials they must go through. I will prepare them, send them forth, give them a definite task and bring their work to a completion, even if this sometimes means their own death.*

*First, I must call them **into my Immaculate Heart**. Many times they are deceived. They do not see the newness of this situation. They go forth as they usually do but encounter only failure, sometimes falling into the very evils which they are trying to overcome.*

Let these words go forth. This is a new and more dangerous situation. Destructive powers have long been at work that have changed the very landscape, not just the individual heart. There is no longer peace. War has broken out and so many of my children are unaware. Many have fallen in battle, not even knowing that a battle is raging.

*That is why I say that before going forth, they **must come into my Immaculate Heart. I must train them in the new ways of warfare.** Otherwise, the enemy will easily destroy them.*[340]

Through Fr. Gobbi, Our Lady says:

Look at my Immaculate Heart, *and there will come down upon you a spirit of joy and of consolation... Why do you doubt? Why are you sad? I am at your side at all times; I never leave you... This is the moment for all to take refuge in me, because **I am the Ark of the New Covenant**.*

*At the time of Noah, immediately before the flood, those whom the Lord had destined to survive His terrible chastisement entered into the ark. In these your times, I am inviting all my beloved children to enter into the Ark of the New Covenant which I have built **in my Immaculate Heart** for you, that they may be assisted by me to carry the bloody burden of the great trial, which precedes the coming of the day of the Lord.*

*Do not look anywhere else. **There is happening today what happened in the days of the flood**, and no one is giving a thought to what is* *awaiting them. Everyone is much occupied in thinking only of themselves, of their own earthly interests, of pleasures and of satisfying in every sort of way, their own disordinate passions.*

Even in the Church*, how few there are who concern themselves with my motherly and most sorrowful admonitions!*[341]

The Father's Secret Plan to Save the World

Mary reveals the great gift of the divine secret that will save all who respond with acceptance:

*****My Immaculate Heart*** – This is **the heavenly Father's secret, his plan for the salvation of the world***. He has placed his Son in my heart. His Holy Spirit has come to abide in my heart. These are the secrets that I am trying to reveal so all might know of this treasury. Some misinterpret this doctrine. They think I am speaking of my own powers and my own prerogatives. Rather, I am speaking of God's powers and where to find them.*

*People search for Jesus. They look, but so many times they do not find. He is in my heart. He abides there. He dwells there. For this reason, **the Father wants all the world to honor my Immaculate Heart***. This is the easiest place to find his Son, Jesus.*

He came the first time through me and he will come the second time through me.[342]

Why Enter the Immaculate Heart?

This might sound too simple, or it may sound as though there is too much focus on Mary. So, what is this all about? Mary explains:

*When you enter my heart, you will receive a **desire to do the Father's will***. As you remain in my heart, that desire will become pervasive and deepen, extending to every thought, word and deed. This is not the work of just one day or one year, but it is the sure and easy way to* *goodness because you will experience a vehement desire to do God's will. I will show the easiest way to accomplish what the Father wants.*[343]

*You need **a hew heart**. Yes, that is what mankind needs – a new heart – **a heart transplant**. That is what I offer you. **Come into my heart and I will give you the heart of my Son**. Otherwise, your intellects will create greater weapons and your hearts will try to solve your problems by destroying the earth. This does not have to happen, but it will, if you do not enter **my Immaculate Heart**.*[344]

Now that we understand the heavenly message and secret to save the world, let us act immediately and go to Mary and enter her Immaculate Heart of safety. This is the divine plan to save the world!

Experience the Triumph & Reign of the Two Hearts

Go to the Two Hearts! As the Angel of Fatima said:

The Hearts of Jesus and Mary are attentive to the voice of your supplication.

Chapter Thirty-Nine

Go & Spread This Heavenly Message NOW!

ॲ

Brothers and sisters:
If you confess with your mouth that Jesus is Lord
and believe in your heart that God raised him from the dead,
you will be saved...
For everyone who calls on the name of the Lord will be saved.
But how can they call on him in whom they have not believed?
And how can they believe in him of whom they have not heard?
And how can they hear without someone to preach?
And how can people preach unless they are sent?
As it is written,
How beautiful are the feet of those who bring the good news!
Romans 10:9f

I ask you to read my messages and to live them.
*Then, **be sensitive to all the help that I will pour down** from heaven.*
Our Lady to the American Locutionist (Locutions.org)

LIVE and SHARE these Biblical and Heavenly Messages!

I wish to share about the conditional aspect of the times we are in the concerning the events to come, about how all this is to come depends on us.

This book has sought to discuss the Good News of the revelations of God to His people for the times we live in today, of the Apocalypse. We now have the mission to share this good news with others and to share our hope. Our mission is to *accept divine peace now and then to spread it, and to spread the heavenly messages of hope.* Our Lady of Medjugorje reminds us of how important our cooperation is, as she says:

*My dear children, I want to collaborate with you, for I need your collaboration... I need you, dear children, to cooperate with me, because **there are many plans that I cannot fulfill without you... I cannot do anything without you**.*[345]

Each of us can hear Jesus speaking to us about our new mission in the Two Hearts, as He says:

Tell the whole world![346]

Thus, dear reader, **Our Lady is calling *you* to do two things: to fully live and urgently spread this heavenly Message!**

Listen, our heavenly Mother, who is being sent by God to us today, says:

*Today I am calling on you to decide whether or not you wish to **live the messages** which I am giving you. I wish you to be **active in living*** *and spreading the messages.*[347]

Our Lady reminds us that they are *the* Message from Heaven in our times, saying:

Live my messages and put into life every word that I am giving you. May they be precious to you because they come from Heaven.[348]

She also says:

Today I invite YOU to become missionaries of my messages... to transmit them to the whole world... to be my joyful carriers of peace...

Through YOU, I wish to renew the world.[349]

Will *YOU* respond now to live and spread this biblical and heavenly message of our times?

Chapter Forty

This Is Your Final Call:
Enter the Two Hearts
and the Divine Will

൪ഠ

*'He shall break the heads of his enemies, that all may know that God
is the king of all the earth,
that the Gentiles may know themselves to be men.'
All this, Venerable Brethren,
We believe and expect with unshakable faith…
Oh! when in every city and village the law of the Lord is faithfully
observed, when respect is shown for sacred things, when the
Sacraments are frequented, and the ordinances of Christian life
fulfilled, there will certainly be no more need for us to labor further to
see all things restored in Christ.*

St. Pius X

My pain and anguish now, as I envisage those poor deluded souls who will be lost to Me, has never been so intense.
*This is why **victim souls**, chosen souls and those who are close to My Sacred Heart, feel such pain right now.*
I suffer through them.

MDM

Become Victim Souls of Love and Truth: This is *the Mission of Missions - the Apostolate of Apostolates*!

In these times, we are being called to be authentic living witnesses of faith, hope, and love – to offer our lives motivated by love. We are being asked to be witnesses (martyrs) of love. Some may be called to a white martyrdom of internal suffering and faithful witness of Christ and to the Faith, while others may be called to a red martyrdom of physical suffering and possibly death for the truth of Christ. The grace of the Lord will be sufficient for us and the Lord will never give us more than we can handle. Our merits will be in the intention of love, in the divine Will, for the glory of God and the salvation and sanctification of souls; and we shall be filled with the joy of the Spirit!

Our Lord wants to begin the restoration of His Peace *now*, in this initial phase *through you*, through *your* life of holiness and self-giving, through your faithful vocation and fruitful apostolate, through your life bound to the Two Hearts and linked to souls in need of her maternal help, by unbroken chains of Rosaries and continuous acts of mercy and love, all united with the Eucharistic Lord. Our Lady is asking us to offer our lives to delay and possibly even prevent some of the prevailing evil and divine justice that is to come and to help save souls who cannot save themselves. Our Lady of Akita said:

*I have prevented the coming of calamities by offering to the Father, together with all the **victim souls** who console Him, the sufferings endured by the Son on the Cross, by His Blood and by His very loving*

Soul. Prayer, penance, and courageous sacrifices can appease the anger of the Father.

What is needed is *your* prayer, penance, and courageous sacrifices – united with the Two Hearts and done in the divine Will – to save the world!

An army of victims of love, even if small, is needed to combat the apostasy, heresy, and compromises, which are currently challenging the Faith. This army will march forward with *joy and love* offering all to Jesus through Mary. These faithful ones will be the greatest power of this age. About this, Our Lady of Good Success says:

*The **small number of souls, who hidden, will preserve the treasures of the Faith and practice virtue** will suffer a cruel, unspeakable and prolonged martyrdom. Many will succumb to death from the violence of their sufferings and those who sacrifice themselves for the Church and their country will be counted as martyrs. In order to free men from the bondage to these heresies, those whom the merciful love of my most Holy Son has designated **to effect the restoration**, will need great strength of will, constancy, valor, and confidence in God. There will be occasions when all will seem lost and paralyzed. This then will be **the happy beginning of the complete restoration**.*

Jesus speaks to us through "Anne", who reportedly receives messages from Heaven by way of interior locution, saying:

*My beloved apostles, please know that **you obtain a constant stream of grace for the world**. You do this by serving so generously. Your generosity obtains for others sublime graces of calm and peace, sublime graces of charity and truth, and sublime graces of conversion and perseverance. When you see how heaven has used your service, you will rejoice that you gave so willingly and consistently... **If I did not wish you to serve, I would not have called you into service**. I need My chosen ones to remain closely tied to their decision to bring My* *light to others. Only in this way will the renewal push further into the world... Please be loyal to your decision for heavenly service as you live your time on earth. If you remain faithful, I can do many things. I am with you. I am directing all that occurs in your life. We walk together and together we will triumph over all temptations.*[350]

Living *in* the Divine Will, *the Sanctity of Sanctities*!

One of the greatest ways to live the call of reparation is to live according to God's will, to embrace His will in everything. Through mystic Luisa Piccarreta, the Little Daughter of the Divine Will, God is asking us not only to seek and obey His Divine Will, but **to live in the Divine Will**, which is *"the most beautiful and the brightest among all other sanctities."* Jesus promises: *"If you put yourself at the mercy of my Will, you will no longer have concerns for anything."*[351] Living constantly in this way, we will have nothing on our own, but everything will be in common with Jesus. In this, Our Lady's *fiat* (*Let it be done to me according to Your Word*) becomes our constant prayer. Our life is now living only in the Divine Will, to *live in* God's Will, by also living united to the Two Hearts. As we commit to living our consecrated lives in Jesus and Mary, let us pray to do so by living in the Divine Will. Our Lord tells Luisa that living in the divine Will will become common in the new era to come; and we are most blessed to be able to begin right now. We can do this by simply asking God each day that we live in His divine Will in all things. As Luisa Piccarreta foresaw, saying:

And precisely in this century, so troubled, the Lord is preparing a new era, which will invade His Church and all men of good will, and in which the triumph of Grace will be the ultimate goal... [So, let us take courage as Jesus reminds us:]

***Do not fear:** I will be with you until the end of time.*

In the new Kingdom that is unfolding before us even now, His Divine Will will be done by all at last. And only His Will can ensure peace among His children. In the new Kingdom, all people will love Him, accept His Love and Gifts, which He wishes to shower upon His children, and live in communion with Him and each other. The final battle that has already begun will see the destruction of evil being finally completed. Then shall come the triumph and reign of the Two Hearts, the era of peace, and the Kingdom of the Divine Will on earth as it is in Heaven.

So, *fight*, the few who can see, for now is the time of all times and the battle of all battles. I say again, courage and *fight*; don't ever give up, until the great victory is won. Praise God! Amen.

COMMENT ON SOURCES

This book relies on only **solid sources that are trustworthy**. It discusses various heavenly prophecies and messages by using three groups of reliable sources:

The Primary Source: the Holy Bible

Other Recognized Sources: the prophecies of the Popes and the Saints; of major and well-known Church-approved apparitions, like Fatima and Lourdes where the Blessed Mother has appeared from Heaven and like where Jesus appeared to St. Faustina.

Various Credible Sources: various reported heavenly prophecies from lesser known or more recent sources which have received positive recognition from the Church, including: Medjugorje, La Salette, Our Lady of America, Garabandal, Akita, Our Lady of Good Success, Our Lady of All Nations, as well as concerning Fr. Gobbi and Luisa Piccarreta and others. Most of these sources are discussed as well in my first book of this subject, *The Secrets, Chastisement, and Triumph,* which received the Church's imprimatur.

New, Solid Secondary Sources: a few additional sources that are secondary, but useful. While these sources do not provide new information as to events that are already known from the primary biblical and heavenly sources, they do provide more details. And when these details are examined, they fit perfectly into the bigger picture together with the other primary sources, to enhance our overall understanding of these times. Thus, they too are judged as credible and rightly believable. This would make sense too, and even be expected, since all the authentic sources have to come from the same Source, God. There can never be a conflict or contradiction in sources and their prophecy and in how they relate to each other. In fact, it is in this latter point that each source is measured for credibility.

So, concerning these secondary sources, I offer a brief introduction:

The American Locutionist
(www.Locutions.org)

Monsignor John Esseff, a diocesan priest of Scranton, Pa., is the spiritual director of a locutionist from the United States who has been reportedly receiving heavenly messages. In 1959, St. Padre Pio became Msgr. Esseff's spiritual director. For many years, he was the spiritual director for Bl. Mother Teresa of Calcutta.

In recent years, he has been director for a special soul who is reportedly receiving heavenly locutions. He has discerned the validity of these locutions. Until now, these locutions were personal teachings given for a small community that gathered in prayer. Beginning on December 10, 2010, a new phase began, namely, some locutions were to be told to the whole world. About them, Msgr. Esseff says: *These are private revelations and there is no need to believe them. If these revelations help your faith, then receive them. If not, you can set them aside. We are called to believe only public Revelation.*

While we do not have to adhere to credible and trustworthy heavenly messages and prophecy that comes from reported heavenly sources, still it is better to have an approach of openness, as long as the Church has not condemned them. Prudence is still needed and prayerful discernment, but also courage and a desire to do God's will.

Maria Divine Mercy
(www.TheWarningSecondComing.com)

Maria Divine Mercy, as she is called, does not reveal her identity as she is to be 'hidden' for a while. She may well go public if and when instructed by Jesus. The Catholic Church is investigating her messages. Her staff says she does not want any attention around herself. She has two spiritual directors and they have not been given the authority by her or with the permission of Jesus to go public. She says that these messages should be spread around the world in order to help save people. Jesus told her that she is *"the seventh messenger"* that is mentioned in Revelation 10. Jesus tells us through her:

The time has come, to inform you, that the prophecies contained in the **Book of Revelation** *are about to unfold before your eyes.*[352] *You are a chosen messenger to deliver, as I have said,* **the most important messages** *for mankind in these times.*[353] **My end time prophet**, *[you are] given the responsibility of the* **opening of the seven seals.**[354]

Jesus says to us today in this situation and in these times, through Maria Divine Mercy:

Do not, however, be afraid to **live your life as you would normally** *as long as prayer and devotion to Me is an integral and important part.*[355]

Blessed Elena Aiello
(www.mysticsofthechurch.com)

Sr. Elena Aiello was declared Blessed on September 14, 2011, Feast of the Exultation of the Holy Cross, by Pope Benedict XVI. Blessed Elena was a Mystic, Stigmatist, Victim Soul, Prophetess, and Foundress of the Minim Tertiaries of the Passion of Our Lord Jesus Christ. She died in the 1960s.

Nancy Fowler
(www.conyers.org)

Conyers, Georgia (USA) is where the Blessed Mother reportedly appeared 49 times to Nancy Fowler on the 13th of the month from 1990 to 1998. Well over a million pilgrims have visited the site, with several gatherings estimated at over 100,000.

This book provides detail concerning the Latter Times and uses reported heavenly messages that are Church-recognized as well as ones that are so recent that the Church has not yet recognized them. In this latter regard, as the author, I submit these messages to the verdict of the authentic Magisterium regarding their authenticity. We are reminded in the meantime that no Church recognition or imprimatur is necessary for the reading, publication, and spreading of private revelations, prophecies, or miracles (so long as they have not been condemned). With this in mind, we wish to move forward with the heart and mind of the Church and thus with her blessing.

It is important to note again that it is not against the Church or her canon law to read and meditate on reliable apparitions and their messages, even on the ones that have not been officially fully approved by the Church, provided they have not been condemned and do not in any way disagree with doctrine and Church teaching. The author recognizes and gladly accepts that the final authority regarding the supernatural character of the apparitions, locutions, and heavenly messages in this book rests always and finally with the Magisterium of the Catholic Church.

Pope Urban VIII also gave sound advice about following reported, reliable heavenly apparitions, saying: *"In cases like this, it is **better to believe** than not to believe, for, if you believe, and it is proven true, you will be happy that you have believed, because Our Holy Mother asked it. If you believe, and it should be proven false, you will receive all blessings as if it had been true, because you believed it to be true."*

May Jesus return quickly in glory! May the grace, love, and peace of the Two Hearts be with you always.

If anyone does not love the Lord, let him be accursed. Marana tha. My love to all of you in Christ Jesus.[356]

ABOUT THE AUTHOR

Dr. Kelly Bowring, received his masters in theology (M.A.) and Christian ministry, with advanced certification in catechetics, from Franciscan University of Steubenville, his licentiate in sacred theology (S.T.L.) from Dominican House of Studies (and the John Paul II Institute) in Washington, DC, and his pontifical doctorate in sacred theology (S.T.D.) from the Pontifical University of St. Thomas Aquinas in Rome.

Dr. Bowring has received the theological *mandatum* to teach theology. He previously taught theology and directed an institute at St. Mary's College of Ave Maria University, and he has been a professor of sacred theology at Southern Catholic College, where he was the Dean of Spiritual Mission and oversaw the theology program. He also served as Dean of the Graduate School of Theology at St. Charles Borromeo Seminary.

Dr. Bowring has published several books including the best-seller, *The Secrets, Chastisement, and Triumph* (Two Hearts Press, LLC), *Dear Children, The Messages of Our Lady of Medjugorje* (with Vince Murray), and *To Hold and Teach the Catholic Faith* (St. Paul/Alba House) and various liturgical and prayer books with W. J. Hirten Publisher. His new book, *Your Life Redeemed*, is also being published with Two Hearts Press, LLC.

Dr. Bowring and his wife, Diana, have eight children.

For more information, go to our website:

www.TwoHeartsPress.com

Email your comments or reviews about this book to:

TwoHeartsPressLLC@aol.com

ENDNOTES

[1] To the Priests #320
[2] Locutions.org (2011-2012) 263
[3] Locutions.org (2011-2012) 274
[4] www.thewarningsecondcoming.com MDM 5/13/11
[5] MDM 4/26/11
[6] MDM 6/11/11
[7] MDM 6/11/11
[8] MDM 3/7/12
[9] MDM 1/18/12
[10] Locutions.org (2011-2012) 16
[11] MDM 3/28/12
[12] MDM 5/18/11
[13] MDM 6/6/11
[14] MDM 5/25/11
[15] MDM 4/17/11
[16] MDM 4/17/11
[17] To the Priests #325
[18] MDM 8/14/11
[19] MDM 2/6/12
[20] MDM 3/5/12
[21] MDM 7/20/11
[22] MDM 8/18/11
[23] #528 September 29, 1994
[24] Signs of the Times Apostolate Newsletter December 2012
[25] Locutions.org (2011-2012) 250
[26] Locutions.org (2011-2012) 208
[27] Locutions.org (2011-2012) 35

[28] Locutions.org (2011-2012) 145
[29] Locutions.org (2011-2012) 142
[30] Locutions.org (2011-2012) 177
[31] Locutions.org (2011-2012) 135
[32] Locutions.org (2011-2012) 72
[33] Locutions.org (2011-2012) 65
[34] Locutions.org (2011-2012) 206
[35] Locutions.org (2011-2012) 205
[36] Locutions.org (2011-2012) 210
[37] Locutions.org (2011-2012) 281
[38] Locutions.org (2011-2012) 36
[39] Locutions.org (2011-2012) 8
[40] Locutions.org (2011-2012) 137
[41] Locutions.org (2011-2012) 106
[42] Locutions.org (2011-2012) 181
[43] Locutions.org (2011-2012) 70
[44] Locutions.org (2011-2012) 244
[45] Locutions.org (2011-2012) 157
[46] MDM 6/11/11
[47] Locutions.org (2011-2012) 75
[48] Locutions.org (2011-2012) 9
[49] Locutions.org (2011-2012) 154
[50] Locutions.org (2011-2012) 174
[51] Locutions.org (2011-2012) 70
[52] MDM 4/26/11
[53] Locutions.org (2011-2012) 6
[54] Locutions.org (2011-2012) 136
[55] Locutions.org (2011-2012) 23
[56] Locutions.org (2011-2012) 209
[57] Locutions.org (2011-2012) 147
[58] Locutions.org (2011-2012) 144
[59] Locutions.org (2011-2012) 91
[60] Locutions.org (2011-2012) 178
[61] Locutions.org (2011-2012) 139
[62] Locutions.org (2011-2012) 134
[63] Locutions.org (2011-2012) 203
[64] Locutions.org (2011-2012) 202
[65] Locutions.org (2011-2012) 200
[66] Locutions.org (2011-2012) 274
[67] MDM 11/30/12
[68] MDM 11/29/12
[69] www.medjugorje.org/overview.htm
[70] Locutions.org (2011-2012) 185
[71] Message of October 13, 1987
[72] Locutions.org (2011-2012) 192
[73] Locutions.org (2011-2012) 264

[74] Locutions.org (2011-2012) 240

[75] Locutions.org (2011-2012) 248

[76] Locutions.org (2011-2012) 95

[77] # 482 November 22, 1992

[78] Message 407

[79] Yves Dupont, *Catholic Prophecy* (Tan Books and Publishers, 1973), 22

[80] Dupont, 29

[81] Dupont, 23

[82] MDM 6/7/11

[83] MDM 6/6/11

[84] MDM 6/1/11

[85] Locutions.org (2011-2012) 30

[86] Locutions.org (2011-2012) 183

[87] Locutions.org (2011-2012) 262

[88] Locutions.org (2011-2012) 119

[89] Locutions.org (2011-2012) 23

[90] Locutions.org (2011-2012) 90

[91] Locutions.org (2011-2012) 34

[92] Locutions.org (2011-2012) 15

[93] Locutions.org (2011-2012) 3

[94] Locutions.org (2011-2012) 4

[95] Locutions.org (2011-2012) 211

[96] Locutions.org (2011-2012) 258

[97] Locutions.org (2011-2012) 79

[98] http://www.vatican.va/roman_curia/congregations/cfaith/documents/rc_con_cfaith_doc_20000626_message-fatima_en.html

[99] The last version of the secret, the longest as it is cited here, that of 1879, received the *imprimatur* of Bishop Zola, bishop of Lecce, Italy. These secrets of Our Lady of La Salette were recently published in April, 2002, in a book, with *imprimatur,* entitled *Discovery of the Secret of La Salette,* by Fathers René Laurentin and Michel Corteville, intended for the general public on authenticity of the Secret of La Salette.

[100] Message 404, May 14, 1989, Feast of the Pentecost

[101] Message 405

[102] Message of May 13, 1976

[103] MDM 5/13/11

[104] MDM 2/19/12

[105] MDM 2/14/12

[106] Message 60, October 29, 1974

[107] Message 405, June 3, 1989, Milan, Feast of the Immaculate Heart of Mary

[108] Message 405

[109] Locutions.org (2011-2012) 23

[110] Locutions.org (2011-2012) 23

[111] Locutions.org (2011-2012) 82

[112] Locutions.org (2011-2012) 74

[113] Locutions.org (2011-2012) 30

[114] Locutions.org (2011-2012) 266

[115] Locutions.org (2011-2012) 126

[116] http://www.ourladyofamerica.com/explanation.php

[117] Locutions.org (2011-2012) 236

[118] MDM 8/29/11

[119] Locutions.org (2011-2012) 246

[120] MDM 8/28/11

[121] MDM 8/22/11

[122] Locutions.org (2011-2012) 182

[123] Locutions.org (2011-2012) 117

[124] Locutions.org (2011-2012) 120

[125] Locutions.org (2011-2012) 237

[126] Locutions.org (2011-2012) 129

[127] Locutions.org (2011-2012) 128

[128] Locutions.org (2011-2012) 69

[129] Locutions.org (2011-2012) 64

[130] Locutions.org (2011-2012) 101

[131] Locutions.org (2011-2012) 68

[132] Locutions.org (2011-2012) 65

[133] Locutions.org (2011-2012) 64

[134] Locutions.org (2011-2012) 222

[135] Locutions.org (2011-2012) 125

[136] Locutions.org (2011-2012) 94

[137] Locutions.org (2011-2012) 51

[138] Message 547 (January 11, 1993)

[139] Message 552 (Mary 6, 1993)

[140] Message 555 (May 25, 1993)

[141] Message 556 (June 1, 1993)

[142] December 29, 1992, Vol III # 516

[143] Message 675 (Dec 30, 1992)

[144] December 30, 1992, Vol III # 452

[145] Message 686 (Aug 25, 1993)

[146] Message 687 (Sept 8, 1993)

[147] Message 525 (Oct 5, 1993)

[148] October 13, 1997 (80th anniversary of the last appearance of Our Lady of Fatima)

[149] July 24, 1992, Vol III # 529

[150] September 13, 1992, Vol III # 640

[151] January 26, 1994, Vol III # 503

[152] March 4, 1994, Vol III # 578

[153] October 14, 1992, Vol III # 537

[154] February 6, 1994, Vol III # 476

[155] August 29, 1994, Vol III # 460

[156] MDM 6/14/11

[157] MDM 12/9/12

[158] MDM 5/23/11

[159] MDM 6/5/11

[160] MDM 5/29/11

[161] MDM 6/8/11

[162] *Diary of St. Faustina*, 83, 1588

[163] MDM 12/9/12

[164] MDM 6/8/11

[165] MDM 4/16/11

[166] Locutions.org (2011-2012) 50

[167] MDM 6/26/11

[168] MDM 6/22/11

[169] MDM 4/16/11

[170] MDM 7/3/11

[171] MDM 9/7/11

[172] MDM 8/10/11

[173] MDM 8/8/11

[174] MDM 7/10/11

[175] MDM 7/30/11

[176] MDM 7/17/11

[177] p. 14-19

[178] MDM 9/12/11

[179] MDM 8/4/11

[180] MDM 4/23/11

[181] http://www.garabandal.org/miracle.shtml

[182] The book, *"Synthesis of the Messages from the Apparitions of the Blessed Virgin Mary Guardian of the Faith"* has received an imprimatur (2009) from the Archdiocese of Cuenca.

[183] http://www.garabandal.us/prph_other.html

[184] July 12, 1982

[185] http://www.sancta.org/eyes.html

[186] Locutions.org (2011-2012) 38

[187] MDM 8/31/11

[188] To the Priests #160-161, 172

[189] Locutions.org (2011-2012) 29

[190] Locutions.org (2011-2012) 29

[191] Locutions.org (2011-2012) 29

[192] Locutions.org (2011-2012) 5

[193] Locutions.org (2011-2012) 99

[194] Locutions.org (2011-2012) 81

[195] Message of October 13, 1987

[196] Locutions.org (2011-2012) 178

[197] Locutions.org (2011-2012) 176

[198] Locutions.org (2011-2012) 157

[199] Locutions.org (2011-2012) 48

[200] Locutions.org (2011-2012) 88

[201] Locutions.org (2011-2012) 104

[202] Locutions.org (2011-2012) 263

[203] Locutions.org (2011-2012) 109

[204] Locutions.org (2011-2012) 134

[205] Locutions.org (2011-2012) 264

[206] To the Priests #315

[207] To the Priests #335

[208] Locutions.org (2011-2012) 196

[209] Locutions.org (2011-2012) 60

[210] Locutions.org (2011-2012) 45

[211] Locutions.org (2011-2012) 151

[212] Locutions.org (2011-2012) 237

[213] Locutions.org (2011-2012) 102

[214] #450 May 19, 1991

[215] #460 November 21, 1991

[216] Message of May 13, 1990

[217] To the Priests #326

[218] MDM 1/21/12

[219] Message 407

[220] MDM 7/3/11

[221] MDM 11/25/12

[222] Locutions.org (2011-2012) 3

[223] Locutions.org (2011-2012) 3

[224] Locutions.org (2011-2012) 2

[225] Locutions.org (2011-2012) 1

[226] MDM 3/31/12

[227] www.thewarningsecondcoming.com 3/4/12

[228] MDM 7/8/11

[229] MDM 4/16/11

[230] MDM 5/31/11

[231] http://www.garabandal.org/punish.shtml

[232] August 7, 1971

[233] On April 22, 1984, after an investigation of over ten years, *"After the investigation conducted up to the present day, I recognize the supernatural character of a series of mysterious events concerning the (weeping) statue of the Holy Mother Mary . . . Consequently, I authorize . . . the veneration of the Holy Mother of Akita."* Bishop John Shojiro Ito of Niigata declared: The Bishop also stated: *"As for the content of the messages received . . . when one thinks of the actual state of the world, the warning seems to correspond to it in many points."* In Akita, Sr. Agnes Sasagawa received messages from her guardian angel and Mary from June 24, 1973, through May 1, 1982. The wooden statue of Our Lady at Akita, which shed human blood, sweat, and tears, is the image of the Church-approved apparition of *"Our Lady of All Nations"* in Amsterdam.

[234] Message 501

[235] Messages 332, 464, 442

[236] 1/24/1926

[237] Locutions.org (2011-2012) 239

[238] #510 January 1, 1994

[239] Matthew 24:29

[240] Dupont, 44-45

[241] The visionaries of Medjugorje have said that Our Lady has not given *them* messages about the three days of darkness. It seems the three days of darkness will take place only *after* the 10 secrets of Medjugorje occur.

[242] The last version of the secret, the longest as cited here, that of 1879, received the *imprimatur* of Bishop Zola, bishop of Lecce, Italy.

[243] To the Priests #313

[244] #438 December 8, 1990

[245] MDM 5/20/11

[246] MDM 12/17/12

[247] Message 435, 186

[248] #431 September 8, 1990

[249] #510 January 1, 1994

[250] Dupont, *Catholic Prophecy*, 29

[251] MDM 5/20/11

[252] #534 December 24, 1994

[253] #603 December 24, 1997

[254] MDM 4/17/11

[255] #435 October 13, 1990

[256] #472 April 19, 1992

[257] MDM 2/14/12

[258] MDM 1/21/12

[259] Locutions.org (2011-2012) 29

[260] MDM 12/10/12

[261] MDM 12/19/12

[262] MDM 12/11/12

[263] # 505 November 21, 1993

[264] Dupont, *Catholic Prophecy*, 33

[265] Message of October 27, 1980

[266] See Messages to Fr. Gobbi, July 3 and August 21, 1987

[267] Message 413

[268] See http://www.mmp-usa.net/arc_defense.html

[269] 546hi

[270] See CCC 1042-1048

[271] See Revelation 21

[272] Message 383, 389

[273] Message 505

[274] http://www.ourladyofamerica.com/explanation.php (August 1957)

[275] *The Life and Kingdom of Jesus in Our Lady*, trans. Trappist Fathers (NY: Trappist Fathers, 1946), 271

[276] *Meditations on Various Subjects* (NY: Trappist Fathers, 1947), 240

[277] Fr. Edgardo M. Arellano, *A Definitive Covenant: The Magisterial Stand on the Alliance of the Hearts of Jesus and Mary* (Two Hearts Media, 1998), Prologue

[278] From the book *Rosary Meditations: Loving Jesus With the Heart of Mary*

[279] Locutions.org (2011-2012) 155

[280] Locutions.org (2011-2012) 143

[281] Locutions.org (2011-2012) 205

[282] Locutions.org (2011-2012) 175

[283] Locutions.org (2011-2012) 216

[284] Locutions.org (2011-2012) 122

[285] Locutions.org (2011-2012) 180

[286] Locutions.org (2011-2012) 13

[287] MDM 5/11/11

[288] MDM 5/4/11

[289] Locutions.org (2011-2012) 129

[290] MDM 8/10/11

[291] MDM 4/17/11

[292] MDM 4/16/11

[293] MDM 5/13/11

[294] MDM 4/30/11

[295] MDM 4/17/11

[296] MDM 6/25/11

[297] MDM 6/13/11

[298] The Good News About Sex (pp. 227, 228

[299] # 2521, 2522

[300] "Christian Courtship in An Oversexed World", Fr. Morrow, Our Sunday Visitor, Huntington, IN, 2003

[301] MDM 6/12/11

[302] To the Priests #330

[303] Locutions.org (2011-2012) 169

[304] www.divinewill.org

[305] #436 November 1, 1990

[306] MDM 5/31/11

[307] MDM 4/28/11

[308] Locutions.org (2011-2012) 66

[309] MDM 4/6/11

[310] Locutions.org (2011-2012) 190

[311] Locutions.org (2011-2012) 33

[312] Locutions.org (2011-2012) 29

[313] Locutions.org (2011-2012) 22

[314] Messages of March 28, 1945, Aug. 15 and Nov. 15, 1951, March 20, 1952, Oct. 11, 1953

[315] On October 4, 1997, the Bishop and Auxiliary Bishop of the Diocese of Haarlem-Amsterdam declared the following: *"I am pleased to support the veneration of Mary under the title "LADY OF ALL NATIONS", which Bishop Bomers and myself have approved for the Diocese of Haarlem-Amsterdam. I am furthermore pleased to encourage the ACTION OF THE LADY OF ALL NATIONS, the goal of which is spreading her image and prayer throughout the world. This prayer has already received more than sixty imprimaturs and is translated into over sixty languages."* Jozef M. Punt, Auxiliary Bishop, Diocese of Haarlem-Amsterdam, Haarlem, Netherlands, October 4, 1997.
On May 31, 2002, Msgr. Jozef M. Punt, bishop of Haalem/Amsterdam, officially recognized the supernatural origin of the apparitions, thereby approving the apparitions, saying: *"In light and virtue of all these recommendations, testimonies, and developments, and in pondering all this in prayer and theological reflection, I have come to the conclusion that the apparitions of the Lady of All Nations in Amsterdam consist of a supernatural origin... The devotion to the Lady of All Nations can help us, in my sincere conviction, in guiding us on the right path during*

the present serious drama of our times, the path to a new and special outpouring of the Holy Spirit, Who alone can heal the great wounds of our times."

[316] June 14, 1980, Feast of the Immaculate Heart of Mary, 201f

[317] July 13, 1980, Anniversary of the Third Apparition of Fatima, 203mn

[318] September 15, 1987

[319] For a detailed explanation of this proposed Marian dogma, see Mark Miravalle, STD, *Mary: Coredemptrix, Mediatrix, Advocate* (Santa Barbara: Queenship Publishing, 1993), 1-24.

[320] 5/31/1979

[321] *Cardinals Lead – Time for Us to Follow,* Catholic Exchange 3/30/2008 http://www.catholicexchange.com/node/71066

[322] 29th Message – March 28, 1951

[323] 47th Message – October 11, 1953

[324] Locutions.org (2011-2012) 107

[325] Locutions.org (2011-2012) 77

[326] Locutions.org (2011-2012) 74

[327] Locutions.org (2011-2012) 100

[328] Locutions.org (2011-2012) 61

[329] Locutions.org (2011-2012) 103

[330] Locutions.org (2011-2012) 243

[331] Locutions.org (2011-2012) 239

[332] Locutions.org (2011-2012) 63

[333] Locutions.org (2011-2012) 269

[334] Cardinal Joseph Ratzinger. "The church will become small" from *Faith and the Future* (San Francisco: Ignatius Press, 2009).

[335] Locutions.org (2011-2012) 270

[336] Locutions.org (2011-2012) 275

[337] *Compendium of Social Doctrine* 488

[338] Judges 6:24

[339] *Compendium* 519

[340] Locutions.org (2011-2012) 58

[341] To the Priests #327-328

[342] Locutions.org (2011-2012) 112

[343] Locutions.org (2011-2012) 26

[344] Locutions.org (2011-2012) 42

[345] January 22, 1989, July 24 and August 4, 1988

[346] Our Lord to St. Faustina, Diary #699

[347] Medjugorje Message 6/5/86

[348] Medjugorje Message 6/25/02

[349] Medjugorje Message of 2/25/95; 6/25/95; 10/25/96

[350] www.directionforourtimes.com Message of 4/1/09

[351] www.divinewill.org

[352] MDM 6/7/11

[353] MDM 4/20/11, 4/6/11

[354] MDM 2/19/12

[355] MDM 6/1/11

[356] 1 Corinthians 16:22-24